Positioning Gender in Discourse

Also by Judith Baxter

SPEAKING OUT: The Female Voice in Public Contexts (*editor*)

Positioning Gender in Discourse

A Feminist Methodology

Judith Baxter
The University of Reading, UK

palgrave
macmillan

First published in hardback 2003
This paperback edition published 2007 by
PALGRAVE MACMILLAN
Houndmills, Basingstoke, Hampshire RG21 6XS and
175 Fifth Avenue, New York, N.Y. 10010
Companies and representatives throughout the world

PALGRAVE MACMILLAN is the global academic imprint of the Palgrave
Macmillan division of St. Martin's Press, LLC and of Palgrave Macmillan Ltd.
Macmillan® is a registered trademark in the United States, United Kingdom
and other countries. Palgrave is a registered trademark in the European
Union and other countries.

ISBN-13: 978–0–333–98635–6 hardback
ISBN-10: 0–333–98635–0 hardback
ISBN-13: 978–0–230–55432–0 paperback
ISBN-10: 0–230–55432–6 paperback

This book is printed on paper suitable for recycling and made from fully
managed and sustained forest sources. Logging, pulping and manufacturing
processes are expected to conform to the environmental regulations of the
country of origin.

A catalogue record for this book is available from the British Library.

Library of Congress Cataloging-in-Publication Data
Baxter, Judith.
    Positioning gender in discourse : a feminist methodology /
Judith Baxter.
        p.   cm.
    Includes bibliographical references and index.
    ISBN 0–333–98635–0 (cloth) 0–230–55432–6 (pbk)
    1. Discourse analysis.   2. Language and sex.   3. Poststructuralism.
    4. Feminism.   I. Title.

P302.B38 2003
401′.41—dc21

                                                        2003049808

Printed and bound in Great Britain by
CPI Antony Rowe, Chippenham and Eastbourne

Contents

To Brian with thanks

Contents

To Brian with thanks

Introduction

This book aims to introduce the newly emerging field of feminist post-structuralist discourse analysis (FPDA) both in terms of its theoretical virtues and its fundamental, practical value for empirical research. FPDA can be defined as a feminist approach to analysing the ways in which speakers negotiate their identities, relationships and positions in their world according to the ways in which they are located by competing yet interwoven discourses. The book explains the theory, reviews antecedents and describes two case studies. It explores the potential value of FPDA as a methodological tool.

FPDA draws upon post-structuralist insights on the nature of order: namely, complexity, plurality, ambiguity, connection, recognition, intertextuality, deconstruction and transformation. All these concepts will be explored fully during the course of the book. The acronym 'FPDA' is used from now on in order to avoid the repetition of a lengthy phrase, which, while being perfectly descriptive, does not exactly 'roll off the tongue'!

While 'post-structuralist feminism' and its close associate 'social constructionist feminism' are increasingly well-recognised concepts within the social sciences, their specific links with discourse analysis are much less widely known. Indeed, many recently published empirical studies adopting a so-called 'discourse approach' (see Litosseliti and Sunderland, 2002), with their focus upon the social construction of gender identities, differences and relationships, accord very broadly with certain key principles of FPDA. But a feminist post-structuralist approach is also rather different from a social constructionist approach. In the spirit of encouraging diversity and textual play, it seeks out the more troublesome issues of working with spoken discourse, high-lighting the unresolved tensions, competing perspectives, shifts of power, ambiguities and contradictions inherent within all texts.

This book addresses the subject of FPDA in five interrelated ways. First, it considers the view (e.g. Francis, 1999) that the emancipatory stance of feminism and the deconstructive purpose of post-structuralism constitute a contradiction in terms. In Chapter 1, I advance the view that this possible dissonance between feminism and post-structuralism may potentially translate into a 'productive contradiction' (Soper, 1993b) for discourse analysis, able to challenge old assumptions and invite the possibility of fresh readings, keener insights and changes in practice. Secondly, I aim to theorise a distinct methodology for FPDA while simultaneously acknowledging that, in post-structuralist spirit, there can never be just *one* but a *plurality* of versions constituting a generally recognisable approach. To this end, in Chapter 3, I propose a broad set of guidelines constituting the FPDA approach for would-be practitioners. Thirdly, I demonstrate 'what an FPDA approach looks like' by conducting a detailed discourse analysis of spoken interactions within two contrasting research settings: a whole class discussion involving a mixed-sex class of secondary/high school students who were being assessed for a public, oral examination (Chapters 4 and 5); and two business meetings involving a team of male and female senior managers (Chapters 6 and 7). The focus of the FPDA approach in this book is therefore very much upon *spoken* rather than written discourse, principally because the method is very suited to identifying and interpreting the fluid and *interactive* ways in which speakers shift between competing subject positions within the course of a conversation, discussion or debate. Furthermore, as Cameron (2001: 1) has remarked, it is also increasingly the case that researchers with an interest in discourse analysis, or indeed social science students handling qualitative research evidence, are likely to have a specific involvement with spoken language data, as they interact with research subjects or with each other. It would certainly be an interesting challenge for future practitioners of FPDA to seek to apply the methods advocated in this book to written, printed or electronic texts.

Fourthly, this book aims proactively to evolve the new genre of FPDA, partly by developing its guiding principles and demonstrating its critical practices, and partly by considering its relationship with two more widely known approaches to discourse analysis: conversation analysis (CA) and critical discourse analysis (CDA). Clearly there are many other varieties of discourse analysis such as the ethnography of speaking, interactional linguistics and pragmatics, but the approaches of CA and CDA are the two most likely to be compared with that of FPDA. In evolving a new approach, I argue that I am not interested in setting up FPDA as a rival critical paradigm (Chapter 2). In my view, FPDA is best perceived as an additional or supplementary mode of discourse analysis to those of the more established approaches. I therefore intend to avoid the use of modernist, adversarial rhetoric that has to *prove* that one approach is necessarily 'better' than the others. Rather, I suggest that developing good practice in the field of discourse analysis depends upon encouraging an interplay between multiple-voices and accounts that only comes into being when each is heard in juxtaposition with others.

The use of FPDA as an additional methodology alongside those of CA and CDA therefore helps to challenge the inertia of 'linguistic orthodoxies' (Billig, 2000: 292), in other words, an unquestioning and overrespectful adherence to methods of discourse analysis associated with certain revered experts. Moreover, as I go on to argue in Chapter 8, FPDA does offer discourse analysts in a variety of fields an *alternative* set of methodological strategies to those of CA and CDA. Such strategies should enable practitioners to produce a complex and penetrating analysis of the fluctuating ways in which gender relations are negotiated within the context of competing yet interwoven discourses, which in turn constitute all textual/spoken interactions.

Finally, I intend to present the case for FPDA in a relatively clear, accessible and user-friendly fashion, avoiding overly esoteric jargon, and aiming to be as self-reflexive in this process as I can. Quite deservedly, post-structuralism has something of a reputation for its use of an alienating, obfuscating terminology. Colleagues and students alike have admitted to me that they 'just don't get it'. This is especially ironic in the light of the post-structuralist quest (Derrida, 1987) to demystify the ways in which both discourse and language 'do power'. However, new concepts are signified by new, specialist terminology and it is often this lack of conceptual/linguistic familiarity which can alienate uninitiated readers. This book intends to contribute to the process of translating and converting potentially off-putting concepts into accessible principles from which practical strategies can be developed for conducting discourse analysis.

In using the theoretically eclectic and loaded phrase, 'feminist post-structuralist discourse analysis', all sorts of questions arise about the range of meanings and definitions intended. I therefore see it as vital to 'set out my stall' at the start of this book by exploring the assumptions implicit within the three separate elements of the phrase: namely, *feminism, post-structuralism* and *discourse analysis*, as well as indicating the possible connections between them. Each of these three elements are expounded in much more detail in the forthcoming chapters, but in order to prepare the ground, I provide brief clarifications here. Further, there are other words and phrases which are used repeatedly throughout this book such as 'gender', 'power', 'discourse' and 'public contexts', as well as common terms associated with post-structuralism such as 'deconstruction', 'intertextuality' and 'self-reflexivity'. Again, the intended meanings of these core terms and phrases are made explicit in this Introduction.

Feminism

Like post-structuralism, feminism draws upon a short but thoroughly diverse theoretical tradition. In her account of 'third wave' feminism, Mills (2002) suggests that it is possible to identify three distinct chronological waves in the history of feminism. Pre-modernist or 'first wave' feminism is generally associated with the original quest for female suffrage in the US and Western Europe in the late 19th and 20th centuries. Modernist or 'second wave' feminism is often identified with the 1960s' political and economic drive to end sex discrimination and promote equal opportunities. As a theoretical force, 'second wave' feminism has been largely preoccupied with celebrating the notion of a universal female nature, and critiquing the structuring influence of the 'big variable' of gender on social relations in order to promote female emancipation. Conversely, 'third wave' feminism is much more concerned to operate at a more mundane, day-to-day, 'bottom-up' level, deconstructing gender identities and relations within specific communities of practice (e.g. Eckert and McConnell Ginet, 1995). According to Mills, 'third wave' feminism refers to the range of theory that incorporates constructivist rather than essentialist principles such as social constructionism (e.g. Crawford, 1995; Hall and Bucholtz, 1995; Gal, 1995; Talbot, 1998) and, of course, post-structuralist feminism. Mills suggests that 'third wave' feminism can be identified by the following six aspects:

- the diversity and multiplicity of women's identities
- the *performative* rather than the essentialist or possessive nature of gender (Butler, 1990, 1991); in other words, gender is something people enact or do, not something they are, own or characterise
- a focus upon context-specific gender issues rather than more generalised questions; terms like 'patriarchy' and 'sexism' are therefore considered out of date
- the importance of co-construction, the process by which identities are negotiated and constructed through social interactions (Chouliaraki and Fairclough, 1999)
- power constructed not as a possession, but as flowing omnidirectionally in a net or web-like fashion, such that powerlessness is no longer considered a feature of all women. Powerlessness may pertain to many women *some* of the time or to a minority of women *most* of the time
- an emphasis upon notions of female resistance to, and a reinterpretation of, stereotyped subject positions rather than notions of struggle against the subordination of women.

However, it is arguable whether feminist history can or should be characterised in terms of chronological stages. Indeed, there is evidence to suggest that feminist writing in different times and places has been imbued with both essentialist *and* constructionist tendencies. Arguably, many 'canonical' feminist writers such as Simone de Beauvoir, Juliet Mitchell, Shulamith Firestone and Germaine Greer have combined aspects of modernist and post-structuralist thinking within a single text. I therefore suggest that we conceptualise 'third wave' or post-structuralist feminism not as a *stage* of historical progression, but as one of several linked but competing theoretical *strands* within feminist history. This profile of 'third wave' feminism will be considered in greater depth in Chapter 1, when I discuss the reasons why feminist post-structuralism is sometimes considered a 'contradiction in terms'.

Post-structuralism

It is clearly important to distinguish 'post-structuralism' from 'postmodernism' as these terms are certainly not interchangeable. *Postmodernism* (e.g. Baudrillard, 1988; Lyotard, 1984) refers to the general philosophical movement (incorporating all fields of knowledge such as art, architecture, critical theory, politics, organisational behaviour and so on) with its sense of scepticism towards all universal causes, its questioning of what 'true' or 'real' knowledge is, and its loss of certainty about all absolutes, whether spiritual, moral, political or ideological. As a branch of post-modernism, *post-structuralism* is not specific to a single school of thought or academic discipline, but is constituted by a plurality of theoretical positions (e.g. Barthes, 1973; Derrida, 1982; Foucault, 1984; Kristeva, 1984). However, the specific locus of its interest is in *language* as a 'site' for the construction and contestation of social meanings. Weedon (1997: 21), who has done much to evolve conceptualisations of feminist post-structuralism, highlights *language* as the common factor in any analysis of power, social meanings and the construction of identities:

> language is the place where actual and possible forms of social organisation and their likely social and political consequences are defined and contested. Yet it is also the place where our sense of selves, our subjectivity is constructed . . . post-structuralism theorises subjectivity as a site of disunity and conflict, central to the processes of political change and to preserving the status quo.

With its focused interest in language, post-structuralism also attends specifically to the *fictionalising* process of any act of research, and the phenomenon that any act of research comprises a series of authorial choices and textual strategies. Fictionalising, according to the post-structuralist view, means that all pursuits of inquiry are concerned with creating a world through language and hence research is itself constitutive or 'world-making'. Post-structuralism sees any act of knowledge generation, such as discourse analysis, as a 'textualising' practice in that no form of knowledge can be separated from the structures, conventions and conceptuality of language as inscribed within discourses and texts. In a post-structuralist approach to discourse analysis, it is in the act of *self-reflexivity* – the practice of calling attention to the constitutive powers of any form of analysis – that the connection can be made explicitly between 'what is being analysed' and 'how it is being analysed'. Furthermore, the role of deconstructive criticism, derived from the work of the post-structuralist Derrida (e.g. 1976, 1987), can inform an analysis of language which does not attempt to identify one, true meaning within a text, but recognises the plurality, multivocality and non-fixity of all meaning.

Discourse, discourses and discourse analysis

Aptly demonstrating the non-fixity of meaning, the term 'discourse' is itself a highly contested term within the field. While it is common currency in a variety of disciplines, 'discourse' is frequently left undefined and therefore carries a kind of multi-accentuality – varying in meaning according to user and context. In this book, the term 'discourse' is used in two particular ways. The first, in my occasional references to spoken or written discourse, is the relatively straightforward, conventional sense of 'language above the sentence' or 'language at text level' (Cameron, 2001: 11). In this first sense discourse refers to stretches of text, spoken or written, monologic or dialogic, which are open to the analysis of 'patterns (structure, organisation) in units which are larger, more extended than one sentence'. This understanding of discourse almost certainly overlaps and intersects with another conventional linguistic definition of discourse as 'language in use': that is, any talk between people, and groups of people, in everyday contexts such as the shopping centre, the classroom, the boardroom or the law courts.

The second and primary use of the term 'discourse' in this book – and generally the way it is theorised by feminist, post-structuralist discourse analysis – is as a form of social/ideological practice (Fairclough, 1992). According to Foucault (1972: 49), discourses are used in the plural sense to denote 'practices that systematically form the object of which they speak'. Thus, discourses are forms of knowledge or powerful sets of assumptions, expectations and explanations, governing mainstream social and cultural practices. They are systematic ways of making sense of the world by inscribing and shaping power relations within all texts, including spoken interactions. Discourses are in turn closely associated with 'discursive practices': social practices that are produced by/through discourses. Indeed, Foucauldian (1984: 61) notions of discourse are always inextricably linked with concepts of *power*, not as a negative, repressive force but as something that constitutes and energises all discursive and social relations:

> If power were never anything but repressive, if it never did anything but say no, do you really think one would be brought to obey it? What makes power hold good, what makes it accepted, is simply the fact that it doesn't only weigh on us as a force that says no, but that it traverses and produces things, it induces pleasure, forms knowledge, produces discourse. It needs to be considered as a productive network

which runs through the whole social body much more than as a negative instance
whose function is repression.

In this book, *power* is conceptualised in this Foucauldian sense, not
as a possession in somebody's hands, but as a 'net-like organisation'
which weaves itself discursively through social organisations, meanings, relations and the construction of speakers' subjectivities or
identities. As Foucault says (1980: 98), 'individuals are always in a position of simultaneously undergoing and exercising this power', located
as they are within different and competing discourses according to
context.

From an FPDA perspective, there are always plural and competing
discourses constituting power relations within any field of knowledge or given context. Within the classroom context, for instance,
we cannot assume that there is simply one discourse determining
gender: there may be dominant discourses constructing stereotypical
assumptions about masculinity, femininity and binary gender differences, but there may also be resistant or oppositional discourses
advocating, for example, gender diversity, inclusion or separatism.
Discourses of gender will themselves be competing with other institutionalised or less formalised discourses within the classroom – such
as discourses constituting peer or teacher approval; discipline and
punishment; or models of teaching and learning – to fix meanings
often in dominant or conventional ways. Such discourses do not
operate in discrete isolation from each other but are always *intertextually* linked, that is, each discourse is likely to be interconnected
with and infused by traces of the others. For example, as we shall see
in Chapter 5, discourses of teaching and learning in the classroom
may be interwoven with discourses of gender differentiation.

The book will explore the way individual speakers are implicated
in the business of negotiating such meanings according to the way
they position themselves, and are positioned, by a specific discursive
context. While certain individuals may be relatively *powerfully* positioned, others will be much less so. The terms 'power' and 'powerfulness' in this book therefore refer to the way in which individual
speakers are often *better placed* than others to benefit from the experiences, interests and goals of a particular context – by virtue of their
more privileged positioning within a combination of dominant discourses. So, for instance, a male speaker in a business meeting may

be more powerfully positioned than a female speaker to make an extended contribution to the meeting, because a dominant discourse of gender differentiation tends to construct 'men as more willing than women to contribute in public or formal contexts' (Holmes, 1992: 132). However, according to an FPDA perspective, individuals are rarely consistently positioned as powerful across *all* the discourses at work within a given context – they are often located simultaneously as both powerful and powerless. In other words, it is possible for a speaker to be positioned as relatively powerful within one discourse but as relatively powerless within another, perhaps competing discourse.

The reason that this book foregrounds speech in *public* or *institutionalised* contexts (the classroom, the boardroom) rather than speech in more informal, intimate, private or domestic settings is that the kind of issues arising from the relationship between discourse and power are arguably more conspicuous. As I discuss in Chapter 6, speakers in public settings are constantly negotiating for positions of power, with a demonstrable duty to 'prove their worth' by accomplishing goal-orientated tasks such as solving problems or making decisions. However, this is not to say that power relations are not equally vigorously negotiated within less obviously public settings, as Simpson's (1997) post-structuralist analysis of a family playing a game in their home demonstrates.

According to an FPDA perspective, discourses are not seen as necessarily all-pervasive, somehow responsible, in the most literal sense, for assembling and constructing an external material reality. But nor are discourses assumed to work through the CDA lens of a *dialectical* relationship by which the discursive event is shaped and thereby continuously able to reconstruct the 'real' or 'material' events, situations, institutions and social structures. As Butler (1991) has surmised, material realities cannot exist outside the range of discourse, and to this extent they are difficult to distinguish conceptually from social realities. Competing discourses work to determine and fix the meanings of the material world and hence our experience of social realities. For instance, while someone's death is an inescapable biological and material fact, the ways in which a culture construes that person's death through competing discourses constitutes the lived reality for the friends and family of the deceased. Thus experience of material or social realities are always produced discursively so that people's identities and subject positions as speakers are being continuously reconstructed and open to redefinition *through* discourse, but never outside it.

In its 'discourse approach' to the analysis of texts, feminist poststructuralism appears to have much in common with social constructionist feminism. Both question gender as an essential and fundamental part of the individual; both conceive language as a culturally constructed 'system of meanings' (Crawford, 1995); both suggest that our identities are 'performed' through language, (Butler, 1990; Cameron, 1997a); and both recognise language to be a potential 'site' of struggle and change. But while social constructionists tend to argue that individuals produce language through the medium of social transactions, post-structuralists argue that language is always *discursively* produced. Thus, speakers produce fluctuating meanings in relation to how powerfully they are positioned within a range of competing discourses.

In this book I highlight a central concern of the FPDA approach: namely to examine the ways in which speakers negotiate their identities, relationships and positions in the world according to the ways in which they are *multiply* located by different discourses. A *feminist* post-structuralist perspective on discourse suggests that females always adopt multiple subject positions, and that it is far too reductive to constitute women in general, or indeed any individual woman, simply as *victims* of male oppression (Jones, 1993). In the majority of cases, females may be simultaneously powerful within certain subject positions but yet distinctly powerless within other subject positions. However, this stance is juxtaposed and counterbalanced by the view that dominant discourses can and do combine systematically to position females as consistently more powerless than males at particular historical moments and within specific 'communities of practice' (Eckert and McConnell Ginet, 1992). The quest of FPDA is not only to identify the ways in which power constantly shifts between different speakers, but also to open up spaces for those female voices which have been systematically marginalised or silenced. It is on this basis that FPDA can justify an interest and involvement in small-scale, community-based, feminist projects leading to transformative action. In Chapter 8, I describe how the use of FPDA within the separate contexts of a classroom and a business meeting ultimately lead to localised acts of transformation. First, as a result of analysing classroom discourse (Chapters 4 and 5), changes were instigated to the school's curriculum policy and practices which specifically addressed the potentially damaging effects of gendered classroom discourse. Second, a key consequence of analysing a series of business meetings (Chapters 6 and 7) was that the dissemination of a 'discourse map' enabled a team of male and female managers to work more effectively together.

A focus on gender

On a conceptual level, it is worth asking upon what grounds gender deserves the particular focus it receives within the FPDA approach. Indeed, the foregrounding of gender for special attention must always warrant a self-reflexive justification according to a post-structuralist perspective. Similarly, within an ethnomethodological paradigm such as CA, gender is also regarded as just one of a number of possible variables which the participants may (or may not) make relevant within their spoken interactions, with no higher claim upon the attention of a discourse analyst than any other variable (Schegloff, 1999; West, 2002). Taking as read that the relationships between gender, language and discourse are always fluid and context-specific, Swann (2002) explores the possible range of 'warrants' for making any claim about gender in a post-modernist research setting. One of the various stereotypes about post-structuralism I challenge in this book is the view that, in an apparently relativist, 'value-free' universe, it is considered hegemonic to identify yourself with a particular focus such as gender, or to support an ideological perspective such as feminism. As I shall argue, post-structuralist theory *does* support the notion of causes, provided that these are small-scale, context-bound, purposeful, critically tuned and short-lived (Elliott, 1996). It is true that local and situated meanings can in themselves be difficult to identify, as Litosseliti and Sunderland (2002) remark. Even when gender seems a salient category to the researcher, it might not necessarily seem so to the participants, an issue I explore in the Management Team study (Chapter 7). Nevertheless the concept of 'warrants' is a useful one for the self-reflexive analyst, and FPDA's own warrants are discussed in more detail at the end of Chapter 1. With its explicitly *feminist* approach to discourse analysis, FPDA has a declared interest in highlighting issues of gender. Indeed, FPDA has its own discursive agenda, namely to 'see the world from woman's place within it' (Callaway, 1981: 480). It is the self-reflexive business of making the feminist perspective *visible*, whilst simultaneously subjecting it to continuous scrutiny, that provides FPDA with a basis for warranting its claims about gender.

Linked to the concept of gender are a range of multi-accentual and potentially contentious terms of reference used in this book such as *woman/man*, *girl/boy*, *male/female* and *mixed-sex*. It has been argued that the use of such terms clearly connoting the biological sex category both foregrounds sex/gender as a superordinate factor in the construction of people's identities and simultaneously legitimises binary gender *differences* as a dominant discourse within feminist linguistics (e.g. Bing and Bergvall, 1998; Butler, 1990; Moi, 2000; West, 2002). Terms such as woman/man, girl/boy and so on are used throughout this book within the explicit context of a feminist post-structuralist perspective, but never unquestioningly. FPDA is able to recognise, for example, that a term like 'woman' is a necessary category within the feminist critique of power relations, but simultaneously to problematise that category in its deconstruction of the multiple but nonetheless limited range of subject positions available to individuals. In other words, FPDA must overtly recognise gender as a potential site of struggle. The extent to which this allows feminist post-structuralists to 'have their cake and eat it too' (Jones, 1997; Davies, 1997) – a modernist rather than a post-structuralist presumption – is something this book goes on to explore.

Conclusion

The urge to make generalisations and transferable explanations within any form of research is understandably pressing, and yet for FPDA, with its emphasis on small-scale, localised transformations, it might seem hard to justify. Yet an FPDA perspective would suggest that the local meanings of talk always work within, represent and reconstitute broader discursive structures, relations and processes. Echoing this, Eckert and McConnell Ginet (1999) have argued that, although making academic generalisations about research has become increasingly problematic within a post-modernist paradigm, it is by no means impossible. They suggest that any commentary on the context-ualised interactions of girls/women or boys/men will inevitably draw upon intertextualised generalisations and broader social explanations. These can potentially produce powerful resonances and rich insights about the intricacies and complexities of human relations.

I hope that *Positioning Gender in Discourse: A feminist methodology* will prove a valuable resource for all researchers interested in questioning the business of conducting discourse analysis. The book is especially relevant for gender and language scholars with an interest in the discourse approach to questions of gender, identity and power. However, I hope that the book will have a broader appeal and relevance to researchers and students in sociolinguistics, education, media studies, sociology and related social sciences because its research methodology *is* transferable. Furthermore, the FPDA approach to positioning gender within discourse should be of particular interest to university and college departments teaching qualitative research methods *across* the social sciences.

1
A Working Partnership?

> The price for giving in to [Foucault's] powerful discourse is nothing less than the depoliticisation of feminism.
>
> (Moi, 1985)

This chapter explores two of the building blocks of feminist post-structuralist discourse analysis (FPDA) – feminism and post-structuralism. It asks *whether* and *how* two such independently powerful and theoretically diverse traditions, with their associated research methodologies, can be connected conceptually and pragmatically under the umbrella of FPDA. I will seek to question the view (e.g. Francis, 1999) that the emancipatory stance of feminism and the deconstructive purpose of post-structuralism should necessarily be viewed as dichotomous. In my view, such a perspective – that feminist post-structuralism is effectively 'a contradiction in terms' – appears to be premised on *modernist* rather than post-modernist presuppositions. This chapter will therefore begin by exploring some of the key principles of modernist feminism, and then move on to examine the principles linking the diverse movement of post-structuralism. I shall conclude by suggesting that a clearer understanding of the possibilities of feminist post-structuralism should provide a bridge for a productive working relationship between these two theoretical traditions. Definitions of the more technical terms used in this chapter can be found in the Introduction.

Principles of modernist feminism

One is not born but *becomes* a woman (italics added).

(Simone de Beauvoir, 1949)

I suggest below that there are three interrelated principles or 'rules of thumb' that might be said to inform modernist feminism. These principles are drawn from a range of international feminist writing (e.g. Beauvoir, 1972; Daly, 1978; Irigaray, 1985; Millett, 1977; Showalter, 1989) as well as from different facets of the movement such as liberal, essentialist, Marxist/socialist and radical feminism (Usher, 1996). Acts of definition such as this inevitably mean privileging certain meanings and marginalising others. The three principles I describe are not intended to exclude others, nor are they intended to 'pigeonhole' modernist feminist theory, which is demonstrably complex and multifaceted. Furthermore, I do not wish to conceptualise feminist post-structuralism as simply the next stage or 'wave' in the historical progression of feminism. This would be to ignore other currently influential and interrelated theoretical perspectives – such as social constructionism, which predominantly informs the 'discourse approach' to textual analysis (as discussed in the Introduction, p. 10). Rather, it can be argued that certain elements of modernism, social construct-ionism and post-structuralism have *always* co-existed in feminist writing. In other words, feminist post-structuralism is a fairly new label but it has important antecedents in earlier work, such as de Beauvoir's *The Second Sex* (1972), usually considered an exemplary text of modernist feminism. Cameron, in a discussion with the author, has pointed out that feminist post-structuralism became aware of itself and named itself as a specific tendency at a particular point in time and was possibly reacting against other tendencies of the time. For example, in linguistics, she mentioned the rise in the work of writers like Bergvall (1999) and Bucholtz (1999) as clearly and directly a reaction to the popular success of Tannen's (e.g. 1992, 1995) 'two cultures' approach to theories of gender difference, rather than as part of a 'new' phenomenon.

The three principles described below thus form an attempt to dis-tinguish some of the key elements of modernist feminism from that of a post-structuralist conception of feminism. These principles are: the foundational belief in *a universal cause* uniting women everywhere;

the notion that *the personal is political* in feminist philosophy and practice; and the search for *a common voice* expressing the cause and symbolising women and womanhood.

A universal cause

Modernist feminism, whether liberal, socialist, radical or whatever, has generally been signified by versions of the Enlightenment dream. In feminist terms, this 'dream' is constituted as the need to resist and subvert the structures of male power. According to this, liberatory knowledge, or the imperative to make women aware of their sub-jugation, is gained by drawing upon the powers of *reason* as the guarantor of truth and freedom, and involves various forms of action such as diverse investigations of the patriarchal order, consciousness-raising and political protest. Such actions would ultimately equip women for the task of freeing themselves from all forms of patriarchal oppression.

In grounding its cause within a liberal-humanist perspective of human progress, modernist feminism has partially shared its heri-tage with other political and intellectual causes such as working-class, Black nationalist and ethnic minority struggles for emancipation and basic human rights. Thus, the feminist cause is perceived as part of a greater social movement towards human equality, authenticity, self-improvement, democracy, freedom and social progress. Under-lying each of these meta-narratives is the assumption that the march of history is evolutionary, rational and progressive, leading ultimately towards the realisation of utopian aspirations. Such a universal cause is considered accomplishable because it is founded upon the view that the human subject has a unified, sovereign, rational conscious-ness which is able to transcend particular conditions of time and place, view the world objectively and gain access to 'true' knowledge. If, according to modernist feminism, all women are fundamentally constituted by the same human nature, they will recognise, by virtue of their reason, the universal nature of their oppression, aspire to the common dream of female emancipation, and grasp the chance to transform their destinies.

Western liberal humanism has tended to privilege a dualistic model of human thought in which sets of concepts, values and experi-ences are counterposed and polarised in a hierarchially structured power relationship. Hence, reason is valued over emotion, objectivity over subjectivity, argument over narrative, masculine over feminine, theory over practice, public concerns over private ones and so on. While ostensibly challenging this patriarchal model of human thought by seeking to overturn such distinctions, modernist feminism itself has in the past tended to fall into a similar trap in the name of the universal cause. In philosophical terms, feminism has appropriated the Self/Other divide for its own purposes by casting males as the 'Other' against which the feminist 'Self' must fight. For, as long as feminism dichotomises the argument and casts the universal female as a *victim* of patriarchal oppression, feminism's power as a voice of protest gives it a compelling political coherence – because there is an 'Enemy'. The liberal-humanist, Self/Other divide has characterised much feminist theory with its emphasis on an unbridgeable chasm between the powerful male and the powerless female. The championing of a universal cause is somewhat ironic, given feminism's goal to reclaim and reinstate women from the realms of 'the Other'. This is because such a cause presents a form of 'reverse discourse' – the Foucauldian phenomenon that any oppressed group will seek to contest its marginalisation by insisting on its 'naturality' – in that the group inevitably invokes the discourse of the oppressor. Post-structuralist feminism has, on the other hand, tended to question the orthodoxy of the universal cause and the essentialist categories of 'woman', 'sex' and 'gender' to which it supposedly applies (e.g. Bergvall *etal.*, 1996; Butler, 1990; Cameron, 1997b; Eckert, 1989; Moi, 1999, 2000). Such writers argue that by reinforcing the Self/Other divide, feminist theory unwittingly upholds male epistemological power structures, which perpetuates differences and inequalities, and excludes the possibilities of more fluid and dynamic interpretations of human identity within women's lives.

The personal is political

This phrase is not simply a banner-waving slogan but rather a founding assumption that has guided modernist feminist theory and practice. It manages to encapsulate the liberal-humanist belief in the centrality of female experiences and the theoretical imperative to gain self-knowledge and give expression to female subjectivity. Thus, self-knowledge and political action are considered to go hand in hand as interrelated and incremental goals. As women have gained more knowledge of themselves and their position in the world, it is presumed that their power to transform social relations should increase accordingly.

The feminist quest to make the personal political is premised on the modernist assumption that each individual woman or man possesses a unique essence of human nature (Weedon, 1997). Classical liberal humanism suggests that this essence is constituted by rational consciousness, which allows us to gain access to the truth about the material world. Thus, in feminist forms of humanism, the central concern is with human nature, the forms of identity it prescribes – both biologically and through socialisation – and, in particular, the essential differences between women and men. It is an important aspect of this view that it is predicated upon humanist assumptions of identity because, if women are unitary subjects possessing a core, female nature, this will transcend differentiating social categories whether of age, class, colour, language, culture or creed. The notion of a 'female' human nature offers a collective bond between all women regardless of history, geography or culture.

According to this perspective, the quest to articulate, reclaim and celebrate the myriad forms of female experience is simultaneously a personal act of self-expression and a political protest against the historical silencing and marginalisation of women. This quest to make the personal political has been conducted through the medium of academic debate, consciousness-raising and collective action, and has various purposes. First, it aims to make visible areas of a woman's world traditionally peripheralised as too trivial, irrelevant, sensitive, threatening or sexually taboo by the world of men. This includes issues of the 'body' such as menstruation, pregnancy, childbirth, mothering, the menopause, rape and domestic violence. Secondly, the modernist quest has sought to liberate individual women from psychological oppression by inviting them to engage in personalised political acts such as consciousness-raising and more recently, psychoanalytic counselling and therapy. Mitchell (1974: 61) has described consciousness-raising, for example, as 'the process of transforming the hidden, individual fears of women into a shared awareness of the meaning of them as social problems'. Thirdly, the value of collective, direct action for feminists (such as the campaign against nuclear weapons at Greenham Common in Britain in the 1980s) is that it can work on both personal and political levels. Women's participation in various forms of political protest is thus viewed as part of a journey towards self-discovery and self-knowledge.

Finally, the aim to make the personal political has been incorporated into some areas of feminist theory. The guiding belief in the centrality of female experiences has led to a feminist hostility, in some quarters, to *theory* as it is conventionally constituted by male academic discourse. Until relatively recently in the history of scholarship, women have been conspicuously absent from the active production of theory. Feminist scholars have criticised rationalist, positivist and empiricist models of theory and research, which they regard as scientistic, exclusionary and sexist. While feminist theorists' resistance to conventional academic discourse has taken a variety of forms, notable among these has been the trend towards making women the *subject* rather than the object of study. This endeavour to transform constructions of and access to knowledge has led feminist theorists to privilege *personalised*, confessional, autobiographical or narrative writing (either their own or that of their research subjects), purportedly unmediated by excess theory and regarded as a conduit to the 'true' expression of female experience. Examples of such alternative feminist approaches to theory construction are plentiful, but two, drawn from an educational context, will suffice here. Miller (1996) has contested the genre of evidence-based rational argument in her book *School for Women* which weaves together anecdotes, autobiography, narrative and writings from teachers, in her overview of the history of women teachers. Similarly, Middleton (1993) uses a life-history approach to analyse women's place within post-war schooling. She effectively blends the personal with the political in her autobiographical approach to the discussion of policy and pedagogy.

A common voice

Modernist feminism has sought to unify women against patriarchal oppression by expressing its arguments and demands for change with a common voice. The rationale for this is that accounts of female subjugation or challenges against patriarchy need to have an unambiguous, univocal coherence so that they simultaneously work internally to address both feminists and the broader category of women, as well as externally to confront male-dominated power structures. In terms of political impact, a unified feminist message is considered to have a greater likelihood of penetrating the monolith of male power than the babble of competing viewpoints. Moreover, armed with the knowledge that women as a social group have been silenced or written out of the histories of culture, language and litera- ture that men have documented, modernist feminists have sought to reinstate the construct of the essential female voice. For example, language and gender theorists, following Lakoff (1975), initiated investigations into the possibility of identifying a common female use of language, which involved the reclamation of styles of speech often associated with females but andro-centrically deemed low status, such as gossip (Jones, 1980), politeness (Holmes, 1995) and co-operative speech (Coates, 1995, 1998).

But in order for the feminist movement to guarantee support for the notion of a common voice representing women's shared inter- ests, it has traditionally had to predicate its assumptions upon the notion of biological sex as a foundational category. Modernist feminists have agonised over the epistemological significance of recognising a female 'pre-discursive reality' – a place where women's experiences can be said to exist prior to their formulation in language or discourse. This notion is important for such theorists to establish, because without it, the foundational category of the female-sexed human nature cannot be presumed to exist outside its discursive construction. As Weedon (1997) points out, the desire to give expres- sion to women's 'essential' subjectivity is a key motivation behind the feminist emphasis on the importance of speaking out for women. In its most radical form, she suggests, this position indicates that what we say as biological females about our experience is what it is to be a woman. In other words, sex determines gender, biology is regarded as the key determining influence on women's language, and women's language can therefore be identified as a separate com- municative subculture. This both strengthens and limits its symbolic value as a common voice. A common female language becomes a strength if it simultaneously reinforces the sense of shared experi- ence and oppression between women from apparently differing backgrounds (in terms of class, race, culture and so on). But, an exclusively female voice may become a limitation if it suppresses vital differences *between* women, thus precluding a belief in the plurality of human identity. As Butler (1990: 325) has said, when the female sex category is understood as representing a set of values and dispositions, it becomes normative in character and thus exclusionary in principle:

> This move has created a problem both theoretical and political, namely that a variety of women from various cultural positions have refused to recognise themselves as 'women' in the terms articulated by feminist theory with the result that these women fall outside the category and are left to conclude that (1) either they are not women as they have previously assumed or (2) that the category reflects the restricted locations of theoreticians and hence fails to recognise the intersection of gender with race, class, ethnicity, age, sexuality and other currents which contribute to the formation of cultural (non) identity.

As a further consequence, the principle of a common female voice potentially distances and alienates the 'Other', that is, those individuals (not always men) and those power structures and processes at which political addresses and actions may be directed. While this may represent a more than legitimate goal for radical feminists and separatists, it may undermine the policies and practices of more moderate feminists for whom engagement and dialogue form a necessary part of the process of resistance and transformation.

These three principles which have featured within modernist feminism – a universal cause, a belief that the personal is political, and its endeavour to achieve a common voice – are at variance with the multi-faceted viewpoints of post-structuralism, as I now go on to discuss.

Principles of post-structuralism

Like feminism, post-structuralism is difficult to characterise in a few pages because it is not a monophonic philosophy or a single theoretical framework. Rather, the history of post-structuralism as a form of textual and discursive inquiry (and the greater cultural movement of post-modernism of which it is a part) has generated diverse, lengthy and competing accounts of itself. However, this does not mean to say that post-structuralism lives up to its popular but negative stereotype (Francis, 1999) of 'anything goes'. Rather, it is associated with a loose collection of common principles that make it identifiably and yet self-reflexively a theoretical discourse in its own right. Below, I outline three of the most significant principles that particularly relate to my previous discussion of feminism: scepticism towards universal causes and 'grand narratives'; the contestation of meaning; and the discursive construction of subjectivity. I shall begin by discussing the first principle within the broader context of *post-modernism* in order to clarify the epistemological origins of post-structuralist theory.

Scepticism towards universal causes

Post-modernism is sceptical of the grand claims and exclusive rights put forward by most paradigms of knowledge, whether these be invested within religion, science, politics, or large-scale social movements. It questions the plausibility of Enlightenment ways of thinking and conducting research that premise their theories on 'grand narratives that unified and structured Western science, grounding truth and meaning in the assumption of a universal subject and universal goal of emancipation' (Elliott, 1996: 19). This is because, in Foucault's (1980: 109–33) terms, the Enlightenment preoccupation with the 'will to truth' is also a 'will to power', and any guiding belief or paradigm of knowledge, however benign, inevitably systematises itself into a 'regime of truth'. In simpler terms, it is like saying that my superior knowledge of the world enables me to hold power over you and your inferior knowledge. Conversely, post-modernist theory questions what 'true' or 'real' knowledge is, expresses a loss of certainty about the existence of absolutes, and is sceptical of all universal claims and causes. In line with this theoretical perspective, post-modernism is likely to be suspicious of any large-scale, emancipatory projects such as feminism.

In terms of research practices, post-modernist theory has challenged the positivist view that there is a determinate, material world that can be definitively known and explained (Elliott, 1996; Foucault, 1972; Lyotard, 1984). Post-modernism does not accept that it is possible to know the world by dissecting it through apparently objective methods of inquiry. Rather, it considers that knowledge is always constructed not discovered; contextual not foundational; singular, localised and perspectival rather than totalising or universal; and egalitarian rather than hierarchical. Post-modernism also questions the way that modernist theories are coded by language and discourse into binary or hierarchical oppositions such as mind/body, masculinity/femininity, theory/practice and public/private. Foucault (1979, 1984) has argued that practices of social regulation and control are rooted in the organisation of knowledge according to irreconcilable binary opposites that are not natural but discursively constructed. In every case, dominant discourses ensure that one pole of opposites is privileged over the other (e.g. objectivity over subjectivity in scientific discourse; masculinity over femininity in patriarchal discourse). This polarising and hierarchial ordering of constructs contributes to the formation of grand narratives that become normalising in character and exclusionary in principle. Thus even the most well-intentioned, humanitarian or egalitarian enterprises (such as Christianity or indeed feminism), in their drive to 'open people's eyes', are *potentially* constituted by elitist, divisive and marginalising practices. In contrast, post-modernist theory advocates the kinetic interplay of multiple but competing theoretical positions, where one form of knowledge is free to enrich, complement, challenge or contest any other.

In the light of its scepticism towards universal causes, feminist theorists (e.g. Balbus, 1987; Davies, 1997; Francis, 1999; Hartsock, 1990) have debated whether post-modernist theory can have any interest at all in social transformation. In consequence, it has been variously criticised as relativist, value-free, nihilistic, cynical, 'a fallacy' and hypocritical in supporting its own 'grand narrative' which specifies sets of insights about the nature of order and meaning. In the later section, 'Feminist post-structuralism?' (p.28), I argue that this is a rather limited and resistant view of post-modernism and post-structuralist theory in particular, which fails to appreciate its transformative potential for social projects which are pragmatic, specific, localised, contextual and issue-orientated.

The contestation of meaning

Post-structuralism, as a branch of post-modernism, has a particular interest in critiquing the ways in which competing forms of knowledge, and the power interests these serve, aspire to fix meaning once and for all. The seminal work of the French theorists Michel Foucault and Jacques Derrida has contributed interrelated yet contrasting perspectives on the ways in which cultural practices are constituted by the struggle to produce, stabilise, regulate, challenge and resist dominant meanings.

Common to both Derrida (e.g. 1976, 1987) and Foucault (e.g. 1972, 1980) is their recognition that social meanings are continuously negotiated and contested through language and discourse. In their view, no form of knowledge can be separated from the structures, conventions and conceptuality of language as inscribed in discourses and texts. Post-structuralism inherits from Saussure (1974), the French structuralist, the principle that meaning is produced *within* language rather than reflected *by* language, and that individual signs (whether in speech, writing or other forms of text) do not have intrinsic meaning but acquire meanings through their relationship with, and difference from, other signs. However, it is from Derrida's (1978, 1987) conception of *differance*, in which meaning is produced through the dual concepts of *difference* and *deferral*, that theorists have developed an understanding of language in a perpetual state of flux. For structuralists, signs are divided into 'signifiers' (e.g. words, sounds, visual images) and 'signifieds' (concepts), neither of which have intrinsic meaning. Rather, their identity emerges in their *difference* from other words, sounds or images, but, as Derrida argues, this identity is in turn subject to endless *deferral*. By this he means that the meaning of any representation can only be fixed temporarily as it depends upon its discursive context. Signifiers are always located within a discursive context, so that the temporary fixing of meaning which comes from the reading of an image, word or text will be dependent upon that particular context. Texts are constantly open to rereading and reinterpretation, both within the particular context and, of course, when/if they are shifted to other contexts. Thus, the meaning of texts can never finally be fixed as knowable and immutable but is always a 'site' for contestation and redefinition by different readings within different contexts. Derrida placed a particular emphasis upon the way any text, by virtue of the range of readings to which it is subject, becomes the medium for struggle among different power interests to fix meaning permanently. Derrida's (1976, 1978) theories on *deconstructive* criticism – which attend to the plurality and non-fixity of meaning – are useful to feminism because they offer a method of questioning and decentring the hierarchical oppositions that underpin gender, race and class oppression, and suggest a way to instigate new, more challenging ways of reading texts.

Like Derrida, Foucault (1984) sought to understand the complex relationship between language and power, but placed a particular emphasis on the notion of *discourses*. His view was that language as a system does not represent experience in a transparent and neutral way but always exists within historically specific discourses. These discourses are often contradictory, offering competing versions of reality, and serving different and conflicting power interests. Such power interests usually reside within large-scale institutional systems such as the law, justice, government, the media, education and the family. Thus, it is a range of institutional discourses that provides the network by which dominant forms of social knowledge are produced, reinforced, contested or resisted. As discourses always represent and constitute different political interests, these are constantly vying with each other for status and power. Foucault (1984: 100), like Saussure (1974), resists a modernist conceptualisation of discourse in terms of dualities or opposites, but prefers a more fluid, dynamic strategic interpretation:

> We must not imagine a world of discourse divided between accepted discourse and excluded discourse, or between the dominant discourse and the dominated one; but as a multiplicity of discursive elements that can come into play in various strategies ... Discourse transmits and produces power; it reinforces it, but also undermines and exposes it, renders it fragile and makes it possible to thwart it.

According to Foucault, one critical site of struggle to determine dominant social meanings is the subjectivity, or socially constructed identity of the individual.

The discursive construction of subjectivity

Post-structuralism has a particular interest in the discursive construction of human identities. This is because it has sought to challenge and decentre the liberal-humanist construct of a rational individual or knowing subject, occupying an 'Archimedean point' that transcends the particularities of history or sociocultural location. As I have noted, humanist discourses presuppose an *essence* at the core of the individual, which is unique, fixed and coherent, and which makes a person recognisably possess a character or personality. Conversely, post-structuralist theory argues that individuals are never outside cultural forces or discursive practices but always 'subject' to them. Their identities are determined by a range of 'subject positions' ('ways of being'), approved by their culture, and made available to them by means of the particular discourses operating within a given discursive context.

So, for example, within the classroom context, students are subject to a range of institutional discourses offering knowledge about 'approved ways to be', in terms of their behaviour, their learning and teacher–student relationships. But of course, not all discourses are institutionally approved or regulated. Competing or resistant discourses will also be constituted by peer value systems and will partly govern peer identities and relationships both in and out of the classroom. These discourses will be interwoven with broader societal discourses, embracing competing perspectives, on age, gender, ethnicity, class and the like. Thus a female student may be subject to various competing discourses within the classroom offering sets of positions relating to her age, gender, ethnicity and so on, as well as her participation as a student and membership of a peer group. Individuals are therefore shaped by the possibility of multiple (although not limitless) subject positions within and across different and competing discourses. Furthermore, the formation and reformation of identity is a continuous process, accomplished through actions and words rather than through some fundamental essence of character. Belsey (1980: 132) has suggested that individuals must be thought of as, 'unfixed, unsatisfied . . . not a unity, not autonomous, but a process, perpetually in construction, perpetually contradictory, perpetually open to change'.

Begging the question within this discussion is the extent to which post-structuralist theory accepts a concept of 'agency': a measure of individual awareness or control over the means by which subjects are 'interpellated' ('called into existence'; Althusser, 1971) into a range of subject positions made available by different discursive contexts. So, what *is* the relationship between discourse and the human subject implied by post-structuralist theory? How much 'control' do individuals have over their ways of being in the world? In a sense, this is a modernist concern, echoing past feminist debates (e.g. Fraser and Nicholson, 1990; Ramazanoglu, 1993) on the implications of Foucault's writings for female subjectivity, in which the human agent exists only in some sort of compliance or resistance to discourse. The question is one to which Foucault appears to have no clear answers. He suggests that it is not the task of the theorist to address the complexity of the world as experienced by the human subject. Moreover, in his discussion of the question, 'What is an author?' in terms of written texts, Foucault explicitly urges theorists that, 'it is a matter of depriving the subject (or its substitute) of its role as originator, and of analysing the subject as a variable and complex function of discourse' (1984: 118). His work has therefore tended to discuss the history and functions of discourse without reference to subjective experience, intentionality or personal aspiration, and furthermore to criticise the constraints that the issue of subjectivity places upon the historical questions he raises about discourse. Unfortunately, Foucault's rather 'macho' approach to the whole question of agency does not help feminists interested in the applications of post-structuralism.

The issue of agency, its importance to feminism and its implications for feminist post-structuralist discourse analysis will be the subject of succeeding sections in this chapter. What is germane to this part of the discussion is that the simultaneous way in which individuals can position themselves and be positioned by power relations is critical to an understanding of how identities are constructed. If Foucault (1980: 87) is coy on the issue of subjectivity specifically, he nonetheless attributes a degree of agency to people's complex relationship with power, which is:

> never localised here or there, never in anybody's hands, never appropriated as commodity or a piece of wealth. Power is exercised through a net-like organisation. And not only do individuals circulate between its threads; they are always in the position of simultaneously undergoing and exercising this power. They are not only its inert or consenting target; they are always also the elements of its articulation.

Post-structuralists have argued that individuals are not uniquely positioned, but are produced as a 'nexus of subjectivities' (e.g. Davies and Banks, 1992; Walkerdine, 1990: 2–3), in relations of power that are constantly shifting, rendering them at times powerful and at other times powerless. Thus, it may be that the same individuals are powerful within one discursive context or powerless within another; or, far more subtly, that people shift continuously within the *same* discursive context so that they experience positions of relative powerfulness and powerlessness either concurrently or in rapid succession. Indeed, Walkerdine (1990) has ably illustrated this in her analysis of a stretch of spoken discourse in the classroom (also see Chapter 2, p. 46), in which two kindergarten boys taunt a young female teacher. In the teacher's embarrassed handling of the boys' sexualised and abusive comments towards her, she is shown to be both powerful in acting out her superior status as a teacher and yet powerless as a woman in her inability to resist their sexist constructions of her. It is precisely for issues such as this that the need now arises for a theoretically precise framework, which draws on a blend of feminist and post-structuralist principles for the purpose of analysing the complexities and ambiguities within much spoken interaction.

Feminist post-structuralism?

It is clear from the preceding discussion that there could be no obvious partnership between modernist feminism and post-structuralism, at least as it is conceived by male theorists such as Foucault and Derrida. There are theoretical contradictions in terms of the conception of the role of emancipatory causes, the individual's place in the world and the relationship between language and meaning. While modernist feminism supports a liberal-humanist belief in a unified notion of woman as an authentic being, post-structuralist feminism has posited that being recognised as female is but one effect of the multiple ways in which individual identities are constituted through discourse. Whereas modernist feminism unifies itself around the Enlightenment cause of freedom from male oppression, post-structuralism has strategically opposed any grand or universalising cause which attempts to appropriate and fix social meanings in its own image. Finally, while it has been a foundational view of feminism that the conditions of women's oppression exist in a bodily, material and pre-discursive sense, post-structuralist theory has, in its most parodic form, suggested that, 'bodies are constructed out of cultural forces in the same manner, that, say, telephones are put together' (Soper, 1993a, b). In other words, controversially, post-structuralism contests the notion that femininity and female oppression have a material or emotional reality *outside* discourse.

At least two of the more dominant themes within recent feminist theory indicate the controversy about feminist post-structuralism that currently exists within the academy itself. The first has been an internally subversive concern with feminist epistemology. Bucholtz (1999) has argued that the theorisation of gender within many areas of linguistics has lagged behind the theorisation of gender and feminist epistemology in other social sciences. This has perhaps accounted for a relatively recent debate on feminism's own conceptual frameworks and basic terminology including the uncritical use of words like 'sex', 'gender', 'woman', 'male' and 'female' (e.g. Butler, 1990; Cameron, 1997b; Eckert, 1989; Gal, 1995; Moi, 1999; West, 2002). It has been suggested in certain cases (e.g. Bergvall *et al.*, 1996) that contemporary feminism may have fallen into patriarchy's own trap of employing the oppressor's own gender-differentiated terms to construct its experiences. The second theme has been a profuse rebuttal (e.g. Francis, 1999; Hartsock, 1990; Moi, 1999; Ransom, 1993) of the feminist post-structuralist quest which is apparently to decentre the female voice, its sense of unique experience, and in particular its need to articulate women's experiences of subjugation. Hartsock, for example, has questioned the timeliness of this (1990: 163–4):

> Why is it, just at the moment when so many of us who have been silenced begin to demand the right to name ourselves, to act as subjects rather than objects of history, that just then the concept of subject-hood becomes problematic? Just when we are forming our own theories of the world, uncertainty emerges about whether the world can be theorised. Just when we are talking about the changes we want, ideas of progress and the possibility of systematically and rationally organising human society become dubious and suspect?

Do comments such as this suggest that a feminist post-structuralist approach to research is likely to be at best an uneasy compromise or at worst a contradiction in terms? Must the attempt by feminists to use the more complex ideas of post-structuralism necessarily lead to 'a paralysing ambivalence for feminist activists' as Jones (1993) has warned? I argue in the next section that the potential for feminist transformative projects and therefore *change* within the post-structuralist paradigm has been both misunderstood and underestimated. But for change to be possible, there must be a readiness for a less defensive, more multi-faceted and resilient version of feminism, that retains connections with its founding principles, yet is simultaneously capable of critiquing, informing and undermining itself with new insights and possibilities. This is very much the social constructionist version, which has many aspects in common both with 'third wave' feminism (Mills, 2002) as well as with feminist post-structuralism. I shall be referring tangentially to Mills' six aspects below (multiple identities, the performative nature of gender, context-specific gender issues, co-construction, power as a net, notions of resistance, see p. 5) as I propose the case for feminist post-structuralism under the following three headings: revisiting the subjective, the role of deconstructive projects, and the potential for transformative projects.

Revisiting the subjective

For feminists, subjectivity, and the ways in which gendered identities are constructed through discourse, has been at the heart of much recent theoretical discussion (e.g. Bergvall *et al.*, 1996; Hall and Bucholtz, 1995; Johnson and Meinhof, 1997; Litosseliti and Sunderland, 2002; Talbot, 1998). As such, the issue of subjectivity should be of critical importance in any form of feminist post-structuralist discourse analysis. While post-structuralist theory does not recognise the category of 'woman' as fixed and unchanging, it is certainly not suggesting that individuals are merely the passive, unstable, fragmented products of competing discourses. Although 'the subject' in post-structuralism is always socially constructed *within* discourses, Weedon (1997) argues that s/he:

> nonetheless exists as a thinking, feeling subject and social agent, capable of resistance and innovations produced out of the clash between contradictory subject positions and practices.

In other words, feminist post-structuralism does not deny women's lived, embodied reality, nor their subjective experiences, since the ways in which individuals make sense of their lives is a necessary starting point for understanding the ways in which gendered discourses continue to structure social relations. Furthermore, feminist post-structuralism concurs with the social constructionist view that identities are continuously *performed*: that is, gender (for example) 'has constantly to be reaffirmed and publicly displayed by repeatedly performing particular acts in accordance with cultural norms...which define masculinity and femininity' (Cameron, 1997b: 49). Identities also have to be *co-constructed*: that is, evolve partially from a process of *affiliation* to particular beliefs and social groups, and partially from the *attributions* or ascriptions of others (Chouliaraki and Fairclough, 1999). However, it is in the conceptualisation of a woman's consciousness, agency or ability to act for herself that feminist post-structuralism differs from modernist and indeed social constructionist versions of feminism by centralising her subjectivity as a *site* contested in discourse. According to this conceptualisation, individuals neither conform to the liberal-humanist conception of the free individual in control of their destiny, nor to the binary notion of a co-constructed subject. Rather, they are positioned in a fluid, dynamic, contextual relation with competing constructs of identity. Constructs such as masculinity and femininity are continuously being contested by dominant social discourses, which vie with each other to fix the meaning of these constructs permanently. But, rather than viewing individuals as being at the mercy of these competing discourses, they can be seen as *multiply* positioned in terms of their agency to adapt to, negotiate or resist dominant subject positions or, alternatively, take up subject positions within a resistant discourse. Ransom (1993: 134) gives an example of how this works in practice by considering the contested site of women who are also mothers:

> discursive constructions of the perfect mother exist, but are challenged by competing feminist conceptions of what women can be or of the ways in which women can be mothers. Women's identity as mothers is contested; a woman can resist the traditional discourse of motherhood by refusing to be a mother, by setting up alternative parenting arrangements, by taking her children on 'reclaim the night' marches or doing an evening course in roofing.

Thus, feminist post-structuralist theory is concerned to identify the versions of subjective reality available to women, and the competing social and political interests which sustain these versions. It aims to describe and critique these different versions of femininity, as well as the multiple but not unlimited range of subject positions pertaining to each version. For individual women, it can offer an explanation of where our experiences have come from, why these are often contradictory or inconsistent, and why and how these can be changed. In other words, the social and historical constitution of the subject is not a limit on women's agency but a precondition for understanding the possibilities for action and change. In Ransom's (1993) words, 'it is because of, not in spite of, women's embeddedness in discursive practices that critical awareness of change is possible'.

Just as feminist post-structuralism critiques the view of woman as a fixed, unchanging category, so it must take issue with the notion of females as the universal *victims* of male oppression. As discussed earlier, Butler (1990), among others, has highlighted the issue of *difference* between women in criticising feminism for its failure to acknowledge the intersection of gender with race, class, ethnicity, age, sexuality and other currents of cultural identity, with the effect that many women fail to empathise with the movement. But it is not simply a matter of differences in the complex construction of identities. Francis (1999), while no fan of feminist post-structuralism, has pointed out that modernist feminism is no longer capable of describing the complexities of the experiences of numerous girls and women who, these days, are often successful both educationally and professionally. In the studies that follow (see Chapters 5 and 7), there are substantive examples of women/girls not only resisting positions of powerlessness but also actively taking up more powerful subject positions relative to men/boys. I shall be arguing, therefore, that theories of females as universal victims of patriarchy no longer *do*. The philosophy of feminist post-structuralism does not share the feminist quest to expose the gendered nature of society or the structural inequalities it produces. This is because feminist post-structuralism appreciates the unevenness and ambiguities of power relations between males and females. Women/girls are perceived to be *multiply* positioned as variously powerful or powerless within and across a range of competing discourses. However, this does not mean that feminist post-structuralism considers males and females to be equivalently positioned in terms of the ways in which power is negotiated through gender relations. Its focus is upon the *pervasiveness* of dominant discourses of gender differentiation which often interact with other discourses to 'fix' women/girls in positions of relative powerlessness, despite 'breakthrough' moments of *resistance* and empowerment. Feminist post-structuralism is thus concerned to equip feminist researchers with the thinking to 'see through' the ambiguities and confusions of particular discursive contexts where females are located as simultaneously powerful and powerless. For example, the classroom study in Chapter 5 shows that there appears to be a range of quite *powerful* subject positions available to girls in this classroom, yet, at the same time, a discourse of gender differentiation is constantly working to undermine the possibilities of such power. A feminist post-structuralist approach to discourse analysis can highlight and critique the contradictions and tensions that girls experience as subjects/speakers in the classroom. It can also fore-ground the ways in which girls take up (or can be encouraged to take up) subject/speaker positions which allow them to contest or resist more powerless ways of being.

The role of deconstructive projects

One of the major enterprises of feminist post-structuralist theory has been the deconstruction of female subjectivity and the analysis of the extent to which women's experiences of themselves as subjects may be constructed within discourses, practices and power relation-ships. Feminists have drawn, for example, on various forms of psycho-analytic theory to try to understand the ways in which 'femininity' and female subjectivity are constructed and shaped (e.g. Irigaray; 1985; Kristeva, 1984; Mitchell, 1974). More recently, this has developed into a parallel interest in male subjectivities and the construction of masculinities (e.g. Benwell, 2002; Johnson and Meinhof, 1997; Mac An Ghaill, 1994) in the light of educational issues such as 'boys and underachievement' in Britain (e.g. Baxter, 1999; Epstein *et al.*, 1998) and hegemonic fears of Western masculinity being in a state of crisis (e.g. Miller, 1996; Skelton, 1998).

Feminist post-structuralist theory is also concerned with decon-structing discourses of gender differentiation in general. Rather than viewing male dominance and female subordination as a universal phenomenon determining all aspects of women's lives, it considers that a dominant discourse of gender differentiation has, at different times and within different places, produced inequalities within gender relations. However, while gender differentiation is, to a large extent, historically accreted and geographically widespread, this discourse is not some kind of fixed, reified, monolithic entity, rather, it is a shape-shifter, taking a multiplicity of forms and guises, and always open to contestation, reconfiguration and redefinition. Deconstruction, as an analytical tool, can be used to identify, describe and explain the plural and diverse forms and practices of gender differentiation within different cultures, societies or communities. For example, discourses of gender differentiation undoubtedly produce widely contrasting subject positions, and different interpretations of inequality, for women within certain repressive, fundamentalist Muslim regimes (such as the Taliban in Afghanistan before 2002), to those of, say, white, British women working in the business world (see Chapters 6 and 7). Clearly, this is not only because discourses of gender differentiation vary from one cultural setting to another, but also because they do not act alone. Discourses are vying with equally powerful, competing discourses (linked with specific cultural practices such as religion or company ethos) to fix meanings within such contexts. Thus, deconstructionist methods contribute to feminist post-structuralist theory by helping to expose the distinctive features and practices of gender differentation within specific, localised contexts, and to reveal how such discourses simultaneously produce tensions between, and connections with, competing discourses in these contexts. In sum, a deconstructionist approach shows how discourses on gender never function alone to fix meaning within any single context but are always interacting with other discourses for control over the production of social meanings.

We noted earlier how the deconstructive tendencies of post-structuralist theory have been received as a mixed blessing by feminists. For example, Hartsock (1990) fears that post-structuralism's untimely quest to turn the deconstructionist spotlight upon feminism's own terms of reference may erode the movement's sometimes precarious sense of unity, voice and purpose. In response to this, Sawaki (1991) makes a robust case to argue that a Foucauldian approach in particular can offer a useful alternative to feminist analyses which adopt over-monolithic notions of male power and male control of women, or which retain utopian visions of attaining female autonomy. She suggests that feminists have at times been blind to their own dominating and oppressive tendencies, and that it is necessary to be aware of this for two reasons. First, women themselves are implicated in many forms of oppression of others, for example white women on southern USA slave plantations in the 1800s, or highly paid business women whose success may be partly dependent upon the exploitation of low-paid male and female workers. Secondly, feminist thinking and practice have at times been guilty of their own divisive and exclusionary tendencies and it is for this reason that the examination of feminist epistemological assumptions is necessary. For example, certain forms of feminist theory have unthinkingly used the concept of 'woman' in a way that generalises, stereotypes and elides differences between individual women. Furthermore, these feminist theorists' very use of such sex-differentiated categories have effectively 'bought into' the male establishment's practice of dichotomising the sexes that has simply perpetuated notions of gender difference, separation and therefore inequality. Also, the feminist tendency to promote female autonomy as an ideal can be seen as suspect, because, according to Butler (1990: 326), it echoes hegemonic constructs where being an autonomous subject is a masculine cultural prerogative from which women have already been excluded. In addition, the construct of the autonomous female may discriminate against certain women in that it sets a 'sheep and goats' standard by which to honour those who apparently achieve autonomy, and to patronise, help or pity those who are deemed not to be 'whole women'.

The post-structuralist recognition that feminism is itself riven with power relations, coupled with the argument that feminism needs to be self-reflexive in regulating its own theory and practices, should not, in my view, be perceived as problematic, dubious or indeed a 'pessimistic' insight (Cain, 1993). Rather, it is to suggest that all forms of knowledge, in their passion to convince, are accompanied by the evangelical tendency to marginalise, silence and exclude. The deconstructive project merely reminds theorists to be more self-aware of the limitations of their particular perspective and to explore the possibilities of self-subversion and the inclusion of more than one perspective within their work.

A transformative project?

An overall aim of this book is to argue that the post-structuralist perspective does have a strong contribution to make to all forms of feminist research. It will challenge the idea that the transformative suppositions of feminism and the deconstructive elements of post-structuralism should be regarded as in any way a contradiction in terms. Alternatively, I am arguing that a feminist post-structuralist stance is able to substantiate a theoretically and politically confident feminism.

Theorists (e.g. Davies, 1997; Francis, 1999; Jones, 1993, 1997; Wetherell, 1998) have debated whether post-structuralism can ever be compatible with a transformative project like feminism, because any such project represents 'a will to power'. While it is certainly the case that post-structuralism can*not* support universalising causes such as the emancipation of all women – even supposing this is still actually necessary – this does not mean that it should conform to the popular, nihilistic stereotype that 'anything goes'. This is because post-structuralism has never claimed to be value-free. Rather, it *is* associated with a loose collection of insights that makes it identifiably yet self-reflexively a theoretical discourse in its own right. For example, it has an interest in connection, recognition, flexibility, richness, diversity, action and transformation, as long as these insights on the production of order and meaning never amount to a grand narrative. Post-structuralist inquiry *can* support reconstructive projects articulating visions of the future, provided that at least two conditions pertain. First, there should be a constant vigilance and readiness to deconstruct a new cause. In other words, feminist theorists must recognise that within any new modes of resistance and self-understanding, or within any intention to transform social relations, there is the danger of reinstating aspects of that 'Other' against which they are struggling. Secondly, theorists should be constantly on guard and self-reflexive about their stated values within different research contexts. It is on this 'deconstructive' basis, I would argue, that feminist post-structuralist inquiry – with its particular interest in the oppressive workings of discourses of gender differentiation – *can* support social transformations because these are implicated in the important task of challenging and eroding grand narratives. Indeed, Foucault (1984: 46) does theorise the possibility of transformative projects within a post-modernist framework, although not consistently and adequately enough to satisfy many feminist theorists (e.g. Francis, 1999; Ransom, 1993; Soper, 1993b). Nevertheless, he does not dispute the importance of transformative social projects such as feminism, as long as these do not claim to be global or radical in the following sense:

> I prefer the very specific transformations that have proved possible in the last twenty years in a certain number of areas that concern our ways of being and thinking; relations to authority, relations between the sexes, the way in which we perceive insanity or illness; I prefer even these partial transformations that have been in the correlation of historical analysis and the practical attitude to the programs for a new man (sic) that the worst political systems have repeated through the twentieth century.

Drawing on the work of Bakhtin (1981), Derrida (1987) and Foucault (1980), I propose that post-structuralist inquiry may indeed support feminist projects with an intent to liberate subjugated groups as long as these aim to promote the free play of multiple voices within diverse contexts. This means that the voices of *minority* or *oppressed* groups need to be heard clearly alongside those of more dominant groups, adding to, undercutting and potentially overturning the status quo. The problem with mainstream discourses is that they seek univocally to silence, displace and suppress the interplay of alternative or oppositional voices. A dominant discourse serves to inhibit and foreclose the possibilities for an interplay of multiple-voices, perspectives and narratives representing the interests and values of diverse groups. This is not just the usual post-structuralist jargon: there is a real message. The post-structuralist 'quest', and I use that word advisedly, is to create spaces to allow the voices of relatively silenced groups such as certain categories of women (or indeed the disabled, the gay community, ethnic minority groups) to be heard with ringing clarity.

A common response to post-structuralist philosophy of this kind runs along the lines of, 'Because post-structuralism cannot be judgemental about *which* minority groups should have their voices heard in the public arena, does it not give a voice to extremist groups (e.g. of a fascist, violent or racist persuasion) who would not normally be tolerated within democratic societies?' The answer to this is quite simple: such groups are rarely concerned with voicing their own views *alongside* those of others; they are driven by a totalising mission to *become* the dominant discourse – to dismantle and overturn other voices, knowledges, discourses and social structures, supplanting them with their own. A much more ambiguous case perhaps can be illustrated by an example I heard recently in the news. A group of anorexic women, who communicate with each other via their own internet website, were arguing that they should have the 'right' to starve themselves to death if they so chose. While such a viewpoint was presented by the news report as 'unhealthy', deviant and a contravention of the common-sense discourse that 'mentally sick people/neurotic women must be helped to get better, by force if necessary', a feminist, post-structuralist perspective would argue that this marginalised group should be, at the very least, allowed the space to make their case alongside and in opposition to other voices. This does not mean that each perspective is equally valid, but each has a point of view and should be interrogated from a stance which accepts that no perspective is producing disinterested knowledge, and each represents particular positions within power relations (Usher, 1996). It is only by welcoming a plurality of opinions on emotive issues such as this that greater recognition, understanding, tolerance, connection and co-existence can be achieved between apparently conflicting viewpoints, interests and experiences.

The notion of 'voice' is particularly associated with Bakhtin's (1981) views on *polyphony*, which call attention to the co-existence in any discursive context of a plurality of voices that do not fuse into a single consciousness but rather, exist in different registers, generating a 'dialogic' dynamism among themselves. Bakhtin's concept of polyphony is supplemented by that of *heteroglossia*, with its support for non-official viewpoints, those of the marginalised, the oppressed and the peripheralised. Bakhtin's views are therefore very much in tune with the feminist liberatory quest both to deconstruct social injustices that permeate gender discourses, as well as to reconstruct spaces in which silenced women can speak. All these concepts are defined and explored more fully as part of the FPDA methodology in Chapter 3.

Foucault offers an alternative perspective on transformative projects which is not expressed in the personalised terms of 'voices', but rather in terms of bringing to light repressed or subjugated *knowledges*. However, there is an interconnected point. He is concerned that certain types of knowledge need to be made more visible by research communities. On the one hand, Foucault refers to 'blocks of historical knowledge which were present but disguised' in academic discourse (1980: 81–2), and on the other hand, 'a whole set of knowledges which have been disqualified as inadequate to their task or insufficiently elaborated' or even 'directly disqualified'. Foucault gives an example of the subjugated knowledge of the psychiatric patient as an example, but there are many equivalent examples within feminist inquiry, for example, the knowledge generated by women artists, writers and musicians from previous ages whose work has been repressed or lost. Foucault (1980: 83–4) suggests that if researchers can bring these localised and popular knowledges to light on behalf of suppressed groups, it allows these groups to engage with power more effectively because at least their knowledge has been named and is therefore rendered more publicly visible. His advocacy of a 'geneological' approach to research, that is, a critical tracing of the descent or 'archaeology' of different discourses, is in order to:

> entertain the claims to attention of local, discontinuous, disqualified, illegitimate knowledges against the claims of a unitary body of theory which would filter, hierarchise

and order them in the name of some true knowledge . . . it is really against the effects of the power of a discourse that is considered to be scientific that geneology must wage its struggle.

From a feminist perspective, it is in line with this kind of transformation that the realist feminist Cain (1993: 90) argues that scholars need to recognise the existence of the 'unformulated experience' among subjugated peoples. She suggests that it is not just that already formed discourses are politically repressed, but also that the play of relations of domination and subordination means that some experiences do not as yet have a voice at all. On the basis of her belief in a 'pre-discursive reality', which opens a door for the possibility of a profoundly female experience within a material world, Cain argues that feminist post-structuralist inquiry should do a 'midwiving job in relation to an emergent discourse'. It should have a mission to reveal the unthought relations and unformulated experiences of 'vulnerable and subjugated people for whose concerns Foucault so passionately wished to create a space for legitimacy' (1993: 84).

From a post-structuralist perspective, I would question Cain's dependence upon a pre-discursive reality in order to press her case for the need to bring emergent discourses to light, in that these must always be constructed intertextually from other discourses at whatever point they emerge into individual or collective consciousness. However, I would go along with Cain's view that feminist inquiry should take an interest in 'discourses in the making'. I have already argued how important it is to promote an understanding of the complex and often ambiguous ways in which women/girls are simultaneously positioned as relatively *powerless* within a range of dominant discourses on gender, but as relatively *powerful* within alternative and competing social discourses. It is in the awareness of the potential for expression and self-empowerment, contained in the spaces *between* conflicting discourses and in the temporary moments of powerfulness *within* discourses, that the opportunities for resistance and transformation lie. In other words, oppressed groups are not permanently trapped into silence, victimhood or knee-jerk refusal by dominant discursive practices; rather, there are moments within discourse in which to convert acts of resistance into previously unheard, but nonetheless intertextualised forms of 'new' expression. Feminist post-structuralist research is not, therefore, just about deconstructive critique, although this should always be part of any transformative project. It must also have a libertarian impulse to release the words of marginalised or minority voices in order to achieve the richness and diversity of textual play that only emerges from the expression of different and competing points of view. In Sawaki's (1991: 44) words:

> Freedom lies in our capacity to discover the historical links between certain modes of self-understanding and modes of domination, and to resist the ways in which we have already been classified and identified by dominant discourses. This means discovering new ways of understanding ourselves and one another, refusing to accept the dominant culture's characterisations of our practices and desires, and redefining them from within resistant cultures.

Here, feminist post-structuralist discourse analysis has a range of specific functions to perform, apart from traditional deconstruction, in its quest to locate and analyse gendered discourse where alternative or oppositional voices may be struggling to be heard. It must be prepared not only to 'press-release' the words of silent groups, but also to advertise and market them in a world saturated by information and with a short attention span. Modernist feminist inquiry has often been constituted by such features as the search for order, hierarchy, bipolarisation, a single, clear vision and planned purposefulness. In contrast, FPDA projects are likely to be more ephemeral, flexible, open-minded, heteroglossic, functional, active and media-orientated. Such projects are more concerned to help *release* the tentative, emergent nature of alternative voices and discourses rather than to supplant a dominant discourse with their own.

In summary, a feminist post-structuralist approach to discourse analysis is a workable partnership if both theoretical traditions are prepared to open themselves to critical self-questioning and supplement their standpoints with alternative or oppositional insights. In post-modernist spirit, I would argue that this complexity should be embraced for its richness of textual play, not disparaged for its lack of univocality. Of course there are theoretical dissonances between modernist feminism and post-structuralist inquiry, but there are also spaces for mutual connection and transformation. As I have mentioned, these points of connection are also apparent in the social constructionist approach to feminist research, also known as 'third wave' feminism. Such versions of feminism have generally embraced the view that women/girls can no longer be appropriately cast as universal victims but should be reconstituted as potentially powerful in terms of their multiple positioning within different discourses. What a specifically *post-structuralist* approach offers feminism, with its emphasis upon specific and localised forms of transformative action, is a politically and theoretically confident approach to all forms of research inquiry. In the following chapters, I shall discuss more fully what feminist post-structuralism has to offer discourse analysis.

2
FPDA – A Supplementary Form of Discourse Analysis?

Introduction

> Post-structuralist theorists, with their more global view, rarely have their noses pressed up against the exigencies of talk-in-interaction. Rarely are they called on to explain how their perspective might apply to what is happening right now, on the ground in this very conversation.

> (Wetherell, 1998: 395)

In this and following chapters, I intend to connect the principles of feminist post-structuralism to the field of discourse analysis in order to explore what constitutes FPDA. In this chapter, I shall consider the relationship of FPDA with two more widely recognised approaches to spoken discourse analysis, conversation analysis (CA) and critical discourse analysis (CDA). Clearly, I recognise that proponents of CA and CDA, such as those mentioned in this chapter, would not necessarily wish to label or limit themselves to one specific 'school' of analysis, or characterise these paradigms as internally unified or mutually exclusive. In addition, there are many other varieties of discourse analysis, such as pragmatics, the ethnography of speaking and interactional sociolinguistics (see Cameron, 2001, for an overview), each with their own distinctive contributions to the field. I have selected CA and CDA for comparative focus for two reasons. First, it seems to be the case that CA and CDA are gaining increasing popularity as approaches chosen for conducting discourse analysis, notably in the field of language and gender. Secondly, there are a number of ways in which I consider the FPDA approach to be intertextually linked with, and *supplementary* to, the methodologies of CA and CDA. The term 'supplementarity' (Derrida, 1976: 27–73) is used periodically within this chapter to convey the built-in dependencies and oppositions of any one theoretical paradigm with any other. In other words, each theoretical approach should be seen as both necessary to and yet simultaneously threatening to the identities of the others. Thus, having observed that FPDA has clear connections with CA and CDA, I shall also be suggesting that it offers the discourse analyst a distinctively *different* epistemological framework, and hence an alternative set of methodological strategies.

My observations about exactly which principles constitute an FPDA approach, and the extent to which FPDA is dependent upon, or contrasts with, CA and CDA, will be drawn from two sources. First, I shall be referring to several prototypical examples from the work of discourse analysts who have drawn upon a broadly feminist poststructuralist approach (e.g. Bergvall, 1998; Davies and Banks, 1992; Francis, 1998; Simpson, 1997; Walkerdine, 1990; Wetherell, 1998). Secondly, I shall be proposing principles and strategies that have evolved in the course of conducting my own research, later demonstrated in the classroom study (Chapters 4 and 5) and in the management team study (Chapters 6 and 7).

While FPDA is emerging in fields such as feminist studies and educational research as an analytical tool with which to investigate and evaluate 'real' samples of text and talk in context, it seems that it is still relatively underused within the broader field of linguistics. The gladiatorial contest in the journal *Discourse & Society* between the two prize fighters of discourse analysis, Schegloff (1999) in the blue corner representing CA, and the discursive psychologist, Billig (1999) in the red representing CDA, revealed this much. Little room is being allocated in the epistemological arena for *alternative* perspectives on discourse analysis, such as feminist post-structuralism, despite its use in other fields.

It is not the primary intention of this chapter to enter into the specificity of the CA/CDA debate, although my aim to situate my case for FPDA between the layers of this ongoing discussion must necessarily include all three perspectives in 'a community of relevance' (Schegloff, 1999: 579). Rather, in the spirit of supplementarity, which argues that no voice should be suppressed, displaced or privileged over another, I shall set my own perspective *alongside* those of other analysts. In so doing, I shall necessarily contest the use of modernist, adversarial rhetoric that has to prove that one method of discourse analysis is 'better' than the others. Rather it will posit from an FPDA perspective that there is room in the epistemological arena for an interplay between multiple perspectives and accounts of discursive practice, which only come into being when each is heard alongside the others.

As an immediate illustration of this principle, I should explain that an earlier version of this chapter exists in article form (Baxter, 2002b; West, 2002) which incorporated a discussion between myself and Candace West about whether or not FPDA offers an *alternative* form of discourse analysis to CA. I was not wholly comfortable with the journal's prescription for the format of this discussion, which had to be constituted as a debate between two opposing points of view. This debate had a tripartite structure: my discussion making a case; West's response to my case; and my reply to her response. The substance of West's reply was essentially cast in adversarial terms, compelling me to adopt a position of defence, if not defensiveness. In my reply, I almost certainly failed to resist taking up an equally oppositional subject position, although the truth of the matter is that I learnt a great deal from West's deconstruction of my argument. This chapter therefore seeks more reflexively to offer a supplementary discussion of the relationship between FPDA and CA/CDA, having appreciated and assimilated West's comments and criticisms.

With this in mind, I shall argue that FPDA is not only a theoretically coherent paradigm in its own right, but also an effective tool for explaining 'what is happening right now, on the ground, in this very conversation'. As both Billig (1999) and Wetherell (1998) have argued, there are too many critical and (feminist) post-structuralist studies which pronounce on the nature of discourses without getting down to the business of what is actually uttered or written. This chapter will seek to argue that FPDA can and should offer a rigorous approach to micro-analysing 'the exigencies of talk-in-interaction'. Moreover, FPDA is a particularly illuminating means of describing, analysing and interpreting an aspect of spoken interaction perhaps overlooked by CA and CDA – the continuously fluctuating ways in which speakers, within any discursive context, are positioned as powerful or powerless by competing social and institutional discourses. Furthermore, it will discuss how FPDA is *not* concerned with the modernist quest of seeking closure or resolutions in its analysis of what discourse means, but rather with foregrounding the diverse viewpoints, contradictory voices and fragmented messages that research data almost always represents.

Links and differences between CA, CDA and FPDA

In this section, I discuss the ways in which FPDA can be perceived as an alternative and supplementary approach to those of CA and CDA. While FPDA is in many ways closer to CDA than CA, there are a number of evident links and differences between all three approaches, as I now discuss. In so doing, it is important once again to stress that both CA and CDA should not necessarily be perceived as internally unified paradigms, but interconnected with a range of different disciplines, purposes and methods. For example, while CA's systematic *methodology* is potentially utilisable by a range of disciplines and theoretical standpoints, CDA is essentially a theoretical *perspective* with a particular value to multi- and interdisciplinary studies. The aim here is to compare the three approaches in terms of higher order principles, namely: definitions of discourse; micro-analysis of discourse; self-reflexivity; text and context; an emancipatory paradigm; and multi-disciplinarity.

Definitions of discourse

While the term 'discourse' is used routinely but not unambiguously within CDA and FPDA, it is not conspicuously a part of the foundational rhetoric of CA. Where the term 'discourse' *is* used by conversation analysts, it is most likely to connote Cameron's (2001) category of 'language in use'. In her terms, this is an overt concern with what and how language communicates when it is used purposefully in particular instances and contexts, and how conversation is negotiated and co-constructed by its participants. More specifically, CA theorists have traditionally been involved with the detailed and systematic examination of short extracts of text or talk in order to identify the intricate patterning in the way these are organised.

For CDA and FPDA, the term 'discourse' reaches well beyond traditional linguistic notions of 'language above the sentence level' (see Introduction) or indeed 'language in use'. According to Foucault (1972: 49), this term is used in the plural sense to denote 'practices that systematically form the object of which they speak'. Thus, discourses are forms of 'knowledge' – powerful sets of assumptions, expectations, explanations – governing mainstream social and cultural practices. They are systematic ways of making sense of the world by determining *power relations* within all texts, including spoken interaction. Both CDA and FPDA view discourses as inextricably linked with concepts of power, not always as a negative, repressive force but very often as something that constitutes and energises all discursive and social relations.

However, within any field of knowledge, there is never just *one* discourse but always plural and competing discourses. Using ethnographic approaches, FPDA in particular specialises in the business of identifying the range of discourses at play within varying social contexts in order to ascertain the interwoven yet competing ways in which such discourses structure speakers' experiences of power relations.

Micro-analysis of discourse

Of the three approaches, CA is traditionally most associated with the micro-analysis of discourse, in other words, the commitment to analyse naturally occurring conversation, or 'talk-in-interaction', within a range of everyday settings. CA has traditionally tended to consider interactive talk (as opposed to monologic sequences, such as narratives) in a range of private, domestic or social settings. However, more recent work has also been conducted on talk in professional and workplace contexts (Drew and Heritage, 1992); media settings (e.g. Hutchby, 1996) and political speeches (Shaw, 2000). CA has been concerned to examine talk that is prototypically a joint enterprise involving more than one person, and involves a rule-governed sequence of conversational turns. Indeed, it is this feature of talk-in-interaction, known alternately as 'a simplest systematics for the organisation of turn-taking for conversation' or as 'the speech exchange system' (Sacks *et al.*, 1974), which has been the focus of much work by conversation analysts.

In fact, CDA and FPDA also have a keen interest in the micro-analysis of text or talk. In contrast to CA, however, CDA has until recently tended to opt for the bigger picture, preferring to conduct larger scale social analyses and critiques of discourses in public or institutional settings. Where CDA *has* adopted the methods of textual micro-analysis, it has tended to focus rather *less* on everyday, interactive talk and rather *more* upon formal, monologic talk (such as political speeches, TV or radio news announcements) or the written word (such as newspaper reports, features, editorials). The fact that CDA analysts are now increasingly working with samples of 'real' talk-in-interaction (e.g. Wodak, 2002) is a self-confessed admission to the charge by conversation analysts that they 'rarely get down to the business of studying what is actually uttered or written' (Billig, 1999: 544).

Despite Wetherell's (1998) concern that post-structuralist analysts, like CDA theorists, 'rarely have their noses pressed up against the exigencies of talk-in-interaction', there are a number of prototypical approaches to FPDA which do get to grips with the micro-analysis of discourse. The four examples that follow all show the ways in which speakers are multiply positioned by competing discourses within any single context, sometimes as relatively powerful, and at other times as relatively powerless. In the first, often quoted example, Valerie Walkerdine (1990: 4–5) makes a detailed analysis of class-room interaction involving a female nursery schoolteacher and two four-year-old boys. She aims to show how the teacher is constituted simultaneously as both powerful as an authority figure, and powerless or disempowered as a woman/sex object, within just a few moments of conversation:

SEAN: Miss Baxter, knickers, show your knickers.

TERRY: Miss Baxter, show your bum off.

(They giggle.)

MISS BAXTER: I think you are both being very silly.

Here, Walkerdine argues from a feminist stance that the teacher has been 'made to signify as the powerless object of male sexual discourse'. Yet, from the greater complexity of a post-structuralist stance, she suggests that the two boys cannot 'simply' be conceptualised as powerless children oppressed by the authority of the teacher, who in turn represents 'the bourgeois educational institution'. Nor can they simply be understood as 'the perpetrators of patriarchal social relations'. In short, these boys have the potential to be produced as subjects in *both* discourses, as simultaneously powerful and powerless.

In the second example, Alyson Simpson (1997: 215) uses 'close linguistic analysis' to show the competing positions taken up by a six-year-old girl (Heather) within a 'family drama' while they are taking part in a board game. She shows, through detailed analysis of the 'dynamics of the negotiation for control' on the dual levels of family relationships and game-playing, that there are continuous *shifts* in the negotiation for power. What is at stake, Simpson argues, is the construction of Heather's subjectivity which is in ceaseless process during the course of the game. Furthermore, Simpson foregrounds *gender* as a cause of feminist concern within this site of competing discourses:

> For Heather, her positioning within the game conflicts with her positioning within the family. She does not have the power to challenge the rules of the game successfully so she chooses to abide by their restrictions. She could resist the gendered construction of her as 'good girl' but she chooses not to . . . It bothers me that she agrees to let [her father] win, positioning herself as 'a good girl'.

In the third example, the social psychologist Margaret Wetherell (1998: 395) argues that both CDA and post-structuralist approaches would do well to 'explain how their perspective might apply to what is happening right now, on the ground, in this very conversation'. She makes the case for a 'synthetic approach' to discourse analysis, which draws upon the combined strengths of CA's interest in the highly situated and occasioned nature of participants' orientations within spoken interaction, and CDA/post-structuralism's more 'sociopolitical' concerns with the assignment of subject positioning through discourse. Wetherell's detailed analysis of a group discussion between three young men also highlights gendered issues but, unlike the work of Walkerdine (1990) and Simpson (1997), does not select a feminist focus for specific analysis. Rather, it fulfils the post-structuralist quest to track:

> the emergence of different and often contradictory or inconsistent versions of people, their characters, motives, states of mind and events in the world – and asking why this (different) formulation at this point in the strip of talk?

While there is certainly a merit in her challenging of theoretical boundaries, I am somewhat at odds with her modernist construction of post-structuralist discourse analysis as something akin to 'social learning' or 'sex role' theory. For Wetherell, subjects have a 'portfolio of positions' at their disposal, which 'remain available to be carried forward to the other contexts and conversations making up the 'long conversation'. These positions may be variously 'troubled' or 'untroubled' by the flow of routine interaction. While there is much to be learnt from her detailed analysis, what is marginalised yet central to post-structuralist inquiry is a conceptualisation of the ways in which shifting power relations between speakers are constantly negotiated through the medium of competing discourses. I would argue that there are essentialist or at least volunteerist implications in the view that speakers have a 'portfolio' of subject positions, troubled or untroubled: namely, that speakers are able to *choose* which subject positions they might adopt or carry forward like acting roles to future conversations. The FPDA perspective would argue alternatively that speakers are able to take up, accommodate or resist relatively powerful or powerless subject positions made available within competing discourses at work within any given moment. The value of a detailed micro-analysis of spoken discourse for the FPDA theorist is that it can fulfil this quest to fore-ground and pinpoint the *moment* (or series of moments) when speakers negotiate their shifting subject positions.

In the final example, Victoria Bergvall (1998) demonstrates, again through close examination of spoken discourse, the complexities and ambiguities of experience for female engineering students in a tradition-ally masculine domain. She argues that women as a minority group in this community of practice are unable to conform to rigid notions of dichotomous gender. They must struggle continuously between multiple gender positions, some relatively empowering and others less so, in order to gain recognition and acceptance from their male colleagues. However, such complex struggles over gender identity are unlikely, in her view, to empower women in the long run, working to limit their success in pursuing an education and a career. The analysis takes the form of detailed attention to the ways in which female speakers co-construct varying identities for themselves according to context. Her methodology prefigures an FPDA approach, but does not demonstrate how subjects constantly *shift* between different positions of power, or different forms of identity, within a given moment or context. In her concluding comments, Bergvall (1998: 194) indicates the need for a form of analysis that is specifically equipped to explore the complexities of constructing and enacting multiple gender positions through discourse. This begins to sound like FPDA:

we need a theory of gender and language that is neither binary nor polarising, but situated and flexible, grounded in research that is based not only on the careful examination of discrete linguistic structures, but also on the social settings in which such structures are embedded.

Self-reflexivity

All three approaches – FPDA, CA and CDA – have in common the conceptual awareness that they are *self-reflexive* about their development as 'knowledges'. In other words, they all challenge the assumption in positivist research that there is an independent, knowable world unrelated to human perception and social practices. All three recognise that social realities are socially (CA) if not discursively (CDA and FPDA) produced. Indeed, as West (2002) points out, CA might be seen as a forerunner in this respect. Back in 1967, the ethnomethodologist Harold Garfinkel demonstrated the 'essential' reflexivity of people's descriptions, including scientific descriptions of practical actions. In so doing, he showed that 'the social constitution of knowledge cannot be analysed independently of the contexts of institutional activity in which it is generated and maintained' (Heritage, 1984: 6). Thus for CA, a raised awareness of the ways in which speakers construct their social world by means of the 'internally grounded reality' of their talk-in-interaction challenges positivist assumptions about an externally verifiable reality as the basis for evidence.

CDA has taken a different direction from CA in its quest to challenge positivist research assumptions that research should necessarily be ideologically neutral in order to represent reality as 'the truth'. In its upfront declaration of its political mission to eschew a spurious objectivity and instead 'choose the perspective of those who suffer most' (van Dijk, 1986: 4), CDA is explicitly self-referential about its value systems. Furthermore, CDA generally flags up and is prepared to meta-analyse its own use of a specialist rhetoric. Likewise FPDA, in post-structuralist spirit, must also draw attention to the constructedness of its own conceptual framework and 'foundational rhetoric' in relation to the subject of study. But in line with feminist ethnography (e.g. Skeggs, 1994), FPDA takes the principle of self-reflexivity one step further by likening the textualising process of research and discourse analysis to a literary form. In other words, the business of text-making will constitute the analyst as almost literally an author, with a certain control (and therefore, ethical responsibility) over his or her work of fiction. However, this 'control' is undercut by the limited number of subject positions made available to researchers according to the range of available discourses determining authorial practices. FPDA practitioners are therefore expected to use 'writerly' (Barthes, 1977) strategies to draw attention to textual constructions as authorising practices by meta-analysing their own role in selecting and orchestrating their subject matter.

Text and context

Bergvall's (1998: 194) comment that discourse analysis should be directed at 'the social settings in which such structures are embedded' highlights the interest of all three approaches in the interrelationship between text and context. Both CA and CDA, for example, accept the fundamentally contextual view of text and talk as being structured under the constraints of the social situation. However, CA, CDA and FPDA all construe the context dependency of discourse in quite contrasting ways.

Conversation Analysis, grounded in ethnomethodological principles, is renowned for its disinterest in the question of external social or natural causes and its 'rejection of the side-step which takes the analyst immediately from the conversation to something seen as real and determining behind the conversation' (Garfinkel, 1967; Wetherell, 1998: 391). Indeed, traditional conversation analysts consider it not just unnecessary but illegitimate to make use of information that the participants themselves have not chosen to 'make relevant' within the course of talk-in-interaction. Schegloff (1997: 166–7) suggests that the main object of CA's investigation is always the 'endogenous constitution' of the conversation sequence itself and what this, and this alone, reveals about the participants:

> ... because it is the orientations, meanings, interpretations, understandings etc. of the participants in some socio-cultural event on which the course of that event is predicated – and especially if is constructed interactionally over time, it is those characterisations which are privileged in the constitution of socio-interactional reality, and therefore have a prima facie claim to being privileged in efforts to understand it.

In other words, contextual categories (such as power or gender) are never *postulated* a priori in order to understand or explain the data until the participants in the conversation sequence *make* them relevant, either in what they say or do. Moreover, Schegloff (1997: 166) claims that the internally grounded 'reality' of talk-in-interaction, made visible by utilising the methodology of the speech exchange system, offers discourse analysts a point of 'Archimedean leverage'. By this he means an indisputable reference point, an objective truth about discourse that provides a vital bulwark against the 'theoretical imperialism' of CDA or the infinite regress of post-structuralist complexity.

This perspective – that text defines context – is avowedly in direct opposition to CDA's mission to bring a 'critical' perspective upon the analysis of text or talk or, in van Dijk's (2001: 96) words, to conduct discourse analysis 'with an attitude'. Like its close associate, critical linguistics (e.g. Hodge and Kress, 1993; Wodak, 1989), CDA has always had an explicitly committed political agenda:

> It focuses on social problems, and especially on the role of discourse in the production and reproduction of power abuse or domination. Wherever possible, it does so from a perspective that is consistent with the best interests of dominated groups. It takes the experiences and opinions of such groups seriously, and supports their struggle against inequality.

Thus, in CDA, the particular concerns relating to an ideologically sensitive context – whether it be the representation of race in mainstream sources such as press reports (van Dijk, 1986) or policies of gender mainstreaming in the European Union (Wodak, 2002) – are brought to bear upon an analysis of the data. But this act of critical discourse analysis is always done in a spirit of self-reflexivity, which makes presuppositions about time, space and setting explicit.

For FPDA, the interrelationship of text and context are conceptualised in terms of the operations of competing discourses. Both CDA and FPDA are interested in the workings of *power* through discourse, although they conceptualise this rather differently. CDA assumes discourse to work 'dialectically' (e.g. Fairclough and Wodak, 1997) in so far as the discursive act – text or talk – is shaped by, and thereby continuously reconstructs, 'real' or material events, situations, institutions and social structures. In contrast, FPDA adopts an anti-materialist stance in its view that discourses operate as 'practices that systematically form the objects of which they speak' (Foucault, 1972: 49). In other words, social 'realities' are always discursively produced, so that, for example, text or talk is being continuously reconstructed and open to redefinition *through* discourse, not outside it. According to the post-structuralist view, therefore, distinctions between text and context are collapsed in favour of the concept of intertextuality, that is, the ways in which texts are always infused and inscribed with traces of other texts.

An emancipatory paradigm?

Which of the three approaches operates within an emancipatory paradigm? The obvious answer appears to be CDA, although not without qualification in the case of each approach. I have discussed how CDA places an explicit emphasis upon emancipatory social theory on behalf of dominated and oppressed groups (Fairclough and Wodak, 1997). This is in clear contrast to FPDA which expresses a loss of certainty about the existence of absolutes, or the benevolence or truth of any single paradigm or knowledge. In Foucault's memorable terms, any theory or research paradigm, by virtue of its emancipatory desire to be 'right', contains a 'will to power' and therefore a 'will to truth'. An emancipatory discourse, as it becomes established as mainstream, would in time become a 'totalising' or imperialist one, marginalising and silencing the voices of other theorists or researchers.

While CDA supports an emancipatory critical perspective, it is nonetheless alert to the possible dangers of its own critical orthodoxy, a point alluded to in a *Discourse & Society* editorial by Billig (2000: 292), who mused that 'the growth of respectability [for CDA] entails the loss of critique as an intellectual activity. Perhaps there is a need for continual intellectual revolution.' This self-reflexive deconstruction of one's own emancipatory position would be entirely in keeping with the FPDA paradigm. Indeed, FPDA has no quarrel with CDA's engaged and committed approach to research theory, provided that it is openly declared and made explicit at all stages of data analysis and interpretation.

It is this failure to declare its own ideological agenda that sets CA apart from CDA and FPDA. On the surface, it might appear that CA has something in common with FPDA in its ethnomethodological mission to eschew an emancipatory agenda. In CA's case, this 'eschewing' is conducted in the interests of 'sociological neutrality' in order to encourage a more egalitarian enterprise to emerge 'naturally' from the data. However, both CDA and FPDA openly recognise this declared act of 'naïve methodological and epistemological naivety' (Schegloff, 1997: 171) to be just that – naive. In his exchange with Schegloff, Billig (1999: 546) drew attention to the ways in which conversation analysts attempted to naturalise their 'foundational rhetoric' in the form of technical terms that describe 'objective' realities in an unproblematic way. He has argued that conversation analysts fail to recognise that there is an 'epistemological or rhetorical difficulty with the ways that CA translates the words of those it studies into its own technical vocabulary'. This, Billig suggests, is the paradox at the core of CA, which on one hand purports to study 'participants in their own terms', yet on the other uses highly technical terms to accomplish this analysis of speakers' own terms. Billig points out that these speakers do not themselves talk about 'adjacency pairs', 'preference structures', 'WH-questions' and so on, a specialist vocabulary to which discourse analysts would need a formalised initiation. It is this lack of self-reflexivity, this failure to acknowledge the sociological and ideological assumptions contained within any research process, this postulation of an 'Archimedean leverage' within texts which clearly distinguishes CA from CDA and FPDA.

For FPDA, does 'truth disappear in a hall of perspectival mirrors' as Schegloff (1997: 166) has suggested about post-structuralist theory? It is certainly the case that FPDA cannot have an emancipatory agenda in the sense that it espouses a grand narrative that becomes its own dominant discourse. Conversely, it must be continuously on guard, openly self-reflexive of its own agendas, values and assumptions. This does not mean, however, that feminist post-structuralist inquiry cannot support small-scale, bottom-up social transformations, which are indeed of central importance in the erosion of grand narratives. As discussed in Chapter 1, FPDA has an interest in the free play of multiple-voices within a discursive context, which means that the voices of silenced, minority or oppressed groups *need* to be heard. As FPDA has an explicitly feminist focus, it has a role to perform in locating, observing, recording and analysing localised, discursive contexts where silenced or marginalised female voices may be struggling to be heard.

FPDA provides new possibilities not only for understanding how language constructs subject identities and for learning how speech is produced, negotiated and contested within specific social contexts, but also for making sense of the relative powerlessness or 'disadvantage' experienced by silenced groups of girls or women. FPDA does have links and parallels with the approaches of both CA and CDA, but it ultimately produces more complex and possibly more troubling insights into the possibilities for transforming social practices, as I shall now explain.

Where I would suggest that FPDA differs from CDA in particular is in its more complex perception of the ambiguities and unevenness of power. While CDA is more likely to polarise the argument casting males as villains and females as victims, FPDA is more likely to argue that females are multiply located and cannot be so dichotomously cast as powerless, disadvantaged or victims. FPDA accepts that girls/women can and do adopt relatively powerful positions within certain discourses and also acknowledges their agency to resist, challenge and potentially overturn discursive practices that conventionally position them as powerless. In Jones's (1993: 164) call for more educational research to be conducted using a feminist, post-structuralist methodology, she suggests that:

> A discursive construction of women and girls as powerful, as producing our own sub-jectivities within and against the 'spaces' provided is useful in offering more possibilities to develop and use a wider range of practices.

The use of FPDA as an alternative methodology alongside those of CA and CDA also helps to challenge the inertia of 'linguistic ortho-doxies' (Billig, 2000: 292), by opening up possibilities for new forms of discourse analysis that 'expose the self-interest and political economy of the sign "critical"'.

Multi-disciplinarity

As well-established fields of discourse analysis, both CA and CDA incorporate a diverse range of approaches to examining text and talk. Apart from their use in all areas of linguistics, both approaches are conducted in and combined with other approaches and sub-disciplines, particularly within the humanities and social sciences.

While CA clearly has a distinct methodology, with its own agenda, conceptual framework and specialist terminology, nonetheless it has proved a useful and flexible analytical tool for researchers in a wide range of fields. Its capacity to be transferable to different disciplines or interdisciplinary contexts is precisely because of the focus it places on *methodology* – a systematic analysis of the mechanisms of turn-taking, rather than the conversational content. In support of its transferability to other fields, Schegloff (1999: 561, 563) has argued that, despite CA's claims to 'sociological neutrality', there is no reason why the approach should not be utilised by those researchers in pursuit of an 'ideological' agenda. In response to Billig's (1999) attack that a 'non-ideological CA' can hardly be deployed to tackle ideological matters such as the indictment of rape or wife-battering, Schegloff (1999: 563) asks:

> How else are we to understand their explosive emergence where they happen/if not by examining ordinary interaction with tools appropriate to it, and seeing how they can lead to such outcomes? ... those [researchers] committed to analysing forms of inequality and oppression in interaction might do better to harness [studies of talk-in-interaction] than to complain of it as an ideological distraction.

For CDA, on the other hand, a methodology is always implicated in the social situations it examines. Indeed, van Dijk (2001: 96) has argued that CDA is not a discrete methodology at all ('not a method, nor a theory that can be applied to social problems') but rather a *critical perspective* on social problems. It does not offer (like CA) a ready-made, how-to-do approach to social analysis. He has suggested that for each study a thorough theoretical analysis of the social issue must be made in order to select which discourse and which social structures to examine. This view, that CDA is a critical perspective rather than a methodology, has led proponents such as Wodak (2002) to argue that it has a particular value in multi- and interdisciplinary studies. This is predicated on the view that the growth of complex new problems in a multinational, globalised world requires more than one expertise. According to Wodak, CDA offers a common perspective that can be utilised by 'critical' analysts in an interdisciplinary way – a shared understanding that they must oppose individuals, groups or institutions who abuse text and talk in order to establish, confirm or legitimate their hegemony.

Where does FPDA pitch in to this debate? Until FPDA is better established as an approach to discourse analysis, it will be difficult to judge how useful it will be within and across a range of disciplines. However, its transformative quest – to represent the complexities and ambiguities of female experience, but within this to give space to female voices that are being silenced and peripheralised by masculinised discourses – must link it to a range of interdisciplinary concerns and contexts. Like CA, it offers principles for a systematic methodology, detailed in the next chapter. The two research studies described in this volume (Chapters 4–7) reveal the versatility of the FPDA approach in its application to two contrasting, institutional settings: the educational context of the classroom and the business context of the boardroom. It is one of the aims of this book to encourage discourse analysts to apply FPDA to a variety of settings where discourses interact with each other to construct unequal power relations within texts or talk, whether domestic, social, public or institutional.

3
Getting to Grips with FPDA

Within the post-structuralist spirit of encouraging interplay between different voices and perspectives, there should never just be *one* version of FPDA, but a whole variety of versions or approaches. Nevertheless, it is the objective of this book to give a clear sense of what constitutes the FPDA approach in order to establish some common ground as a basis for further discussion and developing future practice. In this chapter, I propose a broad set of guidelines for would-be FPDA practitioners, which are explored under the following three headings: principles of FPDA, sources of data and textual analysis.

Principles of FPDA

There are a number of principles constituting the practice of the discourse analyst, which clearly define the FPDA approach but nonetheless overlap with certain aspects of the methodologies associated with CA and CDA. These are: self-reflexivity, a deconstructionist approach and selecting a specific feminist focus.

Self-reflexivity

In Chapter 2, I discussed how different interpretations of the principle of self-reflexivity – or the need to be critical of our assumptions – form an important part of the research practice of CA, CDA and FPDA analysts. Here, I consider three roles for self-reflexivity within the specific context of FPDA research.

First of all, FPDA practitioners should aim to make their theoretical positions clear, and make explicit the epistemological assumptions that are to be applied to any act of discourse analysis. This is based on the way that both post-structuralist theory (Scott and Usher, 1996) and more recent feminist theory (e.g. Butler, 1990; Lather, 1991; Mills, 2002) have challenged the positivist view that there is a determinate world that can be definitively known and explained (Elliott, 1996; Foucault, 1980; Lyotard, 1984). In contrast, both feminist and post-structuralist theories argue that any interpretation of data must explicitly acknowledge that it is constructed, provisional, perspectival and context-driven. A post-structuralist feminism must therefore accept its own status as context-specific, the product of particular sets of discursive relations. It has no more claim to speak the truth than any other discourse but must own up to its own points of view, specific aims, desires and political positions within power relations. Yet, as I discussed in Chapter 1, post-structuralist theory argues that researchers should only temporarily associate themselves with a particular stance for fear that a 'will to truth' will convert into a 'will to power'. Certainly FPDA practitioners should take care not to engage more than temporarily with any single agenda, in order to encourage a wider and richer interplay of ideas and viewpoints in the discursive arena. This is not to say that FPDA practitioners cannot identify with a feminist perspective or take on a particular cause – quite the opposite. FPDA, in keeping with post-structuralist theory (e.g. Elliott, 1996), *does* have a transformative quest; to represent the complexities and ambiguities of *female* experience, and within this to give space to *female* voices that are being silenced or marginalised by dominant discourses. If and when this specific quest is achieved, FPDA should seek to overturn its own dominant discourse by looking to other 'silenced' issues within the field of gender and discourse or cease to function. This in a sense is its particular declared bias; this *is* its *raison d'être*. Self-reflexivity is the principle which governs the business of declaring, monitoring and evaluating the FPDA quest, or any other theoretical/epistemological position, while conducting discourse analysis.

Secondly, an approach to FPDA involves being self-reflexive about the deployment of a specialist technical vocabulary or 'foundational rhetoric' (Billig, 1999: 552). This means an explicit awareness that technical terms cannot describe 'objective' realities in an unproblematic way. Of course, post-structuralist theory has anyway collapsed the distinction between a material reality and a language that describes it, preferring to view language or discourses as 'practices that systematically form the object of which they speak' (Foucault, 1972: 49). From a post-structuralist viewpoint, a specialist rhetoric is always associated with a particular knowledge. As this knowledge becomes more defined, accepted and established, its specialist vocabulary becomes a 'technology' by which it can be transformed into a 'truth narrative'. For this reason, FPDA analysts need to be aware that its own 'foundational rhetoric' can operate as a form of arcane, scholastic discrimination, with the potential to exclude and marginalise uninitiated readers and researchers. Ironically but quite justifiably, post-structuralism has itself become a target for jokes and criticisms directed at the obfuscating nature of its jargon. For instance, McWilliam (1997: 201) has criticised what she calls the 'PMT' (post-modernist tension) of certain feminist post-structuralist writers. She cites Lather (1991) as an example of the kind of writer who argues for openness and self-reflexivity, yet seems quite obscure to other readers because of her use of highly verbose styles of writing. Thus, FPDA practitioners must be prepared to call attention to the assumptions and range of definitions implied in their use of key analytic terms. This is also important because all terms have the potential to be multi-accentual, to be read in plural if context-bound ways. This is why I have explained in the Introduction apparently quite obvious terms such as 'feminism', 'post-structuralism', 'discourse', 'power', all of which are open to a wide range of possible readings and interpretations. I would suggest that it is a legitimate authorial practice for FPDA practitioners to 'close down' the range of readings of terms in this way, provided they are self-reflexive in foregrounding the range of meanings that they are potentially invoking or excluding.

Thirdly, FPDA involves the need to be overtly self-aware of the fictionality and textuality of the research process and the phenomenon that any act of research comprises a series of authorial choices and strategies. According to the post-structuralist view, all pursuits of knowledge are to do with creating a world (Usher, 1996), and hence research is itself a discursive construct and constitutive or 'world-making'. Post-structuralism sees any act of knowledge generation, such as discourse analysis, as a 'textualising' practice in that no form of knowledge can be separated from the structures, conventions and conceptuality of language as inscribed within discourses and texts. The business of textualising will constitute the researcher as literally an 'author', with a certain control over their own work of fiction.

However, the researcher is in turn positioned by the limited range of scholastic discursive practices which legitimate particular ways of recording, analysing and interpreting discourse. Few researchers succeed if they work outside approved discursive practices, and this is a truism barely contested by the scholastic conventions adhered to in this book! However, one of the strengths of the FPDA approach is that it encourages researchers to use 'writerly' (Barthes, 1977) strategies in order to foreground the textualising process of conducting discourse analysis. In simpler terms, researchers need to draw attention to the *choices* they make in determining exactly how they are going to analyse texts, and then be prepared to justify or explain the effects of those choices. Arguably, the FPDA approach to self-reflexivity adds to and enriches other forms of analysis, such as CA and CDA, by the particular focus it places on the authorial role of the analyst and the 'fictionality' or constructed nature of all acts of research.

A deconstructionist approach

In this section, I describe what a deconstructionist approach to the analysis of discourse implies, with its special emphasis on *textual interplay*. Central to *both* a feminist *and* a post-structuralist analysis is the drive to question things, to deconstruct the constructions and structures around us, not in the nihilistic or relativist sense sometimes stereotypically associated with deconstructionism (e.g. Linstead, 1993; Norris, 1990), but in order to release the possibility of fresh juxtapositions and interplay among established and new ideas. This can then become the basis for new insights and small-scale transformative actions. A deconstructionist approach to discourse analysis might combine some or all of the following elements, which are explored more fully below:

- Acknowledgement that the factual is replaced by the representational: that is, that there is no out-there reality that requires sophisticated analytic tools to uncover and predict
- A recognition that the meaning of speech, concepts, people, relationships and so on, can never be fixed permanently, and is therefore endlessly deferred
- An understanding that process is primary to structure (that is, process produces structure, not the other way round)

- The quest against the privileging of something over another, for example, one voice over another (unless in the service of some immediate, localised or short-term cause)
- Avoidance of conceptual closure, or ultimately fixable frames of reference through the continual application of reflexivity, or the need to be critical of our intellectual assumptions
- The existence of a continual *textual interplay* or 'double movement' between concepts so that opposites merge in a constantly undecidable exchange of attributes
- An understanding of the necessary *supplementarity* of meanings in the relationship of opposite terms (for example the terms 'male' and 'female' should be seen as both separately necessary and yet simultaneously interconnecting with and challenging the identity of the other).

The principle of textual interplay derives from Derrida's deconstructive principle of *differance*. As I discussed in Chapter 1, Derrida (e.g. 1976, 1978, 1982) uses the special term *'differance'* to suggest, at the same time, the impossibility of closing off the differing aspects of meaning and the perpetual postponement or *deferral* of meaning. Derrida therefore sees 'differance' as a force of *continuous absence*; that is, where the meaning of something cannot be attained without a continuing recognition of the meaning it defers. He argues that the 'movement of differance' undermines our desire or need to achieve a coherent and singular meaning in a given concept. Hence, the greater the attempt to fix meaning permanently through, for example, the traditional research principles of reliability and validity, the greater the potential for 'slippage' as meaning can only ever be fixed temporarily, located as it is within different discursive contexts. Thus, the effect of any textual representation in which meaning is apparently fixed, such as a work of discourse analysis, is just a temporary and elusive retrospective fixing, always open to challenge and redefinition. In a broader context, the post-structuralist project has sought to challenge and upset all forms of research inquiry that attempts to *fix* meaning permanently as knowledge or, ultimately, as 'truth narratives'.

The hallmark of a deconstructionist analysis is to question the modernist assumption that language is organised in terms of oppositions, each term depending on and being supported by the other in order to signify or *mean*. Such terms of opposition (e.g. male/female;

public/private; subjective/objective) exist or are often treated by modernist analysts as though they exist in a hierarchy, a dualism, a relationship of power, with one term at any moment predominant over the other. However, the social philosopher Cooper (1989) has argued that one term in any pair of oppositions always inhabits and interpenetrates the other term, producing a *supplementarity* of both/ and, – or a kind of 'double movement' between the two. In most forms of research inquiry, modernism pursues the opposition of terms, placing one over or against the other, whereas post-structuralism resists the closure of terms, actively exploring the interconnection or 'supplementarity' of the one with the other.

Cooper (1989: 483) proposes two interrelated deconstructive 'movements' or (in my terms) strategies that might be usefully deployed by FPDA practitioners. The first is that of *overturning*, which focuses on the binary oppositions of terms (subject positions or discourses) and challenges the place of the suppressed term. This, I would suggest, is the approach used in CDA, according to its stated mission that terms associated with the 'oppressed' must be treated as superior to terms associated with the 'oppressor'. But simply centring the marginal and marginalising the central remains an oppositional strategy and itself creates another hierarchy which in turn requires overturning. The hallmark of deconstruction is the second strategy: that of *metaphorisation*, which attempts to go beyond hierarchies of oppositions and sustain the perpetual double movement within the opposition. Metaphorisation recognises that the positively valued term is defined only by contrast with the negatively valued term, and that each inhabit, co-exist and co-evolve with the other. A deconstructionist approach would advocate the need to juggle with sets of oppositions and supplementarities, always keeping one's options open in order to keep a richer, more nuanced range of ideas in play. It is this subtle process of *textual interplay* with apparently opposing or, perhaps, competing terms and sets of ideas which has distinguished the deconstructionist approach from modernist versions of discourse analysis.

But what does all this mean in terms of conducting a feminist post-structuralist approach to discourse analysis? How can we avoid the oft-made criticism (e.g. Linstead, 1993: 109) against deconstructive approaches that 'the idea of a free play of signifiers as a pretext for endless interpretative games without the necessity to pay regard to standards of logic or ideas of truth' makes any analysis from this perspective pointless if not worthless? This charge will be partly addressed in the next section of this chapter when I consider the *feminist* focus upon post-structuralist discourse analysis, and will be specifically addressed by considering the range of strategies below.

I would therefore suggest that there are various strategies by which FPDA practitioners can develop an organised and focused approach to their work whilst simultaneously acknowledging the continual textual interplay of the data arising from their research, *without* being swallowed up by deconstructionist relativism. The *first* is by consciously not developing an overriding authorial argument at the expense of alternative points of view. Those 'alternative points of view' might be represented by the voices of other theorists in the field, the participants in the research study, and/or by different members of a research team in conducting the business of analysing texts. Partly implicated in this is the principle of self-reflexivity: the author/analyst must own up to his/her ideological motives, perspectives and short-comings within a given discursive context. But additionally there is the post-structuralist recognition of a kind of intellectual pluralism that the author/analyst has no more claim to speak 'the truth' and no better right to be heard than any other participant in the study. The purpose of supplementing the analyst's voice with the voices of other participants is different to its role in more traditional ethno graphic terms (e.g. Hammersley, 1990: 606) where the cross-validation of multiple accounts are added to produce 'one true description'. Instead, FPDA's purpose is to pre-empt the imperialism of the author's voice and bring a richer, potentially more imaginative range of ideas and viewpoints into play. In other words, the author/analyst should allow their own voice to be supplemented by voices from a variety of data sources, so that they do not privilege their own readings at the expense of those who may have contributed to, or constituted the data.

Secondly, aiming for textual interplay as a discourse analyst also means resisting the temptation to go for narrative closure, and allow-ing space for an open-ended verdict, or for alternative voices to com-ment on the data. From a deconstructive perspective, this inhibits the possibility of ossification or degradation into hierarchical structure, and opens up the recognition of the subtle, continuous shifts between terms, ideas and perspectives. The job of the FPDA analyst is effectively like that of a juggler who is striving to keep all the batons in the air simultaneously. However, this particular analogy not only implies multiple accounts (the batons) but also an author (the juggler). In self-reflexive spirit, I must therefore acknowledge that the post-structuralist advocacy of open-ended, endlessly deferred meaning goes against the grain for most researchers, trained as they are in the business of having something significant to say from which others might learn. My answer to this is that within an FPDA framework we should attempt to do both: provide opportunities for multiple, open-ended readings of a piece of analysis, but self-reflexively juxtapose our own supplementary accounts alongside those of other participants. Thirdly, we should be self-reflexively open to the incipient irony of what we say and do as authors and analysts: this book represents an attempt to fix meaning, however much it purports to be in the business of destabilising the meanings generated by 'authoritative discourses' (Bakhtin, 1981). Finally, despite the emphasis upon textual interplay and juggling on the part of the analyst, the methodology of FPDA involves a strictly pragmatic, focused, logical and organised process, as I shall demonstrate in the following chapters. This is because FPDA scholarship very much resides in systematically highlighting the diverse voices constituting the data from the cacophony of any research setting. It would be counter-intuitive and frankly daft to expect discourse analysts or their readers to accept a kind of fuzzy, ever-questioning interpretation of spoken discourse where things have no pin-downable meanings.

Finding a feminist focus

In Chapter 1, I explored how 'third wave' or post-structuralist feminism works to defuse and dissolve the oppositions and tensions, which inscribed the emancipatory agenda of modernist feminism. I argued that current versions of feminism are in many ways compatible with, and supplement post-structuralist theory. For example, post-structuralist feminism has been concerned to critique many of the fundamental tenets of 'second wave' feminism, challenging constructs of gender dichotomy (e.g. Bing and Bergvall, 1998) and supplementing them with constructs of diversity and complexity. While it would be wrong to ignore or smooth away the potential contradictions between post-structuralism's advocacy of textual interplay on one hand, and feminism's commitment to privileging the female voice on the other, I have suggested that there *is* space for a partnership between the two perspectives since both support the quest to release the voices of those who have been silenced or suppressed.

As Mills (2002) has argued, feminist research is no longer about exploring the effects of the 'big' sociolinguistic variable of gender on different social groups in a top-down, all-embracing way, nor is it about demonstrating that girls/women are universally subordinated or oppressed. Within a post-structuralist paradigm, a feminist focus is, among other things, 'a form of attention, a lens that brings into focus particular questions' (Fox-Keller, 1985: 6). It is concerned with feminist questions and issues that might arise in the study of specific communities of speakers, and is therefore ideally suited to small-scale, localised, short-term, strategically planned projects which intend to transform some aspects of cultural practice for girls/women. This focus may be preconceived and therefore self-reflexively imposed on the analysis of the data. For example, I applied a preconceived focus to the management study (Chapters 6 and 7) where I chose to study the ways in which one female senior manager negotiated her competing subject positions within the context of a series of male-dominated business meetings. Alternatively, in ethnographic spirit, the feminist focus might arise 'naturally' from extended observations within a research setting. This occurred in the classroom study (Chapters 4 and 5) where I gradually became aware that a dominant discourse of gender differentiation was interwoven with other discourses to position girls as generally more silent than boys in public classroom settings such as whole class discussion.

Thus, selecting a feminist focus to post-structuralist discourse analysis must inevitably move away from the old issues of the oppression and subordination of women, or the effects of gender upon the speech patterns of particular social groups. It involves highlighting key discourses on gender as they are negotiated and performed within specific, localised contexts. It also involves making sense of the ways in which these discourses position female speakers (in particular) as relatively powerful, powerless or a combination of both. It acknowledges the complexities, ambiguities and differences in the experiences of particular female speakers, as well as focusing on the possibilities for resistance and reinterpretation of social practices. It celebrates and foregrounds moments of *strength* in women's interactions with others, whilst self-reflexively pointing up the dangers of becoming complacent about privileging certain (female) voices over those of others.

Sources of data

A powerful source of data for the FPDA practitioner, apart from transcripts of talk or written texts, is that which is gained from a range of different voices: whether those of the research subjects themselves, other members of the research team, theorists in the field or, indeed, the author's own voice. This section explores two interrelated constructs: *polyphony* or multiple-voices, and *heteroglossia* or competing voices and accounts.

Polyphony

We can gain a richer understanding of the concept of 'multiple-voices' for the purposes of discourse analysis by exploring the relevance of the ideas of the Russian formulist Bakhtin (1981) on both polyphony and heteroglossia.

Polyphony involves providing space in an analysis for the co-existence and juxtaposition of a plurality of voices and accounts that do not necessarily fuse into a single authorial account. Bakhtin's music-derived trope of polyphony was originally conceptualised in reference to the complex play of ideological voices in the work of the Russian novelist Dostoevsky. Polyphony refers to the co-existence, in any textual or discursive context, of a plurality of voices which do not fuse into a single consciousness, but rather exist on different registers, generating a 'dialogical' or intertextual dynamism among themselves. According to Bakhtin, this intertextual dynamism doesn't lead to 'mere heterogeneity' but offers an interplay of voices which are juxtaposed and counterposed in order to generate something 'beyond themselves'. For Bakhtin (1981: 60), each cultural voice exists in dialogue with other voices so that 'utterances are not indifferent to one another and are not self-sufficient; they are aware of and mutually reflect each other'. According to this view, social or *discursive* diversity is fundamental to every utterance, even to those utterances which on the surface ignore or exclude other, related voices. This Bakhtinian conceptualisation of multiple utterances or viewpoints is therefore very much in tune with Cooper's (1989) movement of metaphorisation (see above), in which the juxtaposition of dissonant and sometimes contradictory viewpoints brings about a transformative interdependence between them. From an FPDA perspective, this suggests to the researcher the need to investigate a richer, more complex set of possible understandings and readings of the data.

Getting practical, how can the FPDA practitioner achieve a polyphonic approach to the data? Here are three possibilities. First, an analysis can aim to produce multiple perspectives upon a single, centralised event, text or textual extract. In the classroom study (Chapters 4 and 5), I selected just one speech event for the purposes of my analysis – a whole class discussion – from many similar events I had observed and recorded as part of a longer term, ethnographic approach to the data. The selection and foregrounding of this particular discussion was partly fortuitous: it was to be used by the school's English department as a focus for formal coursework assessment, followed by a staff moderation meeting. This offered me the potential for a plurality of voices and perspectives, those of the students in the class, the class teacher, the staff moderating the activity and my own observations. I added the researcher's dimension of a video-recorder in order to capture the non-verbal as well as the verbal interactions of the discussion. Having video-recorded and transcribed the discussion, I showed the video-tape to different groups of participants – the students themselves, the class teacher and the teachers at the moderation meeting – and afterwards tape-recorded their reactions and responses. In the final analysis of the whole class discussion, I attempted to juxtapose the plural and often competing accounts of these different groups of participants alongside my own. Readers will no doubt judge how successful I have been in living up to this principle. But I am more than aware that, however self-reflexive the researcher, it is difficult to resist academic convention and move away from the 'single authoritative account' (Bakhtin, 1981) which, despite all good intentions, does indeed dominate this analysis.

The other suggestions for incorporating polyphony within discourse analysis are more speculative and are suggested as possibilities for future development of the FPDA approach. Thus, my *second* suggestion is where *one* author might produce *multiple* and perhaps competing versions of the same act of discourse analysis, so in a sense there would be no 'original' or authorised version. Similar experimental work has of course been carried out within the broader fields of critical or feminist ethnography (e.g. Skeggs, 1994). Famously, Margery Wolf (1992), the feminist ethnographer, has produced three different narratives of her ethnography in Taiwan. Deploying different frameworks, rhetorical strategies and authorising claims, she exposes the different ways in which her ethnography can be told.

The *third* approach is to make available an initial draft of a given work of discourse analysis available to the subjects within a research study for their feedback, responses and critique. The final draft would be multi-authored to the extent that it aims to juxtapose the researcher's analysis alongside these supplementary accounts. An alternative version might be where a team of discourse analysts are examining a particular phenomenon such as gendered discourse in the classroom. Rather than the modernist approach of a collaborative analysis being produced as a unified, holistic text, multiple readings of the same speech event might be created *simultaneously* by different participants and then juxtaposed with each other like a collage. Either of these two versions would produce a rather different outcome than, for example, collaborative but ultimately monologic analysis. Whereas the single or co-authored account usually aims to produce a clear, unequivocal message and at times an emancipatory action, a polyphonic analysis hopes to disrupt the possibility of neatly packaged solutions, instead provoking unusual combinations of ideas and more thought-provoking if more disruptive insights, which of course can lead to (transformative) action.

While all these approaches are necessarily time-intensive and space-consuming, they have the advantage of producing a multi-faceted discourse analysis of considerable complexity, insight and depth. Furthermore, a polyphonic approach helps to reveal the gaps, ambiguities and contradictions within and between different accounts that are often ignored, masked or glossed over by the single-authored, monologic analysis.

Heteroglossia

An additional source of data for the FPDA analyst is that of differently orientated voices and accounts or, in Bakhtin's (1981) term, 'heteroglossia'. This is the act of making visible the non-official viewpoint, the marginalised, the silenced and the oppressed from other, more dominant viewpoints. Bakhtin's concept of heteroglossia is useful to FPDA because it differentiates the profoundly relational view of post-structuralist theory from its parodic stereotype as an endless free-play of signifiers without reference points. Critics of post-structuralist theory such as Norris (1990: 138–9) have argued that the polyphonic approach appears to deny all standards of interpretative consistency, resulting in 'a kind of pluralist tolerance which leaves no room for significant disagreement on issues of principle or practice'. The concept of heteroglossia provides the FPDA practitioner with a reference point from which to view the world, while recognising that the discursive location of such reference points may be fixed only temporarily.

Bakhtin's (1981) views on heteroglossia have been aligned with the Marxist emancipatory agenda to show:

> The cultural viewpoint of the oppressed, their 'hidden' knowledges and resistances as well as the basis on which their entrapping 'decisions' are taken in some sense of liberty, but which nevertheless help to produce 'structure'. (Willis, 1977: 146).

Bakhtin's specific contribution to post-structuralist thinking, however, was to foreground not the political or economic, but the *linguistic* dimension of social struggle: the ways in which all utterance and discourse are subject to the deforming and transforming struggle for power. In his concept of heteroglossia, Bakhtin locates ideological struggle at the centre of all discourse, whether in the form of political rhetoric, artistic practice or everyday interaction. He suggests that every apparently unified linguistic or social community is characterised by heteroglossia, whereby language becomes the space of confrontation between differently orientated voices, as diverse social groups fight it out on the terrain of language. According to his theory, while the dominant discourse strives to make a given sign, such as 'woman', uni-accentual and endowed with an eternal, reified character, resistant discourses rise up to challenge and disrupt conventional understandings offering multi-accentual readings. In post-structuralist terms, heteroglossia describes the struggle for the control of signifiers such as 'woman', and the process by which discourses compete to fix meaning permanently and irrevocably on behalf of hegemonic interests.

While a Bakhtinian perspective on heteroglossia finds its reference points in committing to an ideological agenda which makes space for the voices and concerns of 'the oppressed', a feminist post-structuralist viewpoint seeks two related reference points. The first is its commitment to spotlight and focus upon (especially) female voices and accounts of participants in a research study who may be relatively *silent* compared to their more vociferous male or possibly female counterparts;

or indeed to make space for voices which show evidence of having been repeatedly *silenced* by others. As an aside, it is worth noting that FPDA would take account of at least two different levels of interpreting the 'silencing' of women, according to feminist linguistics. On a literal level, it is the interpersonal tendency of men to 'silence' women by tactics of interruption, talking over, heckling and so on (e.g. Fishman, 1980; Zimmerman and West, 1975). On a theoretical level, it may refer to the 'dominance' view (e.g. Olsen, 1978; Spender, 1980) of an excluding, 'man-made' language which has constructed females as the 'othered' or 'silenced' sex. An FPDA approach would aim to identify where competing discourses in a given setting seem to lead (temporarily) to more fixed patterns of dominant and subordinated subject positions. Such an analysis would be conducted in the spirit of 'supplementarity' (Derrida, 1976: 27–30) or richer textual play, according to which no single voice is suppressed, displaced by or privileged over any other, but rather, each voice is allowed the space to complement, enhance and, at the same time, undercut or disrupt other voices.

FPDA's second reference point is its quest to challenge any simple dualism between dominant discourses representing the voices of oppressors, and oppositional discourses constituting the voices of the oppressed. It aims to reveal the complexities of participants' interactions, foregrounding the ways in which positions of power are continuously negotiated, contested and subverted, never permanently settling as 'structure'. For example, the FPDA practitioner must embrace the possibility that *male* as well as female speakers are frequently marginalised in such contexts as a board meeting or a whole class discussion, as a consequence of the relative powerfulness of competing institutional discourses other than gender differentiation operating in those settings. Such an analysis must be prepared to take account of the complexity of many mixed-sex spoken interactions. For example, a male business manager may appear to be adopting a quite dominant subject position as a speaker at a board meeting but, is being simultaneously challenged by his colleagues. Or a female manager in the same context routinely comes across as a dominant and influential speaker yet is positioned quite differently from her male counterparts by a discourse of gender differentiation (Chapters 6 and 7).

So, what are the strategies open to the FPDA practitioner for promoting a heteroglossic analysis of the data? The first, most obvious strategy is literally to give a voice to those research participants who appear to be either silent or silenced: the silent girl at the side of the classroom who rarely speaks; or the articulate female manager in the board meeting who appears to have difficulty in sustaining her authority. In my classroom study (Chapters 4 and 5), I gave prominence to both the silent and the silenced. In terms of the more *silent* students, both female and male, I acted as a kind of facilitator or enabler when I interviewed them in groups so that they could have protected access to the floor and develop their views. A better approach, although I did not do this, might have been to have interviewed these students *individually* as well as in groups. (However, my own experience of working with more reserved young people has shown that the one-to-one interview can be a double-edged sword: while some regard it as a welcome opportunity to talk more freely, others read it as a form of unwelcome intrusion from yet another figure of adult authority.) In terms of the *silenced* students, part of my analysis was directed towards ascertaining how and why certain patterns of silence are being actively constructed in the context of oral activities such as whole class discussions. In presenting my analysis, I aimed simultaneously to give space to the competing voices of the participants – juxtaposing the heterogeneous and often conflicting perspectives of the students, the class teacher and the assessors – but yet to give special prominence to those female speakers whose viewpoints might easily have been overlooked or marginalised. This is indeed the core principle of FPDA.

However, the act of silence or silencing should not be read uniaccentually always as a form of marginalisation or submission. It can also constitute a powerful means of *resistance*, in that being silent can sometimes be self-affirming rather than undermining. In Alyson Jule's (2002) study of Amandeep, simultaneously a silent and silenced ten-year-old Sikh girl in the context of a Canadian English as a Second Language (ESL) classroom, the author gives prominence in her discourse analysis to the limited number of speech encounters she observed over a period of two years. We see exactly how Amandeep is constructed as a silent student and how as a consequence she partly *becomes* her construction. But this is not the whole story – her silence becomes a secret weapon in resisting the expectations of her teacher to become a 'good' student and hence a good Canadian citizen. According to Jule, she is refusing to play an active part in the colonising practices of this ESL classroom, which silences, marginalises and threatens to undermine her Sikh cultural identity.

Finally, a word of caution for researchers intending to adopt a 'heteroglossic' approach to the analysis; it is obviously important to be highly self-reflexive about the authoritative researcher position. An analyst must exercise a considerable degree of scrutiny about what constitutes a silent or silenced research subject within a particular location; *who* decides the identity of the silent or the silenced; and upon the basis of *what* evidence. FPDA practitioners must therefore aim to make quite explicit the possible gaps, ambiguities and contradictions in their data on the basis of which they may choose to constitute and represent certain subjects as silent or silenced, and others as doing the silencing.

Textual analysis

The synchronic–diachronic dimension

These terms, borrowed from Halliday's (1989) functional model of language, are used to convey the way in which an FPDA practitioner should ideally adopt two supplementary approaches to textual analysis, which I shall now consider in turn. The first is a *synchronic* approach: that is, a detailed, micro-analysis of short stretches of spoken discourse such as a whole class discussion in a school, or a business management meeting. Indeed, it is this synchronic approach that is especially associated with the approaches of CA and more recently CDA, as I discussed in Chapter 2.

The synchronic approach is of particular relevance to FPDA because of the imperative to capture a moment or sequence of moments when discursive power shifts occur. One of the tenets of FPDA is that speakers are never uniformly powerful or powerless, only temporarily constituted in the same ways by the same discourses within given locations. This is not to say that certain configurations of discursive positioning can and do recur, nor that certain individuals and social groups may be more systematically positioned as powerful or powerless. Nevertheless, where there *are* instances of 'degradation and ossification into structure' (Linstead, 1993: 112), these are always subject to the possibility of resistance by the subject positions offered by competing discourses. Thus the value of synchronic discourse analysis is that it can identify and demonstrate the exact moment or sequence of moments when speakers experience a shift between positions of relative powerfulness and powerlessness. It can show from the analysis of a series of moments that speakers are constantly negotiating for positions of power according to their shifting subject positions within different discourses. It can potentially show why one speaker is likely to be constructed more routinely as powerful and another more consistently as powerless by their responses within a given moment. The next section (Denotation–connotation) discusses *how* such micro-analyses of moments where discursive power shifts occur might be carried out.

The *diachronic* or geneological perspective supplements that of the synchronic by analysing more ethnographically the language of individuals, groups or communities of practice over a period of time. This involves recording configurations, developments and changes in the discursive relationships of individuals or groups for the purposes of discourse analysis. This would not be done in the more traditional sociolinguistic sense in order to record trends, patterns or variations in speech and behaviour according to a variable such as gender. Rather the FPDA approach to long-term observation would be to notice and interrogate the ways in which certain speakers may be more consistently positioned as powerful or powerless, whereas others are subject to more shifting power relations. Such an analysis would be able, for example, to paint a more subtle and complex picture of the differences *within* and *between* girls/women in terms of the ways in which they variously negotiate their positions within competing discourses. It would be able to capture individual moments of resistance and empowerment in the spoken interactions of girls/women who might otherwise be constituted as victims. It would, in short, allow for the possibility of analysing moments where *change occurs* in the form of challenges, contestations, power reversals, perhaps subtle or more direct revisions of the status quo.

The examples of FPDA that I demonstrate in this book constitute 'work in progress'. I do not consider that the studies in this book demonstrate a fully evolved approach to diachronic analysis. Owing to difficulties of access, the management study (Chapters 6 and 7) is largely a synchronic micro-analysis, conducted in a relatively short period of time and failing to track the developments or changes in the discursive relationships of this group of managers. The classroom study (Chapters 4 and 5) also synchronically focuses upon a single speech event, although it does draw upon observations, competing accounts and contradictory experiences from the larger ethnographic study. Future FPDA practitioners might explore beyond the limits of my own version by seeking ways to complement or juxtapose a synchronic analysis with a more diachronic approach. One suggestion is that such an analysis might capture the spoken interactions of a group (such as a class of students), over several separate occasions within a period of time which has significance for them (say, an academic year). This might be supplemented by a comparative analysis highlighting shifts, changes and transformations in the discursive practices of individuals or groups.

Denotation–connotation

Borrowed from the work of the semiologist Barthes (e.g. 1973, 1977) and his followers, this pair of interrelated terms is useful to FPDA because it offers the possibility of an analysis on two discrete but interconnected levels.

The *denotative* level of analysis aims to give a concrete description of what is going on within a text, such as an extract of spoken discourse, by making close and detailed reference to the verbal and non-verbal interactions of the participants. The value of this is that it provides a linguistic analysis of a speech encounter which attends to the obvious, common-sense meanings within any interaction, and therefore forms an apparently uncontroversial basis from which a theoretically driven interpretation can emerge. Here the methods of CA, such as its attention to the turn-taking sequence of participants, may be a useful tool for FPDA practitioners in helping to produce a denotative description of what is going on. Analysts from different fields and with varying theoretical persuasions have adapted the methods of CA in order to produce detailed accounts of gendered discourse. For example, in the field of language and gender, theorists have used CA to produce closely grained descriptions of the ways in which specific linguistic features, such as minimal responses (e.g. Fishman, 1980), interruptions and overlaps (e.g. Zimmerman and West, 1975), directives (e.g. Goodwin, 1990) and tag questions (e.g. Holmes, 1992), are negotiated through a series of turns in single-sex or mixed-sex conversations. (See Appendix 1 for definitions of specialist linguistic terms used in the denotative analysis.)

However, the FPDA practitioner needs to be aware, as a proviso, that however denotative a 'description' aims to be, it is always a culturally specific form of interpretation involving at the very least the selection of a focus, the highlighting of key aspects for attention and the consequent marginalisation of other aspects. Also, many words used to offer a description are 'loaded' words, that is, imbued with the interpretation of the analyst. If the same task of producing a description of a given transcript was asked of ten CA analysts, it goes without saying that each would produce a different reading while retaining certain principles and approaches in common. Indeed, I have already discussed how, within a feminist post-structuralist framework, the implicitly value-laden and interpretative function of any form of analysis is to be welcomed rather than disguised as pseudo-objective. The value of description at the denotative level is that it can offer a preliminary order of quite concrete interpretation which can be readily shared with research participants and theorists alike, but which provides a springboard for more searching and heteroglossic analysis.

The *connotative* level of analysis aims to provide this more searching, interpretative commentary of extracts of spoken discourse, drawing partly from the synchronic, denotative evidence above, and partly from ethnographic or diachronic sources of data. FPDA requires that analysts actively seek to identify institutional or social discourses that appear to be operating in the research setting. This is rarely produced by observing or recording one particular speech event, but is more likely to be achieved by conducting ethnographic observation of a particular social group or community of practice over a period of time. This very much describes the methodology I used in the classroom study on students' assessed talk (Chapters 4 and 5), where I had not initially intended to analyse the data from an FPDA perspective. It was only through extended observation, note-taking and video-recording that I gradually became aware of particular sets of expectations and assumptions that were routinely and consistently at work within the context of this classroom. These often competing sets of assumptions seemed to signify a complex interplay of discourses. These in turn appeared to have a powerful effect in constituting the assessed talk of this class of students. In order that these 'discourses' are *not* perceived as subjective impressions but as 'a materialism of the incorporeal' (Foucault, 1972), it is vital that analysts keep systematic records on how, when and where these discourses occur within a range of contexts. In my own case, I used the following sources of evidence:

- non-verbal language of the participants, such as eye contact, gestures, seating positions
- verbal language, such as constantly repeated keywords and phrases, or regularly used linguistic features by the participants
- metalanguage: the language used by participants in interviews to describe their speech, behaviour and relationships.

By way of illustration, I will give one brief example of how I applied this approach to the classroom study. I identified a discourse of *gender differentiation* at work first of all by carefully noting patterns of non-verbal interaction. For instance, I recorded how girls conformed to classroom rules by putting their hands up in the classroom more often than boys, yet boys were granted far more turns to speak. Secondly, in terms of keywords and phrases, I noted how girls regularly *agreed* with points that boys had made in a discussion by saying, 'I agree with Joe that . . . ', whereas there were *no* instances of a boy naming a girl in this way. Thirdly, in terms of metalanguage, I noted how both boys and girls spontaneously referred to gender difference as a means of generalising about speech and behaviour in the classroom (e.g. 'Girls tend to put their hands up more.'). From these three sources, I was able to gather a body of evidence to suggest that gender differentiation was one of a number of powerful discourses constructing students' talk in this classroom. More detail on exactly *how* different discourses were identified for the purposes of textual analysis is given in the case study chapters.

To sum up, a connotative analysis is concerned to demonstrate how speakers are continuously positioned or repositioned by a range of competing discourses pertaining to a given social/institutional context. It seeks to show how speakers are constantly negotiating for positions of power or resisting positions of powerlessness according to the range of subject positions made available to them. In so doing, the commentary does not simply rely upon the 'authoritative discourse' (Bakhtin, 1981) of the analyst in order to make meaning from the data. It aims to weave together the 'internally persuasive discourses' (Bakhtin, 1981; Skidmore, 1999) or 'supplementary' (Derrida, 1976) accounts of the research participants collected at different stages of the study, in order to represent the multiple, diverse and often dissonant perspectives of the particular case.

Intertextuality

Noting the workings of intertextuality within spoken discourse is an essential part of the craft of FPDA. This involves foregrounding and highlighting the ways in which dominant discourses within any speech context are always inflected and inscribed with traces of other discourses.

Associated with the work of early post-structuralists such as Barthes (1977) and Kristeva (1984), intertextuality applies simultaneously to everyday speech, popular culture and the literary and artistic tradition. In the broadest sense, intertextuality refers to the open-ended possibilities generated by all the discursive practices of a culture, the entire matrix of communicative utterances in which a text is located. To this extent, it can be argued that there are no beginnings and ends between texts, just a boundless fluidity. Eagleton (1983: 138), writing specifically about literary criticism, suggests that utterances reach texts through a quite subtle process of dissemination:

> All literary texts are woven out of other literary texts, not in the conventional sense that they bear the traces of influence, but in the more radical sense that every word, phrase or segment is a reworking of other writings which precede or surround the individual work. There is no such thing as literary originality, no such thing as the 'first' literary work: all work is intertextual.

According to Barthes (1977: 23), intertextuality is not so much a style but a structural property which allows readers to read and texts to be produced. A text only gathers meaning because it is 'woven entirely with citations, references, echoes and cultural languages' and is 'caught up in a system of references to other books, other texts and other sentences'. It is thus both inscribed with the traces of the texts that have gone before it, and formed in the act of reading by the inexhaustible databank of references we all carry with us as participants in a culture.

If this principle is transferred to FPDA, it is possible to analyse the range of discourses shaping spoken interaction within any given context as operating not in a discrete way but always intertextually. For instance, in the classroom study (see Chapters 4 and 5), three key discourses are identified as constituting the talk in this setting: those of gender differentiation; peer and teacher approval; and a model of collaborative talk in English teaching. While it is possible to identify and categorise each as a separate discourse often in competition with the others, they simultaneously appeared to work in intertextualised ways to produce a range of subject positions for this class of students. For example, a discourse of gender differentiation was seen to be interwoven with a discourse of collaborative or 'approved' talk in English, in that girls were expected to be more collaborative than boys. There were clear sets of gendered expectations that girls should listen quietly during a class discussion and conform to the principle of 'hands up', whereas boys could get away with interrupting others and 'chipping in'. FPDA would aim to show how such intertextualisation of discourses may lead to more systematic patterns of gender differentiation, which are then assimilated into the routine practices of the classroom and whole school. However, FPDA would also be concerned to point up instances of the complexities of subject positioning produced by the intertextualised nature of discourses, which provide gaps for agency and resistance, especially among girls.

The principle of intertextuality can be applied not only to the transcripts of spoken discourse within a corpus of data, but also to the polyphonic, supplementary accounts contained in interview data, observation notes, video-recordings and so on. In the next four chapters, I demonstrate how the FPDA practitioner can draw upon the framework of principles discussed in this chapter in order to produce a complex and penetrating analysis of the ways in which intertextualised and often competing discourses constitute all spoken interactions.

4
Developing an FPDA Approach: The Classroom Study

Introduction

In this and the following three chapters, I intend to move from the *theory* of feminist post-structuralism and the principles of FPDA, to consider how such insights apply in *practice* to the analysis of discourse within two very different research contexts. The first of the two research studies to which I shall be applying the FPDA approach is an ethnographic study of school students' classroom talk and, in particular, their speaking and listening skills, which were being formally assessed for a public, oral examination. The second (introduced in Chapter 6) is a study of business managers' talk within a series of management meetings. The purpose of this chapter, therefore, is to set the scene for the school-based research study, highlighting the particular *process* by which I came to identify three intersecting classroom discourses for further analysis. The discourse analysis itself is conducted in Chapter 5.

This research study of classroom talk was conducted over several months in a British secondary/high school. It involved a Year 10 class of 24 mixed-sex students carrying out a range of oral coursework for the General Certificate of Secondary Education (GCSE) in English – a public examination for all students aged 16. The analysis itself focuses on the verbal and non-verbal interactions of two girls and two boys within the larger setting of a whole class discussion. As I describe in more detail below, the original aim of conducting the research study was to analyse what constitutes 'effective' speech in this setting in order to help teachers apply the GCSE assessment criteria. The study was specifically designed to incorporate a broadly feminist, post-structuralist approach to ethnographic research (e.g. Lather, 1991; Usher, 1996). The decision to take up FPDA as a discourse analysis tool was made only during the ethnographic process of collecting the data as I began to discover the significance of the interaction of three key discourses within these students' talk. This is an important point because the decision to apply FPDA was very much a contextualised *response* to the scope and nature of this particular corpus of data, rather than a superimposed, preconceived, theoretical stance.

In the sections that follow, I shall describe the evolution of the process that led to the decision to use an FPDA approach to the data. These sections are: purpose of the classroom study; the research setting; the methodology; and 'identifying the discourses': a description of the process by which the three key discourses were identified in this setting: peer and teacher approval; collaborative talk; and gender differentiation. In the final section of the chapter, I shall discuss what we can expect from a feminist, post-structuralist approach to the data.

Purpose of the study

This section explains the background and original purpose of the classroom study, in order to trace the ethnographic process leading to the emergence of FPDA as an appropriate tool with which to analyse school students' verbal and non-verbal interactions.

The original quest of the study arose as a consequence of two, interrelated perspectives. From an *educational* perspective, I was keen to establish exactly what constituted 'effective' speech in classroom 'public' settings such as whole class discussions, formal talks and debates. There were two reasons for this interest. First, as a former teacher, I have always considered that the ability to speak effectively in a range of unfamiliar, large group, formal or public contexts is potentially empowering for young people socially, academically and professionally. A range of international research (e.g. Coates, 1995; Edelsky and Adams, 1990; Holmes, 1992; 1995; Shaw, 2000; Tannen, 1995) has shown that the agency to speak effectively in public can confer social and professional prestige, and is often a passport to more senior career roles and responsibilities. On a less grand scale, I have argued (e.g. Baxter, 1999, 2002a) that 'effective' speech is also the ability to make a convincing case to a group of peers, to persuade people to your point of view, to resist and challenge the spurious arguments of others, and to make an impact on public opinion.

The second reason for my interest in what constitutes effective speech in classroom public contexts arose from a 'sea change' that had recently occurred within British syllabuses for examining speaking and listening in English. The revised GCSE syllabuses (e.g. EDEXCEL, 1998; NEAB, 1999) provided evidence of a significant *shift* in the criteria – from a model of informal, exploratory, collaborative talk in small groups to that of more public, performance-based talk. This shift was particularly noticeable at the higher grade levels. For example, at grade B, candidates are asked to 'make probing contributions, structuring and organising points for impact on an audience'. But more strikingly at grade A* (the top grade), candidates are required to 'use language in a *dynamic* and influential way' and 'make thought-provoking contributions through *powerful* expression and *command* of the situation' (my italics). Speaking in public contexts has played a relatively undervalued part within the UK national curriculum until this recent shift in the speaking and listening criteria for English.

Thus, from a feminist perspective, it seemed clear to me from the revised criteria that there was more going on than just a simple shift from a collaborative to a performance model of talk. At first glance, such criteria do appear to make gender-related assumptions about the normative voice of public authority, confidence and success that may not be compatible with discursive practices traditionally coded as 'feminine'. 'Effective' talk, according to the GCSE criteria above, appears to be constituted through metaphors of command and control that are stereotypically associated with masculine speech. Thus, I wondered whether exam syllabuses were offering a model of speech in public contexts that would be likely to favour boys rather than girls.

My line of research inquiry was informed by a continuing debate within feminist linguistics about whether gender is a significant factor in determining which speakers are likely to be considered 'effective' in public contexts (e.g. Baxter, 2002c; Edelsky and Adams, 1990; Holmes, 1992; Shaw, 2000; Winter, 1993). At a time in British education when girls are significantly outperforming boys at all levels of schooling, it had puzzled me as a teacher why articulate girls appeared to be more reticent and less forthcoming than their male counterparts in whole class settings, despite many girls' proven oral ability, especially in small group, collaborative work. Nonetheless, a range of international research (e.g. Bousted, 1989; Corson, 1997; Kelly, 1991; Ohrn, 1991; Sadker and Sadker, 1994) has demonstrated that boys tend to dominate the public space of the classroom. My own classroom study was also partially inspired by the recent concerns in Britain about the academic underachievement of boys in relation to girls. Marshall (1998) among others has argued that female examination success is not necessarily a qualification for more senior or highly paid jobs, and I have since suggested that access to 'the public voice' is vital if women are to be as successful as men in the public arena (Baxter, 1999). With the emphasis in recent British government initiatives and research literature (e.g. Frater, 2000; Millard, 1997; OFSTED, 1993; Pickering, 1997; QCA, 1998), very much upon securing boys' success in schools, it seemed an opportune moment to question whether it is right to be quite so complacent about girls' academic achievements.

In sum, the classroom study aimed to find out what constitutes 'effective' speech in public settings at GCSE examination level, and whether there were any differences between girls and boys in meeting such criteria. More specifically, the research aims were:

- to find out what constitutes the ways in which students speak in public contexts
- to explore perceptions of what it is to be an 'effective' speaker in public contexts according to different participants – the students themselves, their teachers, examiners and the researcher
- to consider whether gender is a pertinent discourse for evaluating who is most likely to benefit from the exam syllabuses constructs of 'effective' speech.

The research setting

The research study took place within a co-educational secondary/high school, whose English oral work I observed over a period of three months. The class comprised 24 students of equal numbers of boys and girls (23 Caucasian; one female of Chinese origin for whom English was the home language) from a range of social backgrounds. The class was broadly set for the subject of English within the middle to upper ability range (that is, students were predicted grades A to D out of a possible range A to G/Unclassified). While I would hesitate to describe the class as a homogeneous group, I felt that my awareness of certain commonalities between the students' ethnic background, class, age and ability would allow me to foreground gender for particular observation and scrutiny.

The English department, comprising seven female staff and one male head of department (a not uncommon pattern in many British secondary schools!), were eager to participate as research partners in the study. As a condition of access, they wanted, quite fairly, to know, 'What's in it for us?' Secondary English teachers obviously have numerous demands on their time, and my particular interest in 'the relationship between gender and talk in public contexts', while theoretically interesting to them, was initially perceived to be a tiny slice of the priority cake in terms of curriculum planning and delivery. However, they did share my concern about the more general issue, that 'speaking in public contexts' plays an undervalued part within the English curriculum, and that curriculum reform in this area was long overdue. They were therefore very keen to design a new scheme of work, which would assess students' use of speech in a variety of 'public' contexts. Thus, while the central concern of my research partners was, understandably, a curricular one, my principal focus was more empirical – to observe and gain greater understanding of the gender issues arising from the ways in which students speak and listen in public contexts.

The obvious solution might have been to design and conduct a piece of collaborative action research, targeting curriculum development work on speaking and listening in public contexts. However, as I saw it, the problem with action research into educational practice (e.g. Bryant, 1996; Kemmis, 1993) is that it involves a modernist and therefore an emancipatory quest of identifying a given problem, then jointly seeking to plan, implement and evaluate a course of action (say, through curriculum development work), leading to improved educational practice. For this reason, I felt that action research as the principal research paradigm would not reflect my interest in feminist post-structuralism, nor would it necessarily achieve answers to my research questions.

The eventual answer was to design a case study that managed to combine both observation and action by teaching a unit of oral coursework (constituting a week of English lessons) to the entire year cohort (150 students) which would simultaneously allow for detailed recording of particular activities on my part, and for experimental curriculum work to be implemented. The unit of work, entitled 'The Desert Survival Situation' (Lafferty and Pond, 1989) was tailored by English staff to allow focused opportunities for students to speak and listen in public contexts. In the classroom setting a 'public context' was deemed to be any oral activity involving groups of eight or more students. The analysis in Chapter 5 is based on a teacher-directed whole class discussion, which formed the plenary for a problem-solving exercise conducted beforehand in smaller student-led groups. This unit of work would be followed by an audio-recorded, departmental, cross-moderation meeting. On this occasion, the research partners, acting as teacher assessors, would have the opportunity to watch the video-recordings of the students taking part in the Desert Survival exercise, cross-moderate the students' oral performances, evaluate the unit of work, and comment on their own role within the research process: all as part of developing the multiple-voiced, multifaceted perspective on the case.

Methodology

While the focus of this book is upon discourse analysis, it is evident that the use of such an approach is more feasible if the overall methodology for a research study is designed within a feminist post-structuralist research paradigm. In this section, I discuss how my choice of an *ethnographic* approach to conducting the classroom study has principles likely to be highly conducive to a feminist post-structuralist analysis of the data. I then explain what practical decisions I took to implement a compatible methodology.

There are four ways in which ethnographic research methods are particularly appropriate to this classroom study because of their epistemological parallels and connections with feminist, post-structuralist theory. *First* is the epistemological basis of ethnography: that is, its rejection of the positivist search for universal laws in favour of detailed descriptions of the concrete experience of life within a particular culture, and of the social rules or patterns that constitute it – Hammersley and Atkinson (1995: 8). Both feminist post-structuralist and ethnographic approaches to research often emphasise the localised, microscopic, particular, context-bound features of given settings and cultures. While some branches of ethnography (e.g. Honigmann, 1973) study particular or typical cases in order to generalise to the larger whole (carrying with them modernist constructs of typicality and universal applicability), other branches (e.g Hammersley and Atkinson, 1995) have argued that the job of ethnography is to honour the uniqueness of the individual case. Thus, while the classroom study has an apparently narrow database, the nature of ethnographic study substitutes the advantages of breadth with those of *depth*. From an ethnographic perspective, the advantage of studying a single case is that it allows for a richly detailed picture of a particular group of subjects to emerge, which aims to record the complexity, subtlety and diversity of discursive practices over a period of time. From a feminist post-structuralist point of view, the single case offers the opportunity to *select a feminist focus*, that is, to consider the effects of gender upon the speech patterns of this social group, and to represent this through the multiple and perhaps competing voices and accounts of its various participants.

The *second* way in which ethnographic methods are appropriate to feminist post-structuralist research lies in its preference for deploying plural research methods, combining both qualitative and quantitative techniques. Pat Usher (1996: 132) has posited that feminists prefer to use a multiplicity of methods because they tend to 'value inclusiveness rather than orthodoxy':

> A multiplicity of methods allows women to study the broadest range of subject matters and reach a broad set of goals. Their approaches may include interview and oral history methods, case studies, cross-cultural research, ethnography, surveys or experiments.

In line with feminist post-structuralist methods, Wodak (1996: 23) has also argued for a 'multi-method' approach as part of 'an explicative mosaic' of the case under investigation. In the classroom study, I chose multiple methods in order to capture the contrasting voices and complex interactions of my research participants: myself; the 24 students of the research class; the class teacher and the eight members of the English department acting as teacher assessors, in different speech contexts. First, *observation* and *field-notes* were used to gain a general, *diachronic* impression over three months of verbal and non-verbal interactions of the class in a variety of speaking and listening activities. By allowing space to assimilate diachronic impressions of the data, I was able to record the ways in which speakers engaged in continuously shifting subject positions within and across different speech activities and contexts. Secondly, *video-recordings* were deployed to produce a collection of *synchronic* insights into the verbal and, particularly, non-verbal interactions of the class during the Desert Survival exercise. Thirdly, *audio-recordings* were used for the class teacher and student interviews, as well as for the cross-moderation meeting of teacher assessors, so that a possible range of divergent and competing views would be accurately reproduced for transcription purposes. Finally, my own role as a *researcher-participant* actively ensured that I was contributing to curriculum development work within the school as a condition of access. For example, I worked collaboratively with the research partners to design and produce teaching materials for the Desert Survival exercise, and chaired the cross-moderation meeting of the teacher assessors.

The *third* connection between ethnography and feminist post-structuralism is via the notion of self-reflexivity (see Chapter 3, pp. 58–61). According to Hammersley and Atkinson (1995), the orientations of ethnographers are always shaped by the particularity of their socio-historical locations. Moreover, ethnographic researchers will have an observable effect upon their research context and subsequently on the data gathered. This 'effect' should be regarded as the key to the research act rather than as, in positivist research, a form of 'contamination'. Consequently researchers should be explicitly reflexive or self-referential about how their theoretical assumptions position their research accounts. Furthermore, self-reflexivity, within an ethnographic paradigm, becomes the central issue in drawing attention to the authorial power of the researcher over the researched, particularly in relation to decisions about the *construction* of the research process and the *representation* of research accounts.

One of the key consequences of the principle of self-reflexivity for my own classroom study was that it required a level of honesty, openness and continuous self-criticism between me and my research partners. In other words, it involved a level of *collective* scrutiny in conducting this study where no choice, decision or course of action was assumed or taken for granted. The question 'Why this course of action, not that?' underlay many of the organisational and curricular decisions made, whilst at times imposing a tortuously time-consuming constraint upon the progress of data-collection.

Fourthly, ethnography's emphasis on the inseparability of the 'participant-observer' from their research context also links with feminist post-structuralism's emphasis on the intertextual, interactive and reflexive relationship between traditional dualisms such as theory and practice, subjectivity and objectivity, or male and female. Gold's (1958) widely known typology for 'participant/observer' roles indicates the rather contrasting stances implied by the term. Yet, all four of his categories (complete participant, participant-as-observer, observer-as-participant and complete observer) acknowledge that ethnographers are an intrinsic part of the social world they study, which in turn is intricately bound up with the nature of the research process. As Hammersley and Atkinson point out (1995: 1):

> In its most characteristic form, it involves the ethnographer participating, overtly or covertly in people's daily lives for an extended period of time, watching what happens, listening to what is said, asking questions – in fact, collecting whatever data are available to throw light on the issues that are the focus of the research. Equally though, there is a sense in which all social researchers are participant observers, and, as a result, the boundaries around ethnography are necessarily unclear.

In this study, the role I initially chose to adopt most resembles Gold's (1958) third category of 'observer-as-participant', where, as a researcher, I did not experience the activities for myself but made close and detailed observations. My choice of role was guided by my historical position within the research school. For several years I had visited the school in the capacity of an initial teacher-trainer and tutor to student-teachers, and had occasionally conducted in-service training sessions with the English department. Several of my student-teacher tutees had subsequently been appointed as members of the school's English department, and thus close ties had developed between us. It seemed important as part of ethnographic research that I did not intentionally disrupt the school's day-to-day business, but allowed my role as observer to infiltrate daily working practices, so that my presence might be accepted gradually both by members of staff and students. Thus, I did spend some time in the role of observer, so that the class became used to my taking notes at the back of the class, and learnt to accept me as 'part of the furniture'. However, in self-reflexive spirit, this was not the whole story. There was a consistent level of ambiguity over the exact nature of my role, an uncertainty about where my position as an observer ended and where my position as a participant began. For example, I took an active part in designing the materials for the Desert Survival unit of work, in briefing both staff and students about how the unit of work would run, and how the lessons would be video-recorded for data-collection purposes. I was also asked to chair the audio-recorded meeting of teacher assessors cross-moderating this activity, an act which fully promoted me to Gold's (1958) participant role. From a feminist post-structuralist perspective, such ambiguity caused by the ever-shifting position of the researcher along an observer-participant axis does not matter as long as it is acknowledged and analysed rather than glossed over or excused.

Identifying the discourses

Observing discourse in the classroom

In this section, I shall trace the process by which my decision to use a feminist post-structuralist approach to *discourse analysis* emerged ethnographically from a response to the collected data, rather than as a preconceived decision to use an FPDA approach. My initial plans had been to adopt a multiple methods approach to data analysis in order to judge which communication skills might constitute 'effective' speech within the classroom context. These initial methods included the use of conversation analysis (CA) (e.g. Sacks *et al.*, 1974; Schegloff, 1999); a critical linguistics model of analysing power relations in speech (Hodge and Kress, 1993); and the use of QSR NUDI*ST, the purpose-built qualitative data analysis software program.

However, through the course of my classroom observations, I had periodically noted numerous examples of how students' speech appears to be constituted not by a simple list of speech features or communication skills, but by a complex interplay of discourses and discursive practices. Yet, these discursive practices could *not* simply be accounted for by CA's 'speech exchange system' model of analysis (Schegloff, 1999), or by a model of power relations in which 'context variables are somewhat naively correlated with an autonomous system of language' (Wodak, 2002), *or* by indexing and cataloguing different types of speech features via a computer program.

I began to realise that an 'effective' speaker in public contexts has little to do with common-sense educational notions of whether a student has the ability to acquire and use nationally prescribed communication skills. By way of a parallel example, Swann (1992: 79–80) has criticised past versions of the speaking and listening element of English assessment in the UK national curriculum for its construct of 'communication skills' which she describes as an 'additive model of competence':

> it implies that speakers can simply add on new skills or new ways of speaking to those they already have. It also implies that girls and boys will use the same ways of speaking to similar effect...A 'communication skills' approach suggests that language can somehow be tackled in isolation, as a discrete parcel of skills that speakers have at their disposal. It neglects the fact that, in extending the way they talk, teachers are also challenging the ways girls and boys conventionally relate to others. The issue goes far beyond language.

In the spirit of Swann's comment, it was the significance of the interaction of three particular classroom discourses on students' talk that led me as an educational researcher to take up FPDA both as a theoretically confident framework and as a research tool. Francis (1998) has said that 'writers often fail to explain *how* they have categorised different discourses'. My own categorisations emerged from extended observations of classroom interactions, as these samples of comments from my field-notes and the analysis below illustrates:

> Whenever Michael gets to speak, he looks nervous and anxious as if he feels that he is going to be interrupted. And of course, he usually is. He appears to be under-confident; and this impression is confirmed by the lack of support he gets from his peers when he speaks. If anything, they seem to be out to undermine the little confidence he has.
>
> . . .
>
> When Anne or Rebecca contribute to the discussion, they will often acknowledge a male point of view. 'I agree with Joe's view, but . . .' I have never once heard a boy say they agree with a girl's point of view, but . . .
>
> . . .
>
> In this discussion [group of eight] it's interesting to see how these students 'police' their own talk. They seem to have absorbed the principles of collaborative talk and

are determined to show that they can listen to each other and collaborate without a teacher to 'control' them. But does this make for a less dynamic discussion in the end, when there is no one arguing, provoking, disagreeing, hectoring, confronting?

In the *first* extract, Michael's 'ability' to speak in public contexts seems to be circumscribed by a lack of self-confidence, and by the linked factor of the extent to which he feels supported and approved by his peers. If he is intimidated by their lack of support for him, it is likely that he will feel inhibited from speaking openly or extensively in public settings. In the *second* extract, I noticed that Anne and Rebecca, two relatively dominant female speakers in this class, show a marked tendency to acknowledge the male point of view politely before arguing their own case, rather than arguing openly against it, whereas I did not notice any male speaker showing this particular form of deference. In the *third* extract, the group's ability to operate within a pedagogically approved model of collaborative talk raised questions about whether such a model might again circumscribe rather than enhance the possibilities of that particular speech context. In all cases, it might be argued that there was a lot more going on than just 'language'.

However, in contrast to Swann's (1992: 80) implied assumption that there is a material 'reality' of, for example, gender differentiation beyond the realm of language, I prefer to adopt the post-structuralist perspective that relationships between students are always discursively produced, negotiated and contested *through* language. Furthermore, student and teacher–student relationships are to a large extent governed and organised by the range of discourses available *within* the school and classroom context.

My awareness of the significance of the interaction of certain discourses in the classroom setting was almost subliminal during the course of the research study. It was only upon successive rereadings of my field-notes after the completion of the field study that I became aware that three discourses in particular were actively constructing and mediating the classroom experience. As a self-reflexive researcher, I am aware that these are discursive constructs that I chose to categorise and foreground in this study, and I certainly do not assume them to be, in positivist terms, universally self-evident.

Working in reverse order, it came as no surprise that I chose to foreground the discourse of *gender differentiation*, as this explicitly helped me to address my original research questions above. By this, I mean a conventionalised set of ways of differentiating individuals' identities in the world primarily according to their sex or gender. The discourse of *collaborative talk* particularly struck me as pervading the ways in which students and teachers in this study articulated and practised the subject of English in the classroom. By this, I mean the application of apparent sets of expectations from both teachers and students that most assessable talk in the English classroom should be co-operative, facilitative, supportive and involve active listening. However, the discourse of *approval* – the ways in which social relations in the classroom are governed by the support and approbation of its participants – was perhaps much more of a surprise. This discourse 'discovered me'; as my original research questions testify, I was not looking for it! All three discourses are contextually situated, and therefore, as Fairclough and Wodak (1997: 276) point out, are also inextricably linked to each other:

> Discourses are always connected to other discourses which were produced earlier, as well as to those that are produced synchronically or subsequently ('the intertextuality of a text').

In the next chapter, I shall analyse how these three discourses, both individually and intertextually, work to define, construct, limit or enhance the possibilities for students to use speech in public contexts. Here, I shall define what I understand by each discourse in more detail below.

Discourse of approval

I noticed fairly early on in my observations that this discourse of approval was constructed differently by students and teachers. In terms of the students, *peer* approval denotes the ways in which students' relations with each other are organised and expressed in terms of notions of 'coolness', popularity, personal confidence, physical attractiveness and sexual reputation, friendship patterns, sporting prowess and so on (Francis, 1998). Peer approval was also interwoven with a discourse of *teacher* approval: that is, the extent to which a teacher appeared to favour or privilege one student as a speaker over another. Whereas peer approval was often seen to empower students directly as speakers in public settings, the discourse of teacher approval was much more ambiguous in its effect: receiving special attention or favouritism from the teacher might well be construed negatively by students, particularly those concerned to be positioned by their peers as 'cool' or 'unboffy' ('not a boffin').

My growing awareness of the power of this discourse upon the spoken interactions of students in this classroom setting arose from two sources. First, a particular theme began to emerge in my field-notes, which recorded 'a certain relationship between the extent to which a student is approved and liked by their classmates, and their access to the floor'. I noted how, for example, two 'popular' male students were often not interrupted by their peers and, furthermore, were actively given support for what they said by the use of, say, minimal responses. This appeared to be in contrast with less popular students, male and female, who were often interrupted or heckled when they spoke in a public forum.

Secondly, I became aware of the power of approval from the various interviews I conducted, both with the groups of students and with the class teacher. Many of the interviewees spoke quite spontaneously about the issue of 'popularity', its effects upon class relationships, and its construction of speech prerogatives – the preferential rights of certain students to 'the floor'. A set of constructs seem to be associated with this particular discourse: for example, students who are approved by their peers are usually described as 'self-confident', 'popular' and 'mature'. Indeed, the interviewees' comments seemed to imply that there was a self-fulfilling prophecy at work, a kind of iterative process whereby the more confident a student is, the more popular they are likely to be and, consequently, the more confirmation they receive as speakers. This is a process from which the teacher, when separately interviewed, implied she herself was not immune. It indicated to me that there might be some common ground between those students who receive peer approval and those who earn teacher approval, as indicated by these extracts (analysed more fully in the next chapter) from separate interviews:

CLASS TEACHER: People listen to [Joe]; people actually want to hear what he has to say. . .

. . .

GINA (a female student): I think it is students who are more confident in themselves, like Joe and Damien who are appearing confident, who seem to be more persuasive.

...

CLASS TEACHER: [Joe's] quite witty and sharp, and the way he comes out with witty things is more the reason why people want to listen to him because he is entertaining, and you want to listen to people who are entertaining and I think that is significant.

Considering that the above comments happen to be about male students, it is possible to see how a discourse of gender differentiation intersects with this discourse of peer approval. According to the interview data, what constitutes male popularity does not appear to be the same as what constitutes female popularity, and therefore it is not possible to assume that girls and boys are positioned on an equal basis within the discourse of peer approval, as my analysis reveals in Chapter 5.

Discourse of collaborative talk

I have already mentioned above how a model of collaborative talk has occupied a dominant place in the way that the subject of English has recently been conceptualised in British education (e.g. Howe, 1992; Mercer, 1995; Wilkinson *et al.*, 1990). Swann (2002), in describing the 'authorised' model of collaborative talk as 'designer discourse', has suggested that certain students, and particularly girls, have actually gone beyond their training into the rules of collaborative engagement, actively 'designing' co-operation in their classroom and social practices.

My awareness of the power of the discourse of collaborative talk and its intertextual links with the other two discourses emerged from at least three sources within the data. First, as I mentioned above, it was evident that there has been a recent shift in the English examination criteria for speaking and listening from a model of collaborative talk to one that places a higher value on persuasive, performance talk in public contexts. This is made obvious if we look again at the rubric used to describe the criteria for a grade A* from the *current* generation of GCSE English syllabuses, and compare this with the description of a grade A (the top grade) from the *previous* generation of syllabuses:

Grade 'A':
The candidate will be *sensitively* critical and self-critical in group discussion . . . will take on a variety of roles, and will show a *sensitive* and informed awareness of some

of the factors which influence people's attitudes to the way other people speak. (my italics)

(NEAB, 1996)

Grade 'A*':

The candidate will . . . use language in a *dynamic* and influential way; make thought-provoking contributions through *powerful* expressions and *command* of the situation. (my italics)

(NEAB, 1999)

Setting aside for a moment the considerations about gender I raised earlier, this change in the criteria for a top grade A heralds a distinct move away from the orthodox model of collaborative talk in English teaching. Whereas the first extract connotes the model grade A student to be someone who is rather passive and academic, listening rather than talking, and responding 'sensitively' rather than directly influencing others, the second extract connotes an altogether more active and assertive profile. In the 1996 version, the repetition of the word 'sensitive' signifies the discursive work it performs within the rhetoric of the collaborative talk model.

My observations and interview data indicated that there were tensions in classroom practice between the models of English implied by the 'old' and the 'new' syllabuses. Arguably, the research class in my study represented a generation of students brought up within a culture of collaborative talk, while their teachers saw themselves as purveyors and guardians of this particular culture. The very fact that I was conducting a study focusing upon 'speech in public contexts' foregrounded an underlying *tension* in the English department's discursive practices: on one hand, I heard teachers repeatedly speak (not necessarily in these words) of a continuing allegiance to the model of collaborative talk and, on the other, of a pressure to meet the syllabus requirements for an alternative model of speaking and listening. I therefore had to consider what effects, if any, this kind of discursive tension may have had upon students' spoken performances in classroom public contexts.

The second source from which I identified a discourse of collaborative talk at work was from the frames of reference that determined classroom interactions, often explicitly articulated by the class teacher before an oral activity. For example, in a typical whole class discussion, the class teacher is concerned that the 'rules' of collaborative talk – the ability to listen, take turns and co-operate with each other – are followed by everybody. A discourse of collaborative talk appears to be shaping the teacher's agenda for classroom management as well as the explicit 'rules' for spoken interaction:

32 *TEACHER*: Alright, you are going to have to go one at a time, everybody. Hands up, so
33 you all get a say. OK. One at a time. You won't hear if you all talk at once. Alright, Joe,
34 you started, so carry on. I want everyone else to listen carefully, respect each other's turn, and
35 then put your hands up if you want a chance to speak.

Thirdly, the comments made by different groups of students in their interviews indicated their own awareness of the importance of a model of collaborative talk in designing and regulating their own contributions to classroom discursive practices, as these extracts illustrate:

ME: What makes a good speaker in [a small group] discussion?
REBECCA: Clear reasons for their views.
GINA: They've got to listen to other people when they're talking and not try to talk over them.
HELEN: Politeness, patience, and not coming over as bossy, not taking over and giving everyone a turn.

. . .

ME: What did you think of yourself on the video?
KATE: I think I needed to listen more to what others had to say because Duncan came up with a lot of good points but no one was really listening to him. That's why he couldn't hear himself. Every time he went to talk, everyone interrupted and people weren't really listening, because he was right about quite a lot of stuff. So I think I needed to listen more.

These comments almost echo those of the teacher in setting the rules of engagement for the class discussion, as well as the criteria from the current and previous English examination syllabuses. Nevertheless, in post-structuralist spirit, there was evidence of explicit counteracts of resistance among the students against the authorised discourse:

DUNCAN: I just like a good argument. I will argue with anyone. Everyone was arguing with me. Nobody would believe me.

ME: What was your role in the discussion, Duncan?

DUNCAN: Against everyone.

ROBERT: Chairman Mao.

Discourse of gender differentiation

While the classroom study explicitly foregrounds gender as a discourse worthy of investigation, I found it interesting to learn from my observation and interview data just how much students and teachers constructed and thereby naturalised their experiences in the classroom according to constructs of gender differentiation. I observed this process of naturalisation operating on at least two levels. First, there was the overt level of reflection in the research interview setting, where participants were encouraged to be evaluative about their roles and relationships within the research study. I noticed how a discourse of gender differentiation surfaced unprompted as common-sense thinking in the way both teachers and students generalised about many aspects of their classroom experiences, as these examples illustrate:

GINA: I think the girls were putting their hands up more. They didn't want to speak over somebody, whereas the boys don't mind as much. They are more competitive.

. . .

JOE: You've got girls' views and you've got boys' views then you put them together. They've got different experiences of things.

. . .

CLASS TEACHER: The girls had thought it through and were almost reading it out. With the boys there was hesitation; I don't know whether it was real or just for effect because it often gets a laugh.

Comments such as these, in which generalisations are made about girls' and boys' supposed typical behaviour, were usually offered spontaneously and were very rarely solicited by me. From the start of my collaboration with the research partners, I had tended to highlight my interest in 'speech in public contexts' rather than gender, simply because I didn't want 'the gender question' to govern the ways in which participants responded in interview. I therefore tended to avoid asking explicitly gender-related questions in our conversations, and when students or teachers described their classroom experiences in gender-differentiated terms, I did not consider that they were necessarily saying what they thought I wanted to hear; although from a self-reflexive stance, I can never fully know the extent to which my subtextual agenda may have 'leaked' into the discursive framework of the interviews. Also, and perhaps more significantly, one of the three video-recorded activities, the student groups, was organised on the basis of gender differentiation, although this was simply one out of the many group activities I had observed.

Secondly, I realised that gender differentiation is not only a matter of common-sense thinking that routinely informs 'normal' conversation, it is also deeply embedded within the structures of classroom discursive practice. This is manifest, for example, in the rules of social engagement between boys and girls; in their apparent styles of speaking and listening; in small group and whole class dynamics, and in teacher–student relationships, as I explore in the next chapter. All these are founded at a deeper level, as I go on to explore in this book, by a mythology of gender differentiation within our culture that, as Bing and Bergvall (1998) have argued, is also perhaps unintentionally fuelled by the work of the 'difference' school of language and gender theorists, both populist (e.g. Gray, 1992; Pease and Pease, 2001; Tannen, 1992) and academic (e.g. Coates, 1993; Holmes, 1992). For young adults, the construction of a peer-approved gendered identity (the meeting point of the discourses of peer approval and gender differentiation) is likely to be a critical factor in gaining social acceptance. It is also invaluable, I shall argue, in achieving academic success. Thus, it must take a brave or eccentric young person to resist our culture's prevailing norms of masculinity or femininity.

In terms of the research focus of the classroom study, the potential 'problem' with the workings of any dominant discourse is that it might potentially circumscribe or inhibit the ways in which students feel able to contribute to spoken interactions, by closing down the possible range of ways of being available to them. However, as the FPDA commentary demonstrates in Chapter 5, speakers are always multiply positioned by different and competing discourses rendering them variously powerful and powerless.

A feminist post-structuralist analysis?

Having identified three key discourses at work within this classroom context, my task in the next chapter is to describe and interpret the ways in which such discourses compete and yet supplement each other to constitute the verbal and non-verbal interactions of the student speakers. However, any act of *feminist* research such as this must put the social or discursive construction of gender at the centre of its inquiry – in other words, it must select a feminist focus for analytical attention. Feminism is, among other things, 'a form of attention that brings into focus particular questions' (Fox-Keller, 1985: 6). From an FPDA perspective, this entails the substantial task of considering *gender differentiation* to be a significant discourse in terms of understanding the practices of any group of speakers. Furthermore, FPDA must endeavour to allocate space to those *female* voices, which may have been peripheralised or silenced by discursive practices which produce the effect of constituting male speakers as more powerful than female speakers. As I discussed in Chapter 1, this is not driven by the feminist emancipatory project, but is part of the post-structuralist quest to bring a richer, more diverse range of ideas, viewpoints, voices and readings into textual play.

The potential contradictions inherent in the ways in which feminist principles interconnect with the post-structuralist paradigm have already been discussed in Chapters 1 and 2. The key point here is that feminist post-structuralism takes issue with the traditional feminist view that, for example, female students are uniformly disempowered. It prefers instead to promote an understanding of the complex and often ambiguous ways in which girls/women are simultaneously positioned as relatively powerless within certain discourses, but as relatively powerful within alternative and competing discourses. This ceaseless shape-shifting that speakers experience between different subject positions can occur synchronically within a single speech event or context, or diachronically across a range of speech events or contexts. In other words, girls/women are not permanently trapped into silence, victimhood or oppression by dominant discursive practices;

rather there are moments within competing discourses in which females can convert acts of resistance into previously unheard but always intertextualised forms of 'new' expression. Just how girls achieve these moments of resistance will be demonstrated in the FPDA approach to discourse analysis in the next chapter.

5
The Classroom Study

Introduction

Following on from Chapter 4, I shall now apply a feminist, post-structuralist discourse analysis to transcripts of a whole class discussion involving 24 students and their English teacher. My main intention in this chapter is to demonstrate how the theoretical principles of FPDA translate into the actual practice of analysing stretches of spoken discourse in the natural setting of the classroom.

As discussed in Chapter 4, the transcript material is extracted from a corpus of data forming a much larger study of classroom spoken interaction. To recap briefly, the original aim of the larger research study was to investigate whether girls were considered to be as 'effective' as boys when speaking in public settings such as whole class discussion or debate. An extensive review of the literature (Baxter, 2000b) had indicated that gender differentiation *is* a pertinent discourse in researching speech in classroom contexts, and further-more, while girls are often perceived to be more articulate than boys, they may nonetheless be at a disadvantage in assessment terms (e.g. Cheshire and Jenkins, 1991; Swann and Graddol, 1995; Wareing, 1993). In the extracts below, students were being assessed by their teachers according to new British examination criteria for effective speech in public contexts (EDEXCEL, 1998). The feminist post-structuralist approach used in this chapter aims to analyse the ways in which examination constructs of 'effective' speech are constituted and mediated by the interplay of three interwoven discourses found to be at work within this classroom, namely peer approval, collaborative talk and gender differentiation.

In order to make a close and detailed FPDA commentary, I will focus on just 4 of the 24 students from the research study (two girls and two boys) whom I have called Anne, Rebecca, Joe and Damien, although there are references to other members of the class (such as Helen, Gina, Cathy, Kate, Michael, Simon). Anne, Rebecca, Joe and Damien have been selected here because they all appeared to be relatively effective speakers, according to their class teacher's application of the examination criteria (EDEXCEL, 1998) to their oral coursework. However, I wanted to make comparisons between the supposedly effective female speakers and their male counterparts. Would the purportedly more effective female speakers be able to hold their own alongside the effective male speakers? Would the female students be considered to be at least as effective as the male students in this public speaking context, by themselves, their teacher, a team of assessors and the researcher?

A feminist post-structuralist approach to discourse analysis should give space to the multiple voices and perspectives of an event in order to create multi-faceted, multi-layered insights into the case. In the analysis that follows, my own analysis as a researcher is juxtaposed and interwoven with the accounts of participants in the study: that is, the four students and their peers, their class teacher and a team of teacher assessors.

This chapter is organised in two parts, the first entitled 'Anne and Rebecca' and the second entitled 'Joe and Damien'. Within each part, the format is the same: two extracts have been selected from the transcript of the whole class discussion which I have identified as 'significant moments': pertinent for the ways in which they illustrate and exemplify the positioning of the two selected speakers in relation to the three discourses of peer approval, collaborative talk and gender differentiation. There are two types of analysis: a *denotative* analysis of each extract followed by a *connotative* analysis, in other words, the FPDA commentary. See Chapter 3 for a full exposition of these forms of analysis.

The transcripts are all taken from the same whole class discussion based on the discussion activity, 'The Desert Survival Situation' (Lafferty and Pond, 1989), which consisted of three stages. The first stage required each member of the class individually to rank-order a list of 15 items such as water, a compass, first aid kit and sunglasses in terms of their relative importance to human survival, in the imaginary circumstance that they have crash-landed in a desert. For the second stage, the class was organised into three mixed ability groups in order to agree a group ranking of the 15 items. For the final stage, all three groups were brought together for a whole class discussion in order to agree a common strategy for survival in the desert.

Damien and Joe

I begin my development of a feminist post-structuralist approach to discourse analysis with an exploration of the speech used in a whole class discussion by two male students, Damien and Joe.

Extract one

The following extract starts about ten minutes into the whole class discussion. The class teacher has just identified the controversial issue in the debate: that people have to make a choice about whether the survivors should walk from the crash site to a mining camp some sixty miles away, or whether they should stay put. Anne has just suggested a compromise: that the survivors could do both. (A note on the transcription methods used below is given in Appendix 2.)

TEACHER: OK, OK . . . can anyone see a problem with that? Ssshhh

JOE: Yes, yes . . . (*HE IS USING HIS WHOLE BODY TO ATTRACT THE TEACHER'S ATTENTION, LIFTING HIS BODY OUT OF THE CHAIR AND WAVING HIS ARM. OTHER PEOPLE ALSO HAVE THEIR HAND UP*)

SIMON: If you walk away from it, you may be moving but they would have less chance of finding you.

JOE: Not if you have a compass.

TEACHER: Alright, Joe.

JOE: Um, well, at day, it's quite hot, right, well, very hot in fact, and um, you are going to be walking all this way. There's probably some old people, and

101   they're not really going to manage, so you might end up carrying them . . .

102   *(ONLY REBECCA NOW HAS HER HAND UP. SHE HAS HAD HER HAND UP*

103   *CONTINUOUSLY FOR THE LAST FIVE MINUTES)*

104   **TEACHER**: Alright, and so there's a problem . . .

105   **JOE**: . . . and they're going to need more water, and so, during the day

106   *(TEACHER IS ENCOURAGING HIS COMMENTS WITH 'OK. OK')* you could use

107   the parachute to cover up the wreckage of the plane and that can attract

108   people, the top of it, and you're under shelter. You could look for food or

109   whatever, and then travel when it's colder and use the stars as direction,

110   because there's the North Star, and there's obviously an opposite, so that's

111   south, then there's east and west.

112   **TEACHER**: So, in your view, Joe, what is the best course of action?

113   **JOE**: It's pointless not to travel because otherwise you are certain to die;

114   well, not certain, because someone might find you, but you don't know when

115   they are going to come, and as you've only got a litre of water, um, per

116   person, it's not going to last that long, and so, you need to eat or whatever, so

117   you are going to have to find food, and you are going to have to walk at

118   night, because it's going to be colder . . . *(DAMIEN MAKES OVERLAPPING*

119   *SUPPORTIVE COMMENTS DURING THIS)*

120   **TEACHER**: OK, so in a nutshell, what are you going to do? You don't know?

121   **JOE**: Walk at night and during the day you can attract planes and stuff.

122   **CLASS TEACHER**: *(TEACHER ECHOES 'WALK AT NIGHT' AS IF TO REINFORCE IT)* If you

123   agree with what Joe has said and you can think of reasons to back it up, can you put

124   your hands up?

Denotative analysis

In this sequence, Joe has a series of three lengthy turns followed by one shorter speaking turn. No other student in the whole class discussion has this unparalleled access to 'the floor', and therefore it is worth looking closely at exactly how Joe is able so successfully to get and sustain his four turns. At the very start of the discussion, Joe succeeds in appropriating the most central and visible seating position in the classroom, which is not only in the direct line of the teacher's gaze, but is also exactly equidistant between the two cameras and their operators. Damien sits beside him on the right, and they are the most conspicuous pair in the wide-angle shots of the video-recording. At the beginning of this extract, Joe is using attention-seeking and assertive body language, so much so, that he appears to be almost literally trying to grab the teacher's attention (he is almost out of his chair, and waving his arms in such a way that it invades the body space of Damien on his right and Gina on his left). His tactics work. After an initial false start (another male student chips in to the discussion before Joe is nominated), Joe is granted the first of his four turns.

There are a number of further factors that appear to be contributing to Joe's extended access to the floor. First and foremost, the teacher is instrumental in 'clearing the space' for Joe to speak. She ignores the raised hands of other students, and consequently all except Rebecca put their hands down (l. 102). The teacher encourages and supports Joe's answers in a number of ways: she does not interrupt him; she reinforces his answers with minimal responses and head-nodding (l. 106) as he speaks; she prompts him on three occasions to take further turns by asking questions or rephrasing his points (ll. 104, 112, 120); and when he finally does finish, she legitimates his speeches by summarising the case he has argued in order to prompt further discussion from the rest of the class (ll. 123–4).

Secondly, Joe's access to the floor in this extract is not contested by other students, and appears to be actively supported. His right to speak has clearly been protected by the teacher as shown above, but no one attempts to interrupt, challenge or undermine him. Rebecca and Anne, who have challenged both Joe and Damien at previous points in the discussion, make no attempt to interrupt, but wait patiently with their hands up (e.g. l. 102). Certainly Damien makes no attempt to compete with him, and indeed Damien's body language (occasional head-nodding) and use of overlapping speech as well as minimal responses indicates unequivocal support (ll. 118–19).

Thirdly, perhaps as a result of Joe's assurance that he has a 'protected space' to speak which is not likely to be invaded by other speakers, he is able to make an extended case for his point of view. He builds up his case by developing a scenario that his audience can envisage, using visual language and graphic descriptions of the climactic conditions (ll. 99–101). He uses the second person singular ('you could'), as well as recasting his argument as a story about trying to survive ('you don't know when they're going to come and you've only got a litre of water...' (ll. 115–16)), to enable his audience to enter this imaginary world and engage with the case that he is developing.

Damien, on the other hand, makes no oral contributions to this sequence, but he is seated next to Joe and makes his support for Joe's case very evident, as indicated above.

Extract two

124   **TEACHER**: ... So if you can see that Joe has a point there, OK, let's hear

125   what you think. Damien, Michael, sorry ... (*JOE AND DAMIEN BOTH PUT THEIR*

126   *HANDS UP, BOTH HECKLE AS MICHAEL IS CHOSEN TO SPEAK*)

127   **MICHAEL**: If you walk at night, you are not going to need your supplies as much,

128   you are not going to use them as much.

129   **TEACHER**: Why? Why?

130   **MICHAEL**: Not going to use water as much ... (*SLOW HAND-CLAPPING*

131   *FROM JOE*)

132   **TEACHER**: OK, OK, ... Simon?

133   **SIMON**: Can't you get water from a cactus?

134   **TEACHER**: You have a point there. Damien?

135   **DAMIEN**: I learnt in Geography ...

136   **TEACHER**: (*MOCK SERIOUS*) You learnt in Geography, yes. (*CLASS LAUGHS*)

137   **DAMIEN**: That you *can't* drink water from a cactus, or whatever ... (*ANNE,*

138   *REBECCA AND HELEN HAVE THEIR HANDS UP THROUGHOUT THIS*

139   *SEQUENCE*)

140   **TEACHER AND JOE**: (*IN UNISON*) Why?

141   **DAMIEN**: Because it's *poisonous*.

142   **JOE**: He doesn't know *what* he is talking about. (*CLASS LAUGHS UPROARIOUSLY*)

Denotative analysis

This extract in print does not do justice to its full 'three-dimensional' effect: particularly for the latter part, it is a lively exchange between all participants involving much laughter, joking and engagement from the whole class.

The sequence begins shortly after the close of extract one, where the teacher has chosen to build upon Joe's argument and ask for responses. Even though Joe has arguably had a substantial share of the floor, he seems keen not only to obtain a further turn but is also prepared to thwart other people from obtaining or completing a turn, as is illustrated in his behaviour to Michael. Michael is one of a number of male students who play a fairly inconspicuous role in both the small groups and the whole class discussion. The extract above exemplifies the only occasion in this discussion when Michael chooses or feels able to speak. When he does, Joe and Damien both appear to do their utmost to distract attention away from him and disrupt the progress of his turn. For example, they wave their arms around and heckle him quite loudly (ll. 125–6), and Joe even slow handclaps his answer (ll. 130–1). Neither Joe nor Damien is reprimanded by the teacher for their behaviour. However, Michael does not speak again in this class discussion.

Once Damien is nominated to speak in line 134, the exchange that follows (ll. 136–42) almost has the format of a joky routine between two stand-up comedians, where Damien takes the role of 'fall guy' or 'fool', and Joe delivers the punch line (l. 142). The teacher initiates the sequence by nominating Damien to speak, then echoes his first sentence in a mock-serious, almost affectionate manner, which elicits a laugh from the class (l. 136). Both Joe and the teacher help to prompt Damien into completing his turn (l. 141), which is not allowed to remain a piece of dubiously factual information. Joe exploits the opportunity to 'send up' Damien's ingenuous response which he delivers like a punch line (l. 142), thus provoking a huge laugh from the 'audience'. At the end of this sequence, both boys are smiling broadly, and the class mood seems relaxed and vibrant.

FPDA commentary

The evidence from both extracts suggests that the discourse of *approval* is enormously powerful in constituting who gets to speak and for how long in this public setting of a whole class discussion. It indicates, for example, that students who are recognised to be 'popular' are more likely to receive peer approval and support when they wish to speak, than those who are not. A clear example of this is the difference between a student like Joe, and a student like Michael. In my interviews both with the teachers and with students, there was a considerable degree of concurrence on the extent to which the issue of 'popularity' was connected with constructs of 'self-confidence' and 'strong personalities' as these extracts indicate:

CLASS TEACHER: [Michael] lacks inner confidence. He copes with most situations but he feels unnerved by whole class situations. He gives the appearance of being O.K because he is friendly with Joe, but there is a certain reticence and shyness. He is not as cool and popular as Joe and Damien . . . It's as if he hasn't got the confidence to strike out on his own and be confident about his own view.

. . .

GINA: I think it's people who are more confident in themselves, like Joe and Damien who are appearing more confident, who seem to be more persuasive. The more confident you are to other people, the more people will listen to you. If you're confident, you obviously believe in yourself.

. . .

INTERVIEWER: What makes an influential speaker?
JOE: Someone that's quite loud.
TIM: Puts across a lot of points.
DAMIEN: People who don't get shy or embarrassed easily.
MICHAEL: They make sure everyone knows what they are saying.
TIM: They back each other up a lot. They don't have their hands up for ages waiting to be picked, they just say it out.
JOE: People who don't get embarrassed. . . . Some people just don't like speaking in front of a crowd of people. I reckon Mike doesn't like it.

These comments show that quite a strong association is being made between the way a discourse of peer approval constructs students with confident personalities as popular and what constitutes a persuasive or effective speaker in whole class discussions. In the students' own terms this appears to be the ability to speak loudly; to speak out without embarrassment; to 'chip in' to a discussion without teacher permission; and to make extended contributions.

In this study, a discourse of peer approval appears to construct a link between those students who are deemed 'popular' and those who use humour in their public speech. Popular people use humour to get a laugh and thereby consolidate their class support as Joe and Damien did in their cactus routine. The use of humour can have the effect of 'stealing the show', which may divert attention away from the more serious and substantive points being made by less entertaining students. But, less benignly, humour may be used for more subversive, anti-social ends, such as deriding or mocking those students perceived to be weaker targets, such as girls when they are perceived to be the opposition (see 'Anne and Rebecca' below), or less confident boys such as Michael. Generally it seems that those students who use humour in their speech so that they can get a laugh from both boys and girls, as in the cactus example above, are likely to be approved and therefore listened to. There were snippets of evidence of this perspective in both the teacher and student interviews:

HELEN: When people bring humour into [the discussion] it works quite well as well.

. . .

ASSESSOR J: I would have put [Joe] higher too. Watching Joe and Damien was a bit like watching *The Morecambe and Wise Show*.* I don't think there was actually any negative vibes between them at all. I think they are friends and like each other, and Joe almost gave the other boy a credibility in the group by taking his joking. This may be because I am male but I rather liked the interaction between the two boys.

This teacher's awareness, first that Joe and Damien's comic banter might be more of 'a male thing' and secondly that his own attraction to this kind of verbal display might also be 'because I am male', signifies how the discourse of teacher and peer approval is inextricably interwoven with the discourse of gender differentiation in this setting. In short, if the use of humour is very much a teacher and peer approval thing, it also seems inextricably to be 'a male thing'.

To highlight how the discourse of *gender differentiation* interacts with that of peer approval to position certain boys and girls as

---

* This was a popular British comedy shown in the 1970s

effective speakers in this context, it is first worth noting the apparent differences between boys' and girls' use of humour in the whole class discussion. There is little evidence, for example, of girls using humour in their contributions to the whole class discussion. Indeed, this was so obviously a feature that the class teacher commented that 'the girls weren't there for a laugh; they were there to make serious points in the discussion'. It may also be the case that the boys' use of humour is associated with their apparent tendency, or expectation upon them, to be more non-conformist or subversive than girls. As researchers (Hannan, 1991; Spender, 1982; Walkerdine, 1998) have shown, schools have traditionally positioned boys according to gender-stereotyped discourses which presume them to be, for example, more active, more risk-taking, more non-conformist, more 'naturally' witty and more subversive than girls. Therefore, it might be argued that teachers have developed a much greater tolerance of, and even a greater liking for, male non-conformist behaviour and, by association, their use of humour, as the class teacher's comment here suggests:

CLASS TEACHER: The girls had their hands up and waited and were happier to wait until they were invited, and I think it would have been *a far more tame discussion* had it been all girls because we would have been able to have had all hands up, but the boys would have been able to sustain it a while, but then their eagerness and their desire to be heard meant that they were shooting their mouths off even while I was speaking myself. And even when I hadn't invited them to speak they would be turning to the next person to speak with a joke or to say what they wanted to say ... The girls weren't there for a laugh, they were there to make serious points in the discussion; where they were showing any humour it was in response to what others were saying. (my italics)

Indeed, it seems that the girls weren't simply the more serious ones, they often provided a supportive audience for the more entertaining boys. While the girls did enter enthusiastically into the larger discussion and were prepared to challenge and confront the boys, there were several occasions where the girls also provided Joe and Damien with an appreciative audience backdrop, listening without interruption and laughing at their jokes. However, as we shall see in 'Anne and Rebecca', this was a one-way street, a favour that was rarely returned. In the exchange below, from the student interview with the mixed group, Kate and Cathy unwittingly echo what Fishman (1980) described as 'interactional shitwork', the phenomenon whereby females allow males to dominate any conversation by supporting what they say through their use of minimal responses, whereas, conversely, males use minimal responses for the opposite effect, to silence and subordinate females:

CATHY: When Joe was talking and Damien was talking, Joe had to be right.

KATE: When other people were talking, [Joe and Damien] were trying to distract the class with, 'Don't listen to her, don't listen to her!'

Kate and Cathy have also noted here how the more confident and dominant boys like Joe and Damien *expect* to have a privileged access to the floor. It would be reasonable to extrapolate from my evidence that once boys like Joe and Damien have gained that access, their quest appears to be twofold: to maintain peer approval for their popular status in the class by living up to their reputation as entertainers, and simultaneously to gain both peer and teacher approval by arguing their case impressively, thereby persuading others of the rightness of their point of view. The extent to which peer and teacher approval is actually being constructed through the adept use of verbal humour in public contexts is more than hinted at by the class teacher. Developing her suggestion that people 'wanted to hear what Joe had to say', she commented on this on two separate occasions:

CLASS TEACHER: It's got a lot to do with social relationships, not completely to do with the class situation, but that he is someone who's popular outside the classroom. He's also quite witty and sharp, and the way he comes out with quite witty things is more the reason why people want to listen to him because he is quite entertaining and you want to listen to people who are entertaining, and I think that's more significant.

. . .

CLASS TEACHER: Because other people want to listen to Joe and Damien because they are funny and they make you laugh . . . I find myself doing that too. I do take notice of what they say because it's . . . nice.

Thus, the intertextuality of the discourses of peer/teacher approval and gender differentiation can be clearly discerned in this teacher's comments. It seems that certain more dominant male students have not only found systematic ways through speech in public contexts of constructing themselves as likeable, entertaining and popular, but, from the perspective of the discourse of gender differentiation, have found acceptable and even attractive ways, to both sexes, of preserving that male verbal dominance. For a female to attempt to confront, debunk or silence male humour in a public context would put her into a double bind in the classroom setting. Not only would a female student risk being unpopular and shunned by the dominant male student's peer support group (both male and female); she might also be regarded as somehow less female for challenging the conversational support females are expected to give.

Lastly, true to a post-structuralist perspective on the *competing* ways in which different discourses position their subjects as powerful or powerless, the apparently powerful subject positions of Joe and Damien in class were contested by certain members of the English staff, who viewed these two boys' oral performances through the lens of an alternative discourse, that of *collaborative talk*. During the staff moderation meeting, it became clear that some of the teachers were *not* impressed by Joe's performance in particular. Indeed, both Joe and Damien were criticised for transgressing the norms of collaborative talk by showing little respect for the conversational needs of other classmates:

ASSESSOR P: I was worried about the extent to which he dominated, both him and Damien. Damien was obviously the joker of the group. But I thought with Joe it was very difficult to control his contributions so that other people could have a share. I'm not sure how many favours he did himself. The more he talked the worse he got in a way, whereas the ones who sat back and thought and put in astute observations would perhaps score a bit more highly in terms of engaging others' ideas and structuring their contributions and therefore more challenging thought processes were disclosed, compared to Joe, who tended to talk without thinking.

This teacher's remark is imbued with the philosophy of the model of collaborative talk in British secondary schools, which values listening to others, taking turns, sharing out talk time, not speaking at too great a length, respecting other people's viewpoints and responding to their ideas (Swann and Graddol, 1995; Wilkinson *et al.*, 1990). This may now be an area of contestation for English teachers at a time when the new generation of British examination syllabuses have stipulated a rather different order of speaking skills, particularly at the higher grade levels. These include, as discussed in Chapter 4, being able to 'use language in a dynamic and influential way' and being able to 'make thought-provoking contributions through powerful expression and command of the situation'. Something of the discursive tension between 'the old and the new' was evident in the reactions from these English staff, to be read in juxtaposition with teacher P's comment above, who could not agree on how to grade Joe's performance:

ASSESSOR D: I go along with all the comments regarding [Joe's] lack of sensitivity but I still think he needs to be rewarded for his confidence and for his ability to express his own views quite strongly. And it's always useful in a group anyway so that you can use their ideas to stimulate discussion and argument.

. . .

ASSESSOR L: If you don't rate Joe reasonably well in that, how do you compare others against him? If you put him low down because of the negative things we have said, then what about the people who didn't participate? I would put him reasonably high.

Thus, an FPDA approach has helped to illustrate how difficult it is to define or assess the effectiveness of either Joe's or Damien's speech in public contexts, according to the conventional 'additive model' of language (Swann, 1992: 80) as 'a discrete parcel of skills that speakers have at their disposal'. There is a far more complex and intricate interplay of factors whereby speakers are positioned as relatively powerful or powerless within a web of competing discourses. Joe in particular was variously judged to be both a dominant and an effective speaker among his peers, partly because, as we have seen, his classmates appeared to associate a dominant and confident personality with the ability to speak out. In contrast with certain assessors quoted above, Joe's class teacher also judged his ability to speak in public contexts quite highly, and used the terminology of the examination syllabus (e.g. EDEXCEL, 1998) to support her opinion:

CLASS TEACHER: I think Joe in the end came out quite strongly. Although in the end there were things that were not helpful in what he was doing, he's the one who sticks out in my mind . . . he said a lot, and he was actually *persuasive and influential* in that context (my italics).

But while the other English teachers agreed that he was a dominant speaker, they found it harder to reach a consensus about whether he was an effective speaker, drawing as they did upon competing discourses of oral assessment. Judged solely by the discourse of collaborative talk, it seems that Joe is positioned rather less powerfully as a speaker in public settings than a number of his peers. Yet, judged by the competing criteria of peer approval and gender differentiation, Joe would be regarded as potentially well able to meet the new examination criteria.

Anne and Rebecca

I continue my development of a feminist post-structuralist discourse analysis with an exploration of the speech used in a whole class discussion by two female students in the class, Anne and Rebecca.

Extract one

This extract featuring both Anne and Rebecca is taken from an early point in the class discussion when the teacher has prompted the students to think strategically about whether, as desert survivors, they would choose to walk to the nearest known habitation or remain at the crash-landing site. The discussion has now begun to centre on whether or not the survivors would need a compass:

24 *TEACHER*: Anne?
25 *ANNE*: If you didn't go the, er, habitat (sic), you're not going to be able to
26 survive with just the water and say, the overcoat (*JOE INTERRUPTS FROM*

7   'SAY').

8   *JOE*: You can still go there, can't you?

9   *REBECCA*: Yes.

0   *ANNE*: Not if you haven't got a compass because you are southwest.

1   *JOE*: Yeah, but if you are going to be travelling during the day. . . (*SEVERAL*

2   *OF THE BOYS TRY TO ADD ON, TO REINFORCE JOE; BOYS SPEAK LOUDLY*

3   *WITHOUT BEING NOMINATED BY THE TEACHER; A NUMBER OF GIRLS HAVE*

4   *THEIR HANDS UP*)

5   *TEACHER*: Rebecca.

6   *REBECCA*: But it's pointless trying to stay in one place. You have got to try and

7   survive. You can't just stay in one place. (*GENERAL HUBBUB AS REBECCA*

8   *SPEAKS; SOME HECKLING FROM ONE BOY; DAMIEN ATTEMPTS TO BUTT IN*)

9   *TEACHER*: Hands up, everyone; hands up.

0   *REBECCA*: Until someone will, might come along, you've got to at least *try*. And without a

compass, you don't know where you are going.

DAMIEN: Yeah, but. . . yeah, but. . . (*INTERRUPTS REBECCA FROM 'YOU'VE'*)

TEACHER: Damien

DAMIEN: I think that, sorry, just a minute . . . (*GENERAL LAUGHTER FROM THE CLASS*
AS HE MAKES FACES AND PRETENDS TO FALL OFF HIS CHAIR)

Denotative analysis

Throughout this extract, there is evidence to suggest that both Anne and later Rebecca struggle to complete a sentence or develop a point of view in a sustained way because they experience a series of interruptions and distractions from other speakers, most noticeably from several of the boys. Anne is possibly half way through her point about walking to the habitation (l. 26) when she is interrupted by Joe (l. 28). Having got only the gist of her point, he quickly challenges her. At this point Rebecca signals that she is on Anne's side by answering Joe's question for Anne, who then succeeds in making the second half of her original point. However, if she is about to develop a reasoned case, she is unable to because Joe challenges her (ll. 31–4), supported by heckling comments from several other boys and Damien in particular. During this sequence, Rebecca has kept her hand up, and the teacher apparently supports her conformity to the class rules, by nominating her to speak. In her next two speaking turns, Rebecca tends to assert her point and then repeat it (ll. 36–7), rather than developing a case by drawing on fresh evidence or new insights. It is at this point that she experiences further interruptions from several boys, as well as some heckling from Damien. Having repeated his attempts to interrupt Rebecca (l. 38 and l. 42), he is finally granted a turn (l. 43) by the teacher. Instead of making a contribution to the discussion, he seems to falter and 'lose his thread' (l. 44). This is interpreted by other members of the class as a subversive act of clowning and therefore they laugh. The video-recording shows Damien smiling and making faces (l. 45), clearly pleased at this reaction. He finally pretends to fall off his chair.

Extract two

145   *TEACHER*: Rebecca?
146   *REBECCA*: (*HER HAND HAS BEEN UP A LONG TIME*) I agree with Joe
147   that you should walk at night so that you can cool off, but you need to sleep,
148   otherwise you are just going to, um, run out of energy, but I think it's
149   dangerous sleeping in the day because it's hot and you don't know what to
150   do. (*TEACHER NODS; GIVES SUPPORTIVE MINIMAL RESPONSES.*) I think if you
151   wait at one point you're just going to think, "Oh, we could be doing some
152   thing right now, we could be at least *trying* to get where we want to go.'
153   *TEACHER*: Ummm . . . Anne?
154   *ANNE*: I think that Joe's idea of walking at night and staying put during the
155   day is a good idea, but how many people can actually read the stars?
156   (*GENERAL LAUGHTER AT THIS. JOE IS HECKLING,* 'There's a North
157   Star . . . it's the bright one . . . it's the bright one . . .') Yeah, but who knows which
158   one is the North Star? The point is to get where you want to get . . . (ANNE
159   *PERSISTS WITH HER POINT DESPITE HECKLES AND DERISIVE LAUGHS FROM*
160   *JOE AND DAMIEN*). I'm just putting across the facts . . .
161   *TEACHER*: Thank you very much. Valid point.

Denotative analysis

In this extract, both Rebecca and then Anne show evidence of speaking more extensively within this public context, but not before encountering some difficulties in gaining access to the floor. The video-recording shows that Rebecca has had her hand up almost continuously since she last spoke at line 41. While she has clearly observed the class rules of waiting to be nominated by the teacher, it has not necessarily paid off. When she does speak, however, she has one of the lengthiest turns of any student during the entire discussion. The teacher grants her both the licence to talk and affirms what she is saying as she speaks, by nods and making minimal responses (l. 150). Perhaps because of this overt support, Rebecca is able to speak entirely without interruptions. She goes on to argue her case through the use of a number of rhetorical strategies: strategic agreement with one aspect of the opposing case (l. 146); counterbalancing this with her own argument (ll. 146–8); developing an imaginary scenario (ll. 149–52), and internal monologue (ll. 151–2). Whilst it might be posited that Rebecca's argument isn't strictly coherent, she *is* able to sustain a point of view. On the other hand Anne does not appear to fare so well. Again her speaking turn is authorised by the teacher, but this is not followed up with verbal or non-verbal support. Furthermore, Anne has to withstand an onslaught of heckling and derisive laughter from both Damien and Joe, the latter in particular attempting to interrupt and take over her turn (ll. 156–7). Despite this, she resists their interruptions (l. 157 and l. 160), challenges and sees off their arguments (l. 155 and l. 158), thus achieving an appreciative laugh from the rest of the class and thereby managing to complete her turn.

FPDA commentary

In these extracts, Anne and Rebecca both demonstrate their positions as key players in the whole class discussion, but there is also evidence that the practices that might constitute an effective speaker in this particular context are once again mediated through competing discourses (teacher and peer approval; collaborative talk; and gender differentiation).

Who gets to speak, and to speak at some length, in the secondary English classroom context depends on a complex interplay of subject positions largely governed by these competing discourses. To consider, first of all, the discourse of *teacher approval*, it appears from the above evidence that not all students in the class are treated in exactly the same way. Both extracts foreground, by my very choice of them, moments when Rebecca and Anne get to speak. To this extent, they fail to offer a representative picture of Rebecca and Anne's role in the discussion as a whole; there are longish sequences when neither gets to speak at all. It is observable from the video-recording that both 'putting your hand up' and 'waiting for the teacher to pick you' are rules that are not consistently observed. For example, Rebecca is nominated by the teacher to speak in both the extracts above and gets more turns than several of her peers. Yet she has her hand up for long periods during the discussion as a whole and, indeed, there are sequences where she is the *only* student to have her hand up but, despite this, the teacher elects other students to speak rather than her. In the student interviews, it is clear that Rebecca considers that she had been unfairly overlooked, and has reconstructed this in terms of her subject positions within the competing (sub) discourses of teacher and *peer approval*. When asked what she thought of the whole class discussion, Rebecca replies quite vehemently:

REBECCA: Favouritism. Miss never picked me. I had my hand up about five minutes before Anne did. She just puts her hand up and the teacher went, 'Yes, Anne.' I got really angry then, I can remember.

INTERVIEWER: Who gets picked and who doesn't?

REBECCA: The boffy people. Like the real good people who are real good at work. And the teacher thinks, 'This is on film today, she'll be good to speak.' But she never picked me.

INTERVIEWER: Who are the people who get picked?

HELEN/GINA/REBECCA: Anne, Joe.

Rebecca seems to feel that she herself does not fit the teacher's model of a 'boffy' (from 'boffin') student, while in her view, Anne receives preferential access to the floor because she *does* fit this model. Interestingly, Rebecca constitutes her own position as one in which she is obliged to compete with Anne for the teacher's attention. Thus, the winner is empowered by being regarded as the teacher's favourite but, conversely, peer approval ensures that this victorious position is undermined by the disempowering, put-down tag of 'boffiness', that is, popular or likeable people among their peers in the classroom setting are unlikely to be 'boffy'. Rebecca therefore can be seen as perceiving herself to be relatively *powerless* compared to Anne in terms of the discourse of teacher approval, but to be relatively *powerful* in terms of peer approval. Indeed, her powerful position as a popular student was also demonstrated during the student interviews. Gina and Helen, her quieter co-interviewees, seemed quite prepared to allow her to dominate the floor, manifested by the ways in which they were echoing, supporting or building on her views throughout the interview.

The extent to which either Rebecca or Anne were able to gain speaking turns in the whole class discussion and, having gained them, to speak uninterruptedly, at any length, can also be 'read' in terms of their subject positions within the competing discourse of *gender differentiation*. From a feminist post-structuralist perspective, it can be argued that female linguistic interactions may be limited by the dominant definitions of femininity shaping the subject positions available to girls like Anne and Rebecca. My analysis of the two extracts above shows evidence of how these definitions might be limiting Anne and Rebecca's spoken performances in public contexts in three linked ways. First, both in their speech and behaviour, the girls show a greater conformity (than do the boys featured in these extracts) to the rules of classroom discussion. For example, while Anne and Rebecca wait with their hands up for the teacher to nominate them to speak and thus risk not procuring a turn, several boys, notably Joe and Damien, are prepared to rule-break by 'chipping in' to interrupt and effectively disrupt each girl's turn, and, in at least one case, succeed in taking over the speaking turn (extract one, l.42). Dominance theorists (e.g. Spender, 1982; Swann and Graddol, 1988) might explain this by suggesting that boys have learnt a range of rule-breaking strategies in order to gain control within the public classroom context. Alternatively, a feminist post-structuralist approach would suggest that boys have available to them a range of more powerful subject positions than girls do within this setting. This is made apparent in the student interviews, where both Rebecca and Gina indicate an implicit understanding of how potentially disempowering constructs, such as conformity and good behaviour, are considered to be more compatible with female teenage identity, whereas constructs of non-conformity and misbehaviour are considered to be more compatible with male teenage identity:

REBECCA: I was probably more self-conscious in the bigger group in case I would sound a fool. I had a lot of things to say but I couldn't say them because I wasn't picked.

INTERVIEWER: So you wanted to speak . . .

REBECCA: Yes, I really did. I really wanted to say my view. At one point I was going to shout them out, but I thought, 'No, I better behave myself'.

INTERVIEWER: Was that affected by the camera?

REBECCA: I don't think I would have ever shouted out. That would have been rude and I would have got told off.

INTERVIEWER: Did anyone shout out?

REBECCA: Yeah. Joe and Damien did because they wanted everyone to know what they thought.

. . .

GINA: I think the girls were putting their hands up more. They didn't want to speak over somebody, whereas the boys didn't mind as much. They are more competitive. A lot of the girls were really defensive; they had their arms crossed against them.

Secondly, girls are often constructed as the more supportive sex. This seemed to be evident in the way girls tend to offer boys considerably more interactional support than they receive in return, endorsing previous research by both dominance theorists (e.g. Fishman, 1980) and difference theorists (e.g. Jenkins and Cheshire, 1990). In the second extract, we saw how both Anne and Rebecca pick up on, and build upon an argument introduced by one of the boys:

146   *REBECCA*: I agree with Joe that . . .

. . .

154   *ANNE*: I think that Joe's idea of walking at night and staying put during the day is a
155   good idea. . .

In contrast, at no point during the course of the whole class discussion does any boy ever endorse an idea introduced or developed by a named girl. This feature was so noticeable that it was remarked upon quite spontaneously during one of the student interviews:

KATE: The girls are quieter. The boys say something and the girls just support it.

CATHY: The boys say what they think. It's like the husband and the little wife who has to support them.

KATE: The girls are like hiding their face in shame that they are actually disagreeing with the boys.

Theorists such as Fishman (1980) might read this as a recognition by these students of the way female, verbal subservience helps to reproduce unequal male–female power relationships on a micro-sociological scale. A feminist post-structuralist analysis would alternatively look to the *contradictory* positioning of female speakers here: on one hand, girls appear to be powerfully located according to a discourse of collaborative talk because this values supportive speech and good listening skills. On the other, according to a discourse of gender differentiation, girls are stereotypically *expected* to be good listeners (e.g. Jenkins and Cheshire, 1990; Swann and Graddol, 1995), which consequently might diminish a positive assessment of their contributions.

Thirdly, according to conventional discourses of gender differentiation, males are very often constructed as the wittier, more entertaining sex, while females are constituted as an appreciative audience, as we noted above. In the classroom, these constructions can serve to legitimate the use of male humour as a foil for exercising power in the public context. In both the above extracts, not only did boys appear to use a number of rule-breaking ploys to get access to the floor (heckling, hissing, booing the girls' contributions), but in Damien's case, his final pièce de résistance, a pretence at falling off the chair – enables him to get a laugh, subvert the discussion and simultaneously undercut the rather more serious points being made by Anne and Rebecca. By acting the fool, Damien successfully steals the limelight ensuring that the attention is on him when he wishes to speak. The teacher appears to condone his behaviour. While she is successful in preserving Rebecca's turn (ll. 35–9), she makes no apparent attempt to protect Anne's. Indeed this lack of protection, followed by her legitimation of Damien's disruptive intervention by granting him a speaking turn, adds some weight to the dominance perspective (e.g. Spender, 1980; Swann and Graddol, 1988) that teachers, boys and girls alike appear to collude in positioning males as more powerful within a range of speech contexts such as whole class discussion.

A feminist post-structuralist perspective would alternatively argue that the discourse of gender differentiation works through the institution of the school and the classroom to undermine the possibility of girls achieving powerful subject positions through linguistic interactions. It serves male interests when girls *conform* to the rules of classroom discourse (by putting their hands up, not calling out, listening carefully, providing an audience) because it allows males a greater vocal space in which to struggle for influence over their peers and possibly for approval from teachers. Within such a discursive context, the competing discourses of collaborative talk and gender differentiation, which, as we have seen, both coincidentally place a high premium on sensitive listening and orderly, sequential turn-taking, especially for females, mean that girls may be systematically positioned at a disadvantage.

Nevertheless, such discourses cannot construct the practices of subjects without producing counteracts of resistance, or supplementary challenges according to post-structuralist analysis. In this case, Anne's ability to withstand male interruptions, develop her argument and complete her turn (ll. 154–60) may actually strengthen her aptitude as a speaker in the world outside school, where interruptions, heckling and multiple or parallel conversations are often routine in public settings. This was a point implicitly acknowledged by English staff in assessing Anne's performance as effective:

ASSESSOR J: I thought Anne thought on her feet and tried to develop it, whereas the boys' contributions seemed to be: 'There it is; make of it what you want; I've said it, and in Joe's case, 'because I'm the loudest'.

. . .

ASSESSOR P: I was impressed by Anne though, because since last year I have never seen her perform in such an articulate way – very good at drama and role-play and confident in that way, but I have never seen her so articulate.

An evaluation of the study

Within the context of this particular study, the use of an FPDA approach showed me that speakers who are the most powerfully located within a discursive setting are the most likely to be assessed as effective. In other words, those students who were strongly positioned within and across the three intersecting discourses of peer approval, gender differentiation and a model of collaborative talk were more likely to be awarded a higher grade by their examiners than those who were less strongly positioned. Obviously, a powerful position within each of the three discourses did not necessarily guarantee that one student would be more favourably assessed than another, in that all speakers have some agency to resist, contest or disrupt their discursive positioning. Intriguingly, however, I discovered that examiners were more likely to award higher grades to candidates who were positioned as consistently powerful across all three discourses, than to those who specifically met the examination criteria, but were less powerfully situated overall. By way of illustration, I shall now briefly profile six speakers: Robert, Joe, Anne, Damien, Rebecca and Michael.

The type of speaker most likely to be considered effective by peers, teachers and assessors is one who is male, popular and articulate, equally versatile in their use of the approved model of collaborative talk and the more 'commanding' talk defined by the examination syllabus (EDEXCEL, 1998). This idealised subject position was exemplified by a boy called *Robert*, who is not specifically featured in the data presented in this book. He was listened to respectfully by other members of the class (peer approval); made 'a variety of sensitive contributions' (model of collaborative talk) in a way regarded by his assessors as 'exceptional for a boy' (gender differentiation), and yet had the versatility to use 'language in a dynamic and influential way', and to 'take command of the situation' (criterion for the top grade, A*). Moving on in descending grade order, *Joe* was also deemed to meet the examination criteria of being able to 'take command of the situation' and was awarded a grade A (A* to G grading system). This rating of his speech as very 'effective' was also mirrored by his powerful subject positions within two of the three identified discourses. He was regarded as a well-liked and popular boy (peer approval) who was also approved by his class teacher for his reputation as a 'wit'. However, these relatively powerful subject positions were somewhat undermined by his inability, according to a few of the assessors, to negotiate the discursive practices of collaborative talk regarded as so important within the currently approved model of English teaching in Britain.

Anne was also deemed to be an effective speaker according to her assessors, but again with some qualification. She was considered to meet the criteria for a grade A (rather than an A*) because she made an 'attempt' at commanding talk, but with the compensatory skill that she was prepared to listen and collaborate with others (model of collaborative talk). Her high grade also appears to correlate with her relatively powerful positioning across all three identified classroom discourses. She appeared to receive peer approval in different public settings, and she was praised by her class teacher for her 'leadership skills'. Yet, I would argue that her failure to achieve the top A* grade, unlike Robert, *may* have been simultaneously constituted by her less powerful subject position as a girl. Anne was expected to use 'commanding talk' in a way that is still not socially approved as a means of engagement for females. That this might be so is partly borne out by the reactions of her male peers to her attempts to challenge (particularly) male arguments in the class discussion. I have explored this subject in much greater detail elsewhere (Baxter, 1999, 2002b).

Damien, another popular male student, was awarded a B grade. Again he conforms to the pattern of being relatively powerfully positioned across all three classroom discourses. He received peer approval in the whole class discussion for his antics as the class clown and comic personality (ll. 135–42), although he was clearly overshadowed in this respect by the more dominant Joe. Again, he was singled out by the class teacher for approval because 'he comes out with witty things ... he is quite entertaining and you want to listen to people who are entertaining, and I think that's significant'. Damien's grade again reflects his weaker positioning within the discourse of collaborative talk, where he failed to impress the examiners with his ability to listen and interact. In terms of the lack of weighting placed on the skills of collaborative talk at the higher grade levels, this discourse not only appears to override the official examination criteria for 'commanding talk' at grade A*, but also the competing discourses of peer approval and gender differentiation.

Next, *Rebecca*, able and articulate but only awarded a grade C, appeared to be the least likely of this group of students to benefit from the syllabus's construction of an effective speaker. Again I would suggest that there is a link between Rachel's 'average' grade within this class and her relatively *powerless* positioning across the three identified discourses. In terms of peer approval, she was fairly popular with her peers, who strongly endorsed her more outspoken views in the student interviews. But, in the whole class discussion, her peer approved subject position was undercut by the way she allowed herself to be overshadowed by the more dominant Anne. Her interview comments suggest that she resented having to adopt the less visible position of Anne's supporter. Furthermore, she did not receive the same level of teacher approval as Anne appeared to achieve. Rebecca was perceived by her teacher to be relatively poor at collaborative talk, having been 'obstructive' in the earlier student-led discussion. This in turn reflects an intertextualised expectation that girls should be 'good' at collaborative talk and are penalised when they are not (Cheshire and Jenkins, 1991). In the whole class discussion, Rebecca positioned herself as the rule-abiding female who fails to express her views, and who was consequently rendered silent by the verbal onslaughts of the boys. She failed to receive any real credit for remaining dutifully silent: for the patient way in which she *conformed* to the class rule of 'putting your hand up and waiting for the teacher to select you to speak'.

If, as my study shows, the profile of the kind of student most advantageously placed to mobilise the resources inscribed within mixed-sex classroom discourse is an entertaining but non-conformist, articulate, confident, popular boy, then the kind of student least advantageously placed must logically be a conformist, quiet, under-confident and less popular girl. While the focus of this research was upon the more outspoken students who have demonstrated that they *can* speak in public settings with varying degrees of success, it is essential that future FPDA-driven research in such classroom contexts does not overlook the presence of a small minority of both silent girls and less popular boys who may never provide enough evidence to show whether they can or cannot speak effectively in public settings.

To this end, it is worth mentioning *Michael*, a reticent but highly articulate boy in the small group interviews, who was awarded a

D grade on the basis of his listening skills. If Michael had been a girl, his silence would have been readily explicable according to a modernist feminist analysis, silenced by the dominance tactics of the male sex. But an FPDA approach would alternatively emphasise the way in which Michael's powerless subject position is constructed by *competing* discourses, which tend to offset the presumed advantages of his biological sex identity. In this study it seems that Michael did not know how to enact his gender identity in a way that would be approved by his peers. As a consequence, he was treated with an off-hand lack of respect by his male peers, which meant that when he summoned the courage to speak, he was subject to a repertoire of verbal bullying: interruptions, heckles, jokes, put-downs and slow hand-clapping. Consequently he barely spoke more than a few sentences in the larger group settings. The FPDA commentary demonstrates how Michael's lack of peer approval impacts upon his subject positions within gender differentiation and collaborative talk, rendering him relatively powerless across all three discourses.

To sum up, the value of applying an FPDA approach to educational contexts such as this is that it can help teachers and educational researchers to become more aware of the discursive practices which govern students' interactions with one another in class. This in turn impinges upon crucial matters of pedagogy such as grading and assessment, or upon wider issues of personal and social development. Thus, however, intelligent or articulate a student like Michael might be, if he is unable to enact his masculinity through speaking publicly in peer or teacher-approved ways, he is less likely to be regarded as a student who signifies to his teacher, or as a person who signifies to his peers. Equally, however articulate or confident speakers like Anne or Rebecca may be, there are discursive limitations to the range of subject positions they are able to adopt because they are constructed as *female* speakers in public settings. Yet, girls like Anne and, particularly, Rebecca are far from ineffective as speakers within this classroom 'public' setting. But while they should not be constituted as 'victims', girls are nonetheless subject to a powerful web of institutionalised discourses that constitute boys more readily as speakers in public settings and girls more readily as an appreciative and supportive audience. Teachers and educators do need to intervene to take some form of transformative action. Girls need to learn how to resist certain dominant classroom discourses, so that they can, for example, operate within multiple and competing conversations, or 'run the gauntlet' of male barracking in order to cope with the particular pressures of speaking in mixed-sex, public contexts.

6
Developing an FPDA Approach: The Management Team Study

Introduction

In this chapter, I introduce the second research study to which I apply the method of feminist post-structuralist discourse analysis (FPDA). A case study was conducted over a period of a few weeks in Hook3 (a pseudonym), a small but successful British dotcom company. The study focuses upon the speech and non-verbal interactions of a group of senior managers within the setting of two in-house business meetings. The purpose of this chapter is therefore to set the scene for the management team study, highlighting the particular process by which I came to identify four intersecting discourses at work in this setting which appeared not only to govern the spoken interactions of this group of managers, but also to constitute the business culture of Hook3. The feminist post-structuralist discourse analysis is conducted in Chapter 7.

This chapter will provide a detailed context to this research by outlining: the purpose of the study, the research setting, the methodology, the research process and a description of the four discourses identified in this setting – historical legacy, open dialogue, competing specialisms and masculinisation. These introductory sections pave the way for a *post-structuralist* approach to the data. However, in the final section, I discuss the ways in which a *feminist* post-structuralist analysis enables researchers to be particularly sensitised to the issue of gender when exploring and questioning the discursive interactions between male and female speakers.

Purpose of the study

> Probably the biggest [task for a speaker] is the ability to get your message across, the ability to communicate to the whole group.
>
> (Interview with Richard, a Hook3 manager)

My decision to study the spoken interactions of a group of senior managers arose as a direct consequence of the classroom study described in Chapters 4 and 5. Having discovered that FPDA offers a searching and illuminating tool with which to analyse classroom speech and behaviour, I sought to explore its applicability and trans-ferability to other social and professional contexts. Furthermore, drawing upon FPDA, I wished to examine what constituted effective speech in an alternative public context such as a business meeting. Although there would clearly be no formalised criteria for assessing speech in such a context (as there was in the classroom study), it was likely that there would be unwritten rules determining who would be perceived as an effective speaker, as indicated by Richard's com-ment above. I speculated that, in parallel with classroom talk, who gets to speak, to speak at length and make a noticeable impact upon the views of their colleagues in other settings would again depend upon a complex interplay of competing discourses.

As I have argued, FPDA potentially has a valuable role to play in deconstructing discursive practices within a range of public settings other than the classroom, such as a management meeting, a job interview, a courtroom investigation, an academic conference, a public inquiry or a political debate. This is because, according to the theoretical perspective constituting FPDA, speakers in public settings are constantly negotiating for positions of power, determined by the range of discourses to which they have access, or within which they find themselves positioned. As I have discussed, FPDA might certainly be applied to speech within informal, social or private settings, as Simpson (1997) exemplified in her study of family games. In critiquing the public/private dichotomy as insidious, language and gender theorists (McElhinny, 1997; Ochs and Taylor, 1992) have argued that conversations between married couples, within families or among groups of friends are as much governed by the dynamics of unequal power relations as speech in public settings. However, in more overtly public settings, speakers are both positioned as individuals and also by formally determined subject positions (such as a job role or professional position). Furthermore, speakers are usually brought together in public settings to accomplish specific tasks such as solving problems and making decisions. In order to accommodate their formally designated subject positions, speakers are involved in a constant negotiation of power relations which enables them to prove their worth as effective decision-makers and insight-bringers. In the context of the classroom study, for example, the speakers are not simply positioned as individuals but as students and, more pertinently, as examination candidates. If students fail to speak up, they are less likely to be noticed by the assessors and therefore receive a positive assessment for their oral coursework. In the public setting of the classroom, the ability to speak up and, moreover, to speak effectively is *all*.

Drawing on these findings, I wanted to explore the possibility of applying a similar methodology to adult speech within a public setting other than education or academia, arguably used to excess in sociolinguistic studies for their convenience value. I also wished to explore whether the FPDA approach had any practical value for the research participants themselves, an issue that I had been unable to take further in the classroom study. This time I wished to give direct *feedback* to the participants in the study, that is, the managers themselves, about the findings generated by an FPDA approach. Would these managers find the descriptions and analyses of their spoken interactions helpful in terms of increasing their awareness of their own discursive practices and, if relevant, might this contribute to management change? If increased awareness and possible change were to be the outcomes of this research study, it seemed important to select a setting where people knew each other and met together regularly to solve problems and make decisions. A business setting, such as a small company prepared to accept a roving researcher, seemed to be my best bet. Yet, this in turn led to its own difficulties. Too often the written accounts of research studies appear seamless, rarely dwelling upon awkward and inconvenient matters such as problems of access to research settings. Yet the location of many research studies are as much the outcome of trial and error, persistence, careful networking, accepting compromises and being in the right place at the right time as they are the product of a perfect research design. How could I, for example, readily find a business setting which would tolerate the intrusiveness of an FPDA research intervention requiring multiple accounts of a single case? How would I be able to 'sell the idea' of the work in such a way that it would seem to have some value for future business practices within the company? Furthermore, as I intended to practise a *feminist* approach to post-structuralist discourse analysis, would I be able to find a team of people which regularly met to make decisions – and were therefore more likely to be of managerial rank – which would preferably include both males and females? The company I chose, or rather, which agreed to be chosen, was the only one of several companies approached to match these criteria and, moreover, actively welcome the research intervention I had designed. Their decision to participate in the study led to an invitation by the company's chief executive officer (CEO) to observe selected senior team meetings and interview members of this management team (MT). Full details of the research context are given in the next section.

To sum up, the aims of the research study were as follows:

- To apply an FPDA approach to an alternative public context: managers' speech in the context of senior team meetings
- To consider what constitutes effective speech in this alternative public context, where, unlike the English language classroom, there are no formal criteria by which to produce a set of definitions
- To explore whether an FPDA approach to analysing speech might provide value to the research participants themselves in terms of increasing awareness about the discursive effects of spoken interactions and, as a consequence, potentially help to challenge and transform management practices.

The research setting

Hook3 is a UK dotcom company that markets and sells information about a range of products and services in three main areas – jobs, houses and cars – on its website. The company was founded four years previously by several major shareholders in the UK newspaper and television industries, as a strategic decision to add internet-based advertising and promotion capability to their current media interests. Its first employee was *Sarah*, a website designer, who subsequently became a member of the current senior management team. The company experienced a very rapid growth from a one-woman band to the present size of over one hundred personnel. At an early stage in the launching of the new company, *Keith* was brought in as CEO to develop strategy and oversee the day-to-day management of the company. Sarah was initially responsible for the design and implementation of the technology; the routine operations of the website, but also for making contacts with clients, communicating with shareholders and for sales and marketing. In short, Sarah was in charge of the bulk of the behind-the-scenes work. A few months after the launch, Jack was appointed to take over the sales and marketing function of the business. Within the twelve months prior to my research study, three new members of the senior management team were appointed for the various specialisms within the company: *Richard*, responsible for cars; *Cliff* for homes; *Don* for jobs; and *Pete* was appointed as the financial director. This team of seven people represented the group of managers whose speech and non-verbal interactions I was intending to study.

The company occupies three floors of a modernised, open-plan, Victorian office block on the outskirts of London. Each floor houses a different occupational group within the firm: the sales and marketing team to be found on the lowest floor, the administrative and managerial staff on the middle floor, and the computer operators and programmers on the top floor. Women and men are employed in roughly equal numbers within all three areas of the business. That is to say, even in the more traditionally 'male' areas such as website designing and computer programming, there are a significant number of female employees. The only area of staffing where gender demarkation appeared to be an issue is in the management team (six men and one woman) and among the relatively small number of secretarial staff (all women). The atmosphere in the company appeared relaxed, friendly and welcoming, partly signified by the 'dress down' policy for all staff. Managers, for example, wear jeans and sweaters rather than suits.

Perhaps because the company grew very rapidly in a relatively short space of time, I learnt that there were a number of tensions within the team itself and within management practices that the CEO felt compelled to resolve. At the time I was conducting my study, a management consultancy company was also working with the senior team to implement processes of management change. Given this context, I decided to address the third aim of my study (p. 131) by 'selling the idea' of the research to Hook3 in terms of its capacity to supply useful insights into senior team relationships and management practices. Realising that the notion of an FPDA approach might be something of an anathema to a busy dotcom company, I framed the purpose of the research study to the MT in this way:

Memo to the Management Team

This short study intends to investigate what constitutes power and how this power is negotiated through the spoken interactions of senior managers attending team meetings. Power is normally constituted by means of a number of 'discourses' (ways of making sense of the world) connected to institutionalised power systems that differentiate people such as professional status, seniority, length of service, education, social class, gender, race, language, and so on. Power relations are also constituted by factors particular to an organisation such as company ethos, recent and forthcoming changes in the organisation and personality power battles. Using methods that guarantee anonymity and confidentiality, the study will observe and tape-record the spoken interactions of managers in team meetings. The focus of the study will be upon how individuals negotiate their own positions and their shifting relations with others through their verbal and non-verbal behaviour.

From this study, Hook3 should gain an impression of the varying degrees of influence people have within the management team and exactly how they negotiate that influence through their management and contestation of speaking and listening rights. It might be able to give an analysis of how certain professional, social and personal factors (e.g. status, gender, etc.) constitute the powerfulness or otherwise of each individual speaker on the MT. It might also be able to identify different allegiances in terms of the preferred ethos/culture for Hook3. As a spin-off, it might indicate those participants who are likely to support organisational changes and those who are likely to resist them.

Methodology

The best laid plans of mice and men . . .

Although the management team study set out to mirror and reproduce the best practice of the classroom study, a range of situational constraints led to the need to adapt and improvise my intended methodology. Here, I first explain the four common principles constituting both the studies (a fuller account of the FPDA approach is given in Chapter 3), and then move on to explicate the ways in which I adjusted and adapted the original methodology to this particular business setting. While the need to make adaptations may have produced some limitations upon the data, there were also some unexpected benefits as I describe below.

The four principles

In keeping with the classroom study, I drew upon ethnographic research principles for data-gathering because of their epistemological connections and parallels with feminist post-structuralist theory. This has affected the design of an FPDA methodology for this study in four ways. This section closely echoes the 'Methodology' section in Chapter 4 (p. 85), and therefore keeps the theoretical explanations of the links between ethnography and feminist structuralist inquiry correspondingly briefer.

First, ethnography favours detailed descriptions of the concrete experiences of life within a culture and the social rules and patterns that govern it. These descriptions are gathered by deploying multiple research methods, often including quantitative and qualitative techniques (e.g. Hammersley and Atkinson, 1995: 8). Hence, I planned to spend some considerable time within the research context, observing and recording a number of business meetings, conducting a series of interviews with each of the research participants, and making detailed observations of the fabric of business life within the company.

The second way in which ethnography works in partnership with a feminist post-structuralist methodology is that both emphasise and value the localised, microscopic, particular, context-bound features of given settings and cultures. In other words, both ethnographic and feminist post-structuralist methodologies honour the uniqueness of the individual case, regarding it as an exemplar of the workings of a process, which has its own internal logic. Both approaches seek to uncover, deconstruct and make explicit the internal workings of a given situation or event. Like ethnography, the feminist post-structuralist case study aims to reconstruct a single case from multiple points of view. In the MT study, I clearly had a single case, a group of senior managers using speech in public contexts in a series of business meetings. I intended to draw upon the multiple and possibly competing insights of this team of managers in order to interpret their experiences of this particular business situation.

Thirdly, ethnography has many things in common with feminist post-structuralist notions of self-reflexivity (see Chapter 3, p. 58). This posits that researchers will have a mediating effect upon the research context and subsequently on the data gathered, and consequently should be explicitly reflexive or self-referential about how their theoretical assumptions position their research accounts (e.g. Scott and Usher, 1996). In the MT study, I aimed to draw attention to the (arguably) inevitable ways in which the researcher-author weaves together the multiple accounts of the participants into the authorised genre of academic discussion. In other words, however much the FPDA researcher may wish fairly and equally to represent the mismatching and competing accounts of the research participants within an academic discussion, the monologic voice of the author ultimately prevails. Within FPDA, self-reflexivity becomes the central issue in posing questions about how authors, whether the researcher or the researched, become authors.

Fourthly, ethnography's emphasis on the inseparability of the researcher from the research context can also be linked with feminist post-structuralism's emphasis upon the intertextual, interactive and reflexive relationships between theory and practice, subject and object, and observation and participation. In this study, I was aware that I was likely to be more of an observer than a participant, according to Gold's (1958) typology for participant-observer roles. This was because, unlike my connection to teaching in the classroom study, I was *not* a part of the business world and I had no prior connection to this particular company. In the ethnographic spirit of making a research setting strange in order to observe and understand its discursive interactions, the Hook3 company was almost literally for me an alien environment. However, with all ethnographic research processes, observers gradually assume the characteristics of participants the longer they remain a part of the setting. As I explain in Chapter 7, this increasing element of participation was to be one of the outcomes and, indeed, one of the benefits of the research process.

Theory into practice

With almost any ethnographic study, the business of putting research aims or principles into practice involves a certain measure of adaptation and compromise. In terms of my first aim – to immerse myself in the culture in order to produce detailed descriptions of the concrete experience of life in this setting – I quickly realised that ethnographic research, if imposed from outside rather than being instigated from within, may be perceived suspiciously by insiders as a form of surveillance. Any form of observation of an organisation at work can become intrusive and must be treated as an ethically sensitive experience, raising issues of confidentiality, privacy and the need to protect anonymity. In simpler terms, businesses are full of secrets that they would prefer the outside world, whether suppliers, clients, stockholders, researchers, consultants or the public, not to know. Consequently, it was agreed that I would make a relatively select research intervention, which would involve observing only two MT meetings, and giving interviews with three of the seven managers expected to attend the meetings. This restricted access to the research setting meant that I was unable to deploy a multi-method approach to collecting the data in the way I had hoped. In the event, I was limited to the use of field-notes and audio-recordings of the two meetings (rather than the preferred use of video-recording to capture non-verbal behaviour), as well as four audio-recorded interviews. These semi-structured interviews, lasting about 30 minutes each, were conducted according to a common format: a set of generalised, open-ended questions were used as a starting point for discussion and, in each case, participants were encouraged to speak extensively and with non-intrusive prompts from the interviewer.

In terms of my second aim – to honour the uniqueness of the individual case and generate multiple and possibly divergent accounts of this single case – post-structuralist discourse analysis can *thrive* on relatively limited, qualitative data, provided it is able to capture the interplay of multiple-voices and texts. A single transcript or a group of transcripts of speech extracted from just one business meeting can potentially generate a rich source of data for the discourse analyst, but for FPDA purposes there must also be supplementary accounts of the experience. In the classroom study, I was able to represent the diverse voices of all the research participants: three groups of students, the class teacher and a meeting of teacher

assessors. In the MT study, I did not achieve my objective of inter-
viewing all the participants: ideally, all six participants of the meeting
should have been interviewed including the CEO. (However, I did
have an unrecorded discussion with the CEO, on which I made notes.)
Furthermore, it would also have been useful to have interviewed less
senior staff for their perceptions of organisation culture. This last
intention was partially fulfilled by an interview with Pam, the personal assistant to the management team. While not actually present
at the two meetings observed, Pam provided the ancillary service of
organising the meeting, setting up the meeting room and typing the
agenda. Her perceptions of the relationships between members of
the MT and of organisation culture and practices more generally, do
indeed bring supplementary insights to the case, as the analysis in
Chapter 7 shows.

In terms of the third aim – that researchers should be explicitly
reflexive or self-referential about how their theoretical assumptions
position their research accounts – the reader must be the judge of
how effectively I fulfil this in forthcoming chapters. With regard to
the fourth aim, my role as an observer gradually metamorphosed
into that of a participant, thus eroding the dualistic observer/partici-
pant divide in much research practice, as I became increasingly
involved in shaping suggestions for transforming management practices and culture within the company (see Chapter 8).

Identifying the discourses

With the three particular aims of the MT study in mind (see p. 131),
my approach to identifying discourses from the data gathered was to
be somewhat different from that used in the classroom study. With
the latter, my decision to use FPDA constituted an *inductive* approach,
that is, inferring a general set of principles from particular circum-
stances. This decision was more of an accidental discovery than a
preconceived plan, having applied a range of better known analytical
models to the classroom data, and found these to be inadequate for
the purpose. With the MT study, I would be broadly taking a *deduc-
tive* approach to the data, that is, applying an inference gained from
a general set of principles to a particular setting. In other words,
I explicitly intended to reapply the FPDA approach developed in the

classroom study in order to assess its value to other speech contexts. On the one hand, I was conscious of the potential for authorial fictionalising, that I must not go out *looking* for discourses where they might not exist; on the other, I knew that, as I gathered the data this time, I would be especially sensitised to the existence of discourses operating both overtly and subtextually within this business setting. In any form of ethnographic research, there is always the fear that a researcher only sees what she wants to see. It was for this reason that I considered it important this time to feed back my analysis to the participants themselves and learn their response.

Nevertheless, on the level of identifying discourses, I considered that I was adopting a classic ethnographic approach (e.g. Hammersley and Atkinson, 1995) to gathering information, because categories were generated *from* the data rather than imposed *upon* the data, albeit within the prescribed methodological framework of FPDA. The point about identifying discourses is that they are rarely obvious to a researcher on first encountering the data, but only emerge in the process of engaging with multiple accounts of a particular case. It was only after successive rereadings of my field-notes, and after repeatedly replaying the various audio-transcripts, that particular discourses came to my attention. However, in many ways, the discourses were actually much easier to identify than in the classroom study, because the interviewees were relatively more articulate, reflective and self-aware of relationships, tensions and power struggles within the team. This was probably a result of their participation in the concurrently run management development programme, which appeared to call for a high level of reflection and self-appraisal.

In locating the discourses, I found that it was useful to ask the following four questions:

- Which words, terms or phrases were repeatedly used in the speech contexts and by whom?
- Which themes, issues and preoccupations were common to all the transcripts?
- What connections, links and associations were apparent in what people were saying to each other?
- What contradictions, oppositions or competing viewpoints were apparent in what people were saying to each other?

As a result of this research process, I gradually became aware of the significance of the interaction between four discourses in the Hook3 context: historical legacy, open dialogue, competing specialisms and masculinisation. While each is separately named and described below, they should not be viewed as static or tightly compartmentalised, but rather as overlapping, intertextualised and in constant process. In the next chapter, I analyse how these four discourses, work together to define, construct, limit, or enhance the possibilities for effective speech in the business meeting context. Here, I consider the provenance of each of these discourses in turn and what I understand by them.

Historical legacy

> There is a dividing line between Richard, Don and myself, and Sarah, Jack and Keith. Richard, Don and myself seem to have a lot more arguments with Keith than do Sarah and Jack and the reason is historical.
>
> (Interview with Pete)

My initial awareness of the power of this discourse to constitute spoken interactions emerged while observing the two management meetings. During these meetings, both of which appeared on the surface to be good-humoured and urbane, I sensed some underlying tension between certain members of the team. For example, Pete, the financial director, made a few jokes at the expense of Jack, the sales and marketing manager, and Jack, in turn, appeared to 'have a go' at Richard, director of cars. However, the significance of these 'spats' were lost on me until I conducted the interviews.

Two themes or preoccupations were apparent in the comments of all four people I interviewed. The first was a clear perception that a distinction existed between those managers who helped to found the company, and develop it in its early days (Sarah, Keith and Jack), and those managers who were more recently appointed to the team (Richard, Pete, Don and Cliff). In real time, this 'historical divide' appears barely worth commenting on, the founder members having set up the company four years prior to the research study and the newer managers having been appointed within the previous twelve months. However, conceptually, it was apparent that time had become 'stretched' as a result of the very rapid expansion of the company from a staff of three to its present 100 or so employees.

The historical divide between the two groups of managers appeared to have a philosophical significance in terms of a contrast in attitudes towards how the company should be run. For the founder members, the company was not just a means to an end, but part of a personal mission and an entire way of life:

> Keith is absolutely committed to team, beyond this being a job, probably the most important thing he does in his life is run the business. Therefore to come in at 7.00 o'clock and to leave at 10.00 o' clock at night is doing the job . . . For some people its just a job and there's nothing wrong with that.
>
> (Interview with Richard)

> I have a strong personal drive to see this company succeed. I was in at the beginning and I hope that one day it will be very successful.
>
> (Interview with Sarah)

For the newer members of the MT, there appeared to be a more pragmatic, focused, functional approach to work, as a means of making a living or developing a career. Richard, for example, felt that there was too much pressure on employees to take on extra responsibilities for the ultimate 'good' of the company, and not enough understanding that people are also motivated by a degree of self-interest.

Managers I interviewed also suggested that the historical divide between founder and newer members of the MT determined attitudes towards management practices. One substantive example of this was the issue of how decisions were made. Owing to the very rapid growth of the company, founder members had grown used to contributing to almost every managerial decision regardless of whose responsibility this was. Yet this was obviously a source of irritation and confusion to the newer members of the team, as these extracts typify:

> Until Keith turned up, Sarah ran the company, so Sarah finds it quite difficult to hand over the reins to different areas of responsibility. Sarah had my department

reporting to her up until six months ago at which point it switched to me and that was quite difficult for her.

(Interview with Richard)

I like to be involved in decisions at all levels. It is what I'm used to. But I know I have to learn to back off. It's one of the things I'm working on.

(Interview with Sarah)

It emerged from the interview data that one dominant feature of this historical legacy – the practice of collective decision-making – was construed by the newer managers to be an inability of the founders to delegate or trust their colleagues.

In sum, the discourse of historical legacy denotes a set of perceptions that the three founder members of the MT have the right to intervene in making decisions across management specialisms. The unintended consequence of this is that decisions are not always clearly delegated to their more recently appointed colleagues, who therefore feel undermined and devalued.

This discourse of a historical legacy, which supports a company culture of collaborative decision-making at the expense of delegating decisions to specialist managers, intersects with two further discourses: those of open dialogue and competing specialisms, which I now consider in turn.

Open dialogue

What is regarded as freedom at one level is regarded as a lack of direction at another.

(Interview with Richard)

Of the four discourses found to be at work in this business setting, the discourse of open dialogue was the most clearly identifiable. This is because constructs of 'open dialogue' were frequently referred to as part of an authorised company ethos, both in the meetings I observed and in the interviews. In a statement of 'core values' describing and, in effect, personifying the Hook3 culture, the 'target brand personality' is described as 'friendly, accessible, reliable, fun to be with, useful and trustworthy'. The guiding principles which form part of the company mission statement are as follows:

- We build trust and respect through personal development, responsibility and accountability
- We are open, honest and frank
- We are customer-driven
- We have a win-win mindset
- And we have FUN!

In my field-notes, I was interested in how often the word 'open' was used in conversation and how this generally connoted positive, idealised qualities. The word 'open' was applied to spoken exchanges, relationships between senior and junior staff, business practices and the company culture. It appeared to connote a collection of values suggesting that the company either *is* or *should be* non-hierarchical, democratic, non-bureaucratic, self-regulating, co-operative and freethinking. This collection of values was symbolised in at least two ways. First, in architectural terms, the company had an open-plan policy. Managers were not allowed to have their own separate offices, but instead were required to work side by side in large, open-plan spaces, which, I discovered, was a bone of contention among the newer managers. Secondly, there was a particularly strong emphasis on 'open' communication, which denoted the right of anyone within the organisation to freedom of speech. In other words, employees were encouraged to voice their opinions frankly on any aspect of company practice, regardless of job role or rank.

The meetings I observed manifested signs of a discourse of open dialogue in a different way. In both meetings, the atmosphere was generally polite, relaxed and informal, with occasional outbursts, although Keith, the CEO, told me later that my presence, combined with the tape-recorder, ensured that people were 'on their best behaviour'. Both meetings conformed to a fairly egalitarian discursive format: Keith as chair apportioned each manager some uninterrupted time to report on their area of responsibility, drawing out any issues for discussion that were of general concern to the whole team. Keith appeared to take a low profile throughout the meeting, unobtrusively steering each contribution and moving the agenda along. People were generally respectful of each other's protected turn and, consequently, each speaker held the floor for at least ten minutes. These were followed by free-for-all discussions in which issues were explored and decisions were reached collaboratively. In short, a discourse of open dialogue seemed to govern the structure of the meeting, arguably privileging a 'feminised' approach to discussion and decision-making (e.g. Coates, 1993; Holmes, 1992; Tannen, 1995). However, it was also during these free-for-all discussions that tensions between speakers were seen to surface, and it is these 'significant moments' that I have chosen to analyse in Chapter 7 for the discursive contradictions they reveal.

However, this discourse of open dialogue never acted autonomously but always intersected and competed with other discourses identified in this setting. For example, in line with the company ethos, managers were expected to encourage staff to be independent and make decisions for themselves, rather than being told what to do. However, such an expectation was in contradiction with the discourse of historical legacy, which, as we have seen, continued to support collaborative decision-making, reconstituted by certain more recently appointed managers as senior team interference. In the interviews, these managers overtly expressed their resistance to open dialogue as an authorised company discourse:

> People often say, 'that's not the Hook3 way', and I find that an absolutely unsatisfactory phrase. I've often questioned people with, 'What do you mean, 'that's not the Hook3 way. Says who?' One of the key guidelines we seem to operate as a senior team is that people in Hook3 don't like being told what to do. But sometimes there are situations in companies where frankly you just have to be told to do things.
>
> (Interview with Pete)

This resistant view, that 'what is regarded as freedom at one end is regarded as lack of direction at another', is tied up with the way these managers are also positioned by two oppositional discourses: those of competing specialisms and masculinisation, as I discuss below.

To sum up, the discourse of open dialogue denotes an authorised company view that employees at all levels should be able to speak openly to their colleagues without fear of censure. This was part of a wider philosophy that the company should be run according to non-hierarchical, egalitarian and democratic principles which involves the workforce in collective rather than top-down decision-making.

Competing specialisms

We tend to wind each other up. It tends to happen along lines of job demarkation.

(Interview with Pete)

While both meetings I observed were generally non-argumentative, the tensions that did surface seemed partly to do with the different and competing responsibilities held by this group of senior managers. Both meetings were organised in such a way that they foregrounded and reinforced the way in which each manager's subject position was defined by his or her professional role: each manager was expected to report back on the 'state of play' within their business specialism. While the intention of each meeting was clearly to *integrate* the different areas of the business through the sharing of information, one of the contradictory effects of this process was to emphasise and even promote difference and opposition between knowledges or specialisms.

My awareness of competing specialisms as a powerful discourse shaping speakers' contributions to the meeting evolved from a close observation of the sources of tension between members of the MT. Three brief examples will suffice to illustrate this point. The first was the way in which certain members of the team used highly specialised and often mystifying language to describe issues relating to their area of responsibility, and the effect this produced on their colleagues. For example, Sarah, the operations director, described a highly complicated technical problem to the meeting and explains how she intended to solve it. The following is a more accessible example of her use of specialised technical jargon:

From the beginning of the New Year, we'll be building an internal system to hold a replica of the live database and set up a system for taking central amendments, additions and deletions here, matching them up against the database, classifying them to the live service and feeding those amendments back to [X company] to go back into the system. There is a translation table that will map street codes to our classification codes . . .

After an extended monologue along these lines, Sarah was then subjected to quite stiff interrogation by Jack, the sales and marketing manager, about its implications for his area of the business. His unfriendly, interrogative stance appeared to be designed to demystify the specialist language Sarah had used, in order to turn it into shared, common-sense knowledge. When I asked certain interviewees to comment on this incident in the meeting, it was conceptualised in terms of competing specialisms, using images of conflict and territorial defence:

> When Sarah is under pressure, she becomes more and more technical. If she feels she is being attacked by the others she takes this as a slight on her competence and becomes more and more defensive. In effect she is putting up the barriers and saying, 'Look, you don't know how to do this, but I do, so leave me alone.'
>
> (Interview with Pete)

The second example from the data was the way in which newer members of the team appeared to resent intervention and interference in their specialism from their colleagues. They felt that they had been appointed as experts within their particular field and were frustrated that others did not recognise the boundaries between one job role and another. Here, the discourse of competing specialisms is intertextually linked with that of historical legacy. In his interview, Richard described the difficulties he faced in taking over an area of responsibility from Sarah:

> What I bring is a knowledge of consumer publishing and delivery of information to an audience, and what Sarah has a particular strength with is the mechanics . . . not the way in which you formulate the front end of the delivery. But she found this very difficult to let go and I have felt quite uncomfortable with that.
>
> (Interview with Richard)

The third example from the data of how a discourse of competing specialisms appeared to shape verbal and non-verbal interactions at the meetings was in the use of jokes and put-downs, particularly between the male members of the MT. While both the meetings were generally quite serious, teasing and banter became a more noticeable feature in the closing stages. Indeed, humour appeared to be a means of masking and defusing tensions 'along lines of job demarkation' between the MT. However, the substance of the humour was clearly to do with deprecating the skills associated with a colleague's specialism, as this interview comment endorses:

> There is an element of power struggle, an element of tension between Pete and Jack. He made one absolutely killing snipe at the meeting about whatever it was, was all bull-shit, because it came from a salesperson and that's all they ever do.
>
> (Interview with Richard)

To sum up, the discourse of competing specialisms denotes a set of perceptions that other members of the MT are as much competitors and rivals as colleagues.

According to this discourse, managers' subject positions are largely defined and constituted by their particular professional expertise, which they have a proprietorial interest to protect and develop. Typically, they regard their area of responsibility as vital to the business, highly specialist and too complex to explain. They are unhappy about intervention and interference from other members of the team, and believe they should be allowed to get on with making their own decisions within given parameters established from 'the top'. In apparent good spirit, they like to project impatience and contempt for the value and practices of other specialisms in the business.

Masculinisation

> Since the beginning of the year, I've noticed that the atmosphere in the team has become very boysy. We're going through a very boysy phase and we've got some very boysy characters, actually.
>
> (Interview with Sarah)

While this book has explicitly foregrounded *gender* as a discourse worthy of investigation, I did not wish to assume that simply because there was a woman present on the MT, I should go looking for evidence of discourses of gender differentiation or discrimination. In the case of the classroom study, the research participants, both students and teachers, conceptualised their experiences in the classroom from a clear perspective of gender differentiation, justifying its choice as a discursive frame of reference. In the case of the Hook3 study, ironically Sarah was the *only* member of the MT to make gender explicit in her comments and terms of reference, perhaps subliminally aware of her 'othered' status according to the androcentric principle (Coates, 1993) governing social relations. Evidence that gender differentiation was inscribing the discursive practices of the two meetings I observed was therefore far more subtle, nuanced and ambiguous than in the classroom study. Sarah herself was a dominant, assured and articulate figure in both meetings, perhaps based upon her historical legacy as the original founder member of the company. Thus, from a feminist perspective, she was no obvious 'victim' (Jones, 1993) of a discourse of gender differentiation.

What emerged from the data after repeated rereadings was a strong sense that a discourse of *masculinisation*, rather than gender differentiation, was governing the interactions of this group of managers. By 'masculinisation', I mean a set of ways of making sense of the world and inscribing its discursive practices which harness *stereotypical* constructs of masculinity such as hierarchy, order, structure, dominance, competitiveness, rivalry, aggression and goal-orientated action. This clearly differs from a discourse of gender differentiation which I defined earlier as 'a conventionalised set of ways of differentiating individuals' identities in the world primarily according to their sex or gender'. In this case study, masculinisation largely appeared to cut across sex category differences, interpellating all members of the team, both male and female. In broad terms it was a discourse that constituted a kind of resistant subculture within the organisation, affecting the team's relationships, terms of engagement, management practices and ultimately contesting the company ethos.

Evidence of this discourse was manifested in the research data in the following ways. First, a discourse of masculinisation, intersecting with that of competing specialisms, appeared to shape a number of tense encounters between members of the MT. In one example, analysed in detail in the next chapter, Sarah is confronted quite forcibly by Jack for experiencing an operations problem that was affecting his own area of responsibility. Rather than 'caving in', Sarah is very assertive in defending the reasons for the actions she had taken to sort the particular problem. The choice of a confrontational approach to other people's problems rather than the more feminised conciliatory approach was noted by Richard here:

> With that relationship with Jack and Sarah, she would say, 'I'm sorry the site is down' and he would say, 'that's not good enough, tell me what's happening.' If there was an element of trust there, you would just say, 'You must be having a shit time there,' but that's not what happens.
>
> (Interview with Richard)

Secondly, and closely associated with this confrontational approach to discussion, several members of the MT, including Sarah, were conspicuous for their use of a stereotypically masculinised speech style (e.g. Coates, 1993; Holmes, 1992; Tannen, 1995; Zimmerman and West, 1975). In the meetings, this was characterised by, for example, lengthy turns, use of interruptions, talking over others, blocking statements, refusals to comply, bald assertions and interrogative questions. The adjective 'aggressive' was used on several occasions by speakers who were referring to particularly difficult clients or suppliers, or to describe people's behaviour. In addition, the imagery used to describe the relationships between managers in the interview data was indicative of violent power struggles, drawing upon the boxing ring, target practice and the battlefield:

> He made one absolutely killing snipe at the meeting . . .
> It's more Jack drilling Sarah than the other way round . . .
> Jack will attack quite hard when he has Sarah on the ropes . . .

There was therefore a strange sense of dissonance in the data between the collaborative approach to discussion in the meetings, and the often masculinised style of engagement between the 'combatants'. This sense of dissonance was also apparent in the third way in which the discourse of masculinisation appeared to shape spoken interactions: a disagreement over the management of decision-making in meetings. I have already considered how a discourse of open dialogue favoured an exploratory, collaborative approach to decision-making which might be described as 'feminised' (e.g. Coates, 1993; Holmes, 1992; Tannen, 1995). However, in practice, not all members of the team collaborated in making decisions at the meeting and, in particular, Cliff (publisher of homes, who was not interviewed) and Pete (the financial director) said very little. When I asked Pete about his relative silence, he confessed that he considered the 'open' approach to decision-making to be unfocused, time-wasting and unproductive:

> What it needs is for Keith to take a stronger lead in steering the discussion so we make decisions quickly and effectively. There are many occasions in discussion where you feel he could exercise his authority more forcibly and we would get a lot more work done.
>
> (Interview with Pete)

According to Pete's masculinised model of discussion and decision-making, the chair should be more overtly prepared to take control of the meeting by both 'steering' the discussion to produce outcomes and by making 'top-down' decisions where collaborative decision-making is perceived to be time-wasting. Richard separately advocated the need for a more direct, goal-orientated, action-driven model of running a meeting by describing his preferred approach in which a discourse of masculinisation intersects with competing specialisms:

> I try to get the information across as quickly as possible in a way that does not imply debate. If there are big issues to get across then talk about them but don't talk about the smaller issues. Don't have a debate about one person's area of expertise unless there is real value in that; it's not the forum for that. As I can see that Keith isn't going to, I try to steer that. I try to shut things down.
>
> (Interview with Richard)

Despite Richard's evident disagreement with the party line, a discourse of masculinisation is not necessarily always in conflict with that of open dialogue, according to a post-structuralist model of analysis. There are, of course, competing value systems at play. Where open dialogue values exploratory discussion and debate, masculinisation prefers information-giving, action and outcomes. Where open dialogue foregrounds collaboration and shared decision-making, masculinisation opts for either an authoritative, top-down approach or decisions delegated to individuals. Where open dialogue welcomes conciliation and forgiveness, masculinisation goes in for the kill. However, when masculinisation supplements or intersects with open dialogue, the result might be an approach to information-sharing that is organised, logical, involving, collective, but also decisive and action-orientated.

In the next chapter, I draw upon these four competing yet interwoven discourses – historical legacy, open dialogue, competing specialisms and masculinisation – to analyse the speech and non-verbal behaviour of this group of managers in two team meetings.

A feminist post-structuralist analysis?

Any act of feminist research such as this must put the social or discursive construction of gender at the centre of its inquiry. Feminism is, among other things, 'a form of attention that brings into focus particular questions' (Fox-Keller, 1985: 6). This entails the substantial task of considering gender to be a significant discourse in terms of understanding the practices of a group of speakers.

In the Hook3 context, I have already argued that gender differentiation does not overtly appear to organise the interactions between this group of male and female managers, although it may work in less obvious ways. As the ethnographic evidence suggests, Sarah is seen to occupy a number of powerful subject positions within the course of both meetings as the forthcoming analysis demonstrates. There are two important consequences of this for a feminist post-structuralist analysis. The first is that her very show of strength does not negate the need for a feminist analysis, rather, the opposite is true. A feminist analysis should acknowledge, if not celebrate, the considerable achievement that Sarah has succeeded and is succeeding in this otherwise all-male environment of the MT. The second is that Sarah's apparent show of strength should be simultaneously questioned and deconstructed. The reason for this, as I have suggested, is that Sarah is as much a party to the constitution of a discourse of masculinisation within the company culture as her male colleagues, but she is the only one to make explicit in her interview comments the view that gender differentiates her from the other members of the team (see above). This dissonance between the way Sarah speaks/behaves in meetings and the way she reflects in interviews suggests a complex interrelationship between sex and gender, as raised in the Introduction. The feminist focus of FPDA will therefore seek to address the following questions in the next chapter:

- To what extent is Sarah assimilated within the 'boysy culture' of the senior MT?
- Do her insights about gender differentiation within the MT alternatively signify that she feels a sense of distance from the 'boysy culture'?
- Does Sarah adopt competing subject positions in this context such that she is both assimilated within the 'boysy culture' and simultaneously separated from that culture?
- Does her possible sense of distance or difference cause her to take up positions of acquiescence or resistance within management meetings?

7
The Management Team Study

I continue my demonstration of a feminist post-structuralist approach to discourse analysis by examining the speech of five senior managers of a successful dotcom company in the public context of two senior management team meetings. Following on from Chapter 5, I show here how the theoretical rationale for FPDA can be transformed into a workable methodology.

Two senior management meetings are featured in this chapter. Both meetings lasted for just over an hour and took place in a private meeting room in the company offices. Both fell under the heading of 'Bogs and Boilers meetings', which meant that they were largely concerned with non-confidential, day-to-day issues. Both meetings conformed to a standard format: each manager in turn was apportioned some uninterrupted time (about ten minutes) to report on their area of responsibility, drawing out any issues that were of general concern to the whole team. While there were seven members of the management team (MT), only six, the same six, were present on both occasions. These were: the chief executive officer (CEO), Keith, who also chaired the meeting; Sarah, the operations manager and the only woman present; Jack, sales and marketing manager; Richard, manager of cars; and Pete, the finance director. While present at the meeting, Cliff, manager of the site for homes, did not speak in the extracts featured in this chapter. The director missing from the two meetings was Don, manager of the site for jobs.

The chapter is divided into two sections, entitled 'Meeting one' and 'Meeting two'. Within each section the format is the same. Two extracts have been selected from the transcript of each meeting, which I have identified as 'significant moments': pertinent for the ways in which they illustrate and exemplify the positioning of the five speakers in relation to the four discourses of historical legacy, open dialogue, competing specialisms and masculinisation (see Chapter 5).

After each extract, there is a detailed, denotative description of the verbal and non-verbal interactions of the key participants within both extracts. Once again, I shall iterate here that however denotative a description aims to be, it is always a form of interpretation involving at the very least the selection of a focus, the highlighting of certain aspects for attention and the consequent marginalisation of other aspects. Also, many words that are used in discourse analysis are 'loaded'; that is, they are imbued with the interpretation of the analyst. However, it has been part of this book's thesis that the implicitly value-laden and interpretative function of discourse analysis should be made explicit and if possible welcomed rather than disguised as pseudo-objectivity.

Following the derotative analysis, there is the connotative analysis, that is, the FPDA commentary of the data. As expounded in Chapter 3, this aims to weave together or juxtapose the voices or 'internally persuasive discourses' (Bakhtin, 1981; Skidmore, 1999) of the research participants: those of the three members of the MT (Pete, Richard and Sarah), the personal assistant to the management team who was not present at the meeting (Pam), and, of course, the researcher.

Meeting one

Extract one

The following extract is taken from an early stage in this senior management meeting. Richard is the first member of the senior team to be asked by the chair to speak.

Prior to the start of this extract, Richard has spoken for about five minutes, without interruption, on his area of responsibility, that of selling space on the Hook3 website to advertisers of cars. The first line (211, below) '... and that's just about it', signifies that the floor is open to other speakers, and that anyone can now join in a free-for-all discussion. (A note on the transcription methods used below is given in Appendix 2.)

211   **RICHARD**: . . . and that's just about it.

212   **JACK**: Going back to cars, do you have any clarity yet on the launch date?

213   *Richard*: No we don't. Kirsten is the person who is pulling together the project plan. She's

214   desperately uncomfortable with pulling together a date at this stage. It's not the work isn't

215   moving ahead very quickly. She understands the value of the final date, but she just doesn't have

216   enough information because there's a bottleneck with the analysts to understand the scale of some of

217   the developments that are being done, so if pushed, it would be the same date as we had before . . .

218   **JACK**: (*INTERRUPTING*) What's that, what's that? April . . . (*APPEARS TO BE SPEAKING OVER*

219   *RICHARD FROM* 'She understands . . .')

220   **RICHARD**: I think April is what we are talking about. Beginning of April, end of April. The

221   same date as we had before. April is the time they're looking at . . .

222   **JACK**: (*OVERLAPPING FROM* 'April is the time . . .') We've launched two sites haven't we?

223   **RICHARD**: We have, yes.

224   **KEITH**: You've got to be careful you don't end up at the sharp end of not being able to deliver cars.

225   **JACK**: No, no, this is quite amazing because we've launched two sites.

226   **RICHARD**: Yes.

227   **JACK**: So we know what to do.

228   **RICHARD**: They're just not top level sexy sites, so they're not something we've been

229   shouting about quite as much, is it . . .

230   **JACK**: (*SHOWING INCREASING FRUSTRATION BECAUSE RICHARD APPEARS TO BE*

231   *MISSING THE POINT.*) No, no, we've launched jobs and we've launched homes.

232   **RICHARD**: Oh right, we're talking about the latest launches now?

233   **JACK**: No, no, no, we've launched jobs and we've launched homes.

234   **RICHARD**: (*VERY LONG PAUSE*) Yes. Yes.

235   **JACK**: We know what to do, hopefully.

236   **RICHARD**: (*LAUGHS BUT SOUNDS HESITANT*) Yes. The site was down. We had this

237   conversation before the site was down yesterday.

Denotative analysis

In this extract, Jack appears to become increasingly irritated with
Richard's initial response to his opening question (l. 212). Richard
responds to Jack's question directly, by providing a negative answer,
but, perhaps realising that this is *not* what Jack wishes to hear, goes
on to justify and explain the lack of a positive response. Jack's
appears to become irritated by Richard's continuous repetition of

a vague rather than a precise date (ll. 220–1). Jack's irritation is indicated by the way that he interrupts Richard mid-flow (l. 222) and talks over him with a rhetorical question that is almost certainly intended as a statement. Indeed he goes on to repeat the point, 'We've launched two sites', three more times (ll. 227, 230, 233) in the extract. This repetition signifies both his rising level of irritation with Richard's failure to grasp a simple point, but may also indicate a case of professional 'one-upmanship'. Jack's wrapping up line, 'We know what to do, hopefully' suggests that he regards himself as more experienced than Richard in setting up launches, and that Richard would do well to take advice from him and other more experienced colleagues.

To consider Richard's speech in more detail, while he is fluent, eloquent and organised at the start of the extract (ll. 213–18), there are signs that he becomes increasingly flustered as he fails to grasp Jack's point. In lines 220–1, he repeats the word 'April' four times as if to reassure Jack that, contrary to his initial negative, he *does* have a definite date in mind. From this point, Richard becomes increasingly less vocal and virtually monosyllabic (ll. 223, 226, 234) as he appears to sense that he is being challenged and missing the point. His relative silence serves to suggest that he is trying to second guess what Jack has in mind, rather than expose himself to the possible ridicule of his colleagues by saying, 'I don't understand you', or risking a more direct confrontation with Jack by saying, 'What are you getting at?' On the two occasions Richard does attempt to feed back into the dialogue, it is made clear by Jack's dismissive responses ('No, no, no . . .', l. 233) that he has got it wrong. His final response in this extract is difficult to make sense of, and may be a reference to an earlier conversation on the same subject between them. In other words, it is likely that this 'spat' has a history.

Extract two

This extract comes towards the end of Sarah's allocated speaking turn, during which she has spoken more or less uninterruptedly for ten minutes or so. Prior to this extract, Sarah has given a lengthy and quite technical explanation of a short-term, but nonetheless serious problem that was affecting the company at the time of the meeting – the 'networks were down' for a temporary period, meaning that the company's website was unavailable to both Hook3 employees and customers. Jack's first question to Sarah (l. 532 below) implicitly opens up the floor to all the participants of the meeting.

532   *JACK*: Does everyone in the company know that the system was down?

533   *SARAH*: Yes.

534   *JACK*: And single node was what it was on yesterday which meant that . . .

535   *SARAH*: No, it was . . . it's really, really complex. I'm sorry, I can't explain it any simpler . . .

536   *JACK*: OK, then, the question really is . . .

537   *SARAH*: (*OVERLAPPING*) No, no . . . I really can't explain it.

538   *JACK*: Is . . . is the way that it comes up going to mean that performance is less than . . .

539   *SARAH*: (*INTERRUPTING*) The way . . . no.

540   *JACK*: So yesterday was . . .

541   *SARAH*: (*INTERRUPTING*) We are aiming . . . we are aiming that it will come up on the

542   database server with 12 CPUs on it, rather than the standard 6 anyway.

543   *JACK*: Right, so it won't mean that . . .

544   *SARAH*: (*INTERRUPTING*) Last night, it was screaming, it was screaming through.

545   *JACK*: So when it really does come up, it won't be performance issues, it's just that it's going to be . . .

546   *SARAH*: (*INTERRUPTING*) We had different issues yesterday afternoon as I said, in that we had,

547   one, a database issue which shouldn't have affected performance at all. But we had a problem with the

548   networks falling over, and it's hard to correlate the two. I can't guarantee . . .

549   *JACK*: (*INTERRUPTING*) No, no, no . . . all I'm concerned about is that, when an e-mail is sent out

550   that says, 'Hurrah, it's back up' that if necessary we say, 'It's back up but at the same time there will

551   be some performance issues, so if you're talking to customers and you are taking people through the

552   site, that they may well experience difficulties.

553   *KEITH*: There's a sort of user interpretation of 'back up' and a technical interpretation.

554   Yesterday afternoon I thought it was down because I couldn't get to it but there was a

555   different reason, I understand that.

556   *SARAH*: I didn't understand you were having those experiences, and I sit next to you

557   (*LAUGHS*) I knew what we were doing, I knew we were having issues, but I did not

558   understand that user issues were absolutely appalling. (*WITH EMPHASIS*) Nobody told me.

559   (*SILENCE AMONG WHOLE MEETING FOR SEVERAL SECONDS.*)

560   *JACK*: Well, I just thought the site was down all day you see . . .

561   *SARAH*: (*INTERRUPTING*) We did communicate to everybody when it was back up.

KEITH: Could we have some way of making sure when the site is back up . . .

SARAH: Yeah, well, the guys upstairs would have been aware, but I'm just saying that I

wasn't. It isn't as if they would get it back up and ignore it. You know, get it back up and just walk

away, it doesn't work that way.

JACK: That's why I just assumed that if the guys upstairs, if they were having problems with it,

they . . .

SARAH: (*INTERRUPTING AND OVERLAPPING*) The guys upstairs understand it but you're

asking (*CONTINUING TO TALK OVER THE OTHERS*) you're asking for a different

interpretation to different people, which is fine, but I just need to be aware of that and this

discussion is absolutely fine. (*SILENCE AMONG WHOLE MEETING FOR SEVERAL*

SECONDS)

Denotative analysis

During this extract, Jack again takes on an interrogative stance by subjecting Sarah to a series of testing questions. His second question (l. 534) appears to indicate that he hasn't quite assimilated the earlier technical explanation. At the same time, he is keen to show that he shares her technical knowledge and is therefore on her wavelength by using technical jargon ('single node', l. 534). However, he seems concerned to establish that there may still be less technical but substantive 'performance issues' affecting colleagues and customers that Sarah has not fully considered. Jack's interrogative stance is indicated by his more or less complete dominance of the floor as questioner (until l. 552); his use of definite question markers at the start of sentences such as 'so', 'right' and 'OK', and his attempts to demystify Sarah's more technical explanations by translating them into more down-to-earth language (ll. 545, 549–52). The only other speaker to contribute to this part of the discussion is Keith, the CEO. Both his contributions (l. 553 and l. 562) appear to be in keeping with his role as the meeting's Chair. His first comment merely clarifies a possible confusion by contributing a point of information to Jack and Sarah's discussion, and his second is an attempt at producing 'an action' from the discussion of a problematic issue; he does not obviously take sides.

There is evidence in this extract that Sarah feels she is being unfairly held to account by Jack for the operations failure, but that she is determined to resist taking the blame. Sarah's response in lines 535 and 537, where she flatly refuses to explain further and apologises for her inability to do so, may also indicate some irritation that she is being forced to defend her actions. After this point, she repeatedly interrupts and speaks over Jack when he continues to question her about what happened, to the extent that he rarely completes a sentence (e.g. ll. 538, 540, 543, 545). Her emphasis is not upon what went *wrong*, but on what she has been doing to put the matter *right* (ll. 541–2, 544). She resists the position of 'scapegoat', not simply by defending her own actions but by criticising those of her colleagues. For example, she indicates that other people must take some responsibility for the consequences of the operations failure. In lines 556–8, she admonishes her colleagues for a contributing factor – their inability to communicate their experience of the problem to her ('Nobody told me.'). Unlike Richard in the previous extract, Jack's questioning approach does not reduce Sarah to silence. On the contrary, she herself causes the meeting to fall silent for a significant few seconds on two occasions during this extract (ll. 559 and 571). This might either indicate an embarrassed acceptance on the part of her colleagues of some of the blame, or, in line with Zimmerman's and West's (1975) research on delayed responses in mixed-sex settings, might signify a sense of withdrawal or lack of support from her male colleagues. There is a hint that Sarah feels that she may have alienated her colleagues by overreacting to Jack's questions when she says meta-analytically, 'I just need to be aware of that and this discussion is absolutely fine' (ll. 570–2).

FPDA commentary

I have argued so far that, according to feminist post-structuralist analysis, speakers in public settings are constantly negotiating for positions of power, determined by the range of discourses to which they have access, or within which they find themselves positioned. In parallel with classroom talk, the question of who gets to talk, to speak at length and make a noticeable impact on the views of their colleagues within a business meeting is dependent upon a complex interplay of subject positions governed by competing, intersecting discourses. Each of the four discourses identified in this particular business setting – historical legacy, competing specialisms, open dialogue and masculinisation (see Chapter 6) – make a significant contribution to the ways in which speakers are constituted as persuasive or influential through their spoken interactions. However, these discourses are never constant: they are continuously shifting, fading and reforming in relation to each other. Thus, while there are six speakers of roughly equal status (with the exception of the CEO) at the meeting, they occupy constantly shifting positions of powerfulness and powerlessness in relation to each other, as the first half of this commentary aims to show. The second half will address the *feminist* perspective raised at the end of Chapter 6, which considers the competing subject positions of Sarah: the extent to which she appears to be assimilated within, and/or distanced from the 'boysy culture' of the management team.

In extract one, the interaction between Jack and Richard is particularly shaped by two intersecting discourses – those of historical legacy and competing specialisms. During the course of this extract, we have seen how Richard, who is initially so vocal, is gradually silenced by Jack. I would argue that Jack's ability to disempower Richard at this point in the discussion is partly to do with the former's subject position within the discourse of historical legacy. In simple terms, Jack considers that he is an experienced Hook3 manager whereas Richard is less so. In aiming to assert that he has 'been there and done that', Jack is seen progressively to assert his authority over Richard who, by the end of the extract, is effectively reconstituted as 'a new boy'. My interview data supplemented this observation by discovering that the management team was informally divided into two 'camps': the founder members (Sarah, Keith and Jack), and the more recently appointed staff (Richard, Pete and Don). This historical division in terms of recruitment and experience, is also mirrored by the management team's *attitudes* to company ethos. The founder members have developed a particular managerial style and company culture that is not wholly shared by the more recently appointed members:

PETE: There is a dividing line between Richard, Don and myself, and Sarah, Jack and Keith . . . [Some of the differences can be put down to] the way the company has grown and the fact that Sarah, Jack and Keith were here from the start. Culturally they are attuned to having an input on every decision, but as the company has grown, they need to be able to say, 'here's my colleague in Cars. I know he may not be doing things in the way I might have wanted him to, but we have to rely on him to do his job.'

. . .

RICHARD: There is a very difficult subculture here, which is that people who were here at the start used to do everything because it was a company with five people in it; everyone did everything . . . But it is surely a question of trust. Wherever there is a question of trust in belief in competence, there you start to see people needing to drill for information.

. . .

SARAH: I don't feel I have many allies among the new people. One thing that has always been good about [Keith and Jack] is that we understand where we are all coming from. You don't get that same shared sense of where we're coming from, from the others.

In extract one, the tension between Jack and Richard is less about divided attitudes and more about relative experience. Jack's repeated assertion, 'we have launched two sites . . . so we know what to do' *might* be read charitably as an attempt at offering reassuring support and back-up for Richard from an experienced colleague who can help him. But the impatient and insistent manner in which these assertions are delivered ('No, no, this is quite amazing because we've launched two sites') suggests that Jack is annoyed that Richard is failing to register his/the company's repository of experience.

Jack's powerful subject position within a discourse of historical legacy ('We know what to do, hopefully') is intersected by a discourse of competing specialisms. While Richard's job role entails that he is in charge of launching the cars site, Jack's job remit is more overarching and wide-ranging. As sales and marketing manager, he is responsible for publicising and selling the products of *all* the individual departments: homes, cars and jobs. When Jack repeats, 'We've launched jobs and we've launched homes', he is almost literally marketing his own job role. In other words, the products of other departments are largely dependent on the work of the sales and marketing team to launch a site or 'to get the show on the road'. Jack's repeated assertion throughout this extract is like a kind of mantra reminding Richard (and, indeed, the others) of each publishing department's ultimate dependency upon the responsibility of sales and marketing for the 'sharp end' of the business. Interestingly, this is endorsed by Keith, the CEO, when he warns Richard (l. 224), 'You've got to be careful you don't end up at the sharp end of not being able to deliver cars.'

The discourses of open dialogue and masculinisation both supplement those of historical legacy and competing specialisms in positioning Jack as increasingly more powerful than Richard during this first extract. As I have discussed in Chapter 6, open dialogue is an official company discourse in so far as it is seen to govern the rhetoric of company documents, conferences, meetings and conversations. Pete's comment above about the founder members ('culturally they are attuned to having an input on every decision'), while an aspect of historical legacy, also signifies the authorised value placed upon open dialogue: that any matter, relating to any department is 'open' to discussion among the management team. Thus, when Jack questions Richard about a departmental matter, this is *not* regarded as time-wasting, unnecessary interference or, from Richard's perspective, 'a question of trust in belief in competence'. Richard's plans for the launch of his cars site are a quite legitimate topic for the whole of the MT to discuss, and Richard is therefore expected to listen and respond to the questions and advice of others. However, in their interviews, both Richard and Pete expressed resistance to this authorised discourse, typified by Pete's comment here:

PETE: Let's assume we have a group of managers, all the interested parties are here in the room. You get the feeling that, even if the decisions are delegated to them, other people may feel they have a right to chip in to any type of discussion in any area of the organisation. Even when a decision's been made by the relevant people for the right reasons, someone else, often a more senior manager may come and just change it.

In extracts one and two, Jack exercises his 'right to chip in', which potentially enables him to 'do power' over other speakers. However, while Jack's *intent* – to open up the subject of the cars launch to a general discussion of key issues – is authorised by the company's discourse of open dialogue, the closed and peremptory *manner* of his delivery is more positioned by the competing and unauthorised discourse of masculinisation. I have discussed above how the company's constructs of 'open dialogue' may be equated more with the co-operative and facilitative features associated with a stereotypically 'feminine' speech style (e.g. Coates, 1995; Holmes, 1992; Swann and Graddol, 1995; Tannen, 1995). Jack's speech here (use of negatives; repeated, bald assertions; talking over other speakers; a refusal to elaborate his message or engage Richard in fuller discussion) seems more compatible with a stereotypically 'masculine' speech style conducted in public settings than with open dialogue. In sum, Jack may be using the company's authorised discourse to his personal advantage in order to score points, as well as a means to generate broader discussion of the issues.

In extract two, we experience something of a shift in the power relations between the more voluble speakers in the meeting. Although the second extract begins in a similar way to the first, with Jack asking Sarah a question in order to gain information and open up a topic for discussion, and follows with a dialogue between just two participants, it is Jack, rather than Sarah, who is gradually silenced through the course of the discussion. However, it is evident that there is a greater sense of struggle for the retention of power than in the first extract. Here, Sarah can be seen as progressively more dominant in relation to Jack according to an interplay of all four identified discourses, but not unambiguously so. With regard to historical legacy, the interview data revealed that Hook3 was originally Sarah's brainchild and that she was single-handedly responsible for founding the company:

SARAH: For all the day-to-day work, I was more or less a one-woman band . . . I will admit that because of this, I have found it very difficult letting go of certain areas of the business, because I am still actively interested in everything. But it is something I am working on. I see it is as one of my greatest challenges.

. . .

PAM: Until Keith turned up, Sarah ran the company, so I think Sarah finds it quite difficult to hand over the reins to different areas of responsibility.

One of the areas of the business Sarah has had to let go is that of sales and marketing. While Jack is considered a founder member in so far as he was appointed at an early stage in the company's short history, he nonetheless inherits the legacy of Sarah's knowledge of, and original responsibility for, his job role. However, it must remain speculative whether the tension that emerges between them in this extract may be a result of Sarah's powerful position in terms of historical legacy. Certainly, the way in which she is prepared to repeatedly cut in and talk over Jack (over five times in this extract), and the corresponding way in which he accedes to her interruptions, are linguistic manifestations of power (e.g. Fishman, 1980; Holmes, 1992; Zimmerman and West, 1975) which indicate an exercise of authority on her part and a deferral to authority on his. Of course, language and gender literature has traditionally attributed such speech strategies to the *male* dominance of women. The fact that there is a role reversal in this case points to the anti-essentialist explanation that a variety of competing discourses are governing Sarah's shifting subject position as a speaker.

Thus, Jack's deferral to Sarah in this context might also be explained by her apparent empowerment within the discourses of masculinisation and competing specialisms, which seem to supplement each other here. However, Sarah is ambiguously powerful as we shall see by considering two aspects of her use of language. First, Sarah's job role as operations director gives her a highly specialised, technical knowledge of computing hardware and software – areas traditionally associated with masculine expertise – which appears to empower her. This is apparent in the second extract as well as in other parts of the transcripts, where Sarah uses an abstruse, technical jargon to denote her specialist work. At the start of the extract, for example, Jack makes several tentative attempts to demystify her specialist vocabulary in order to spell out the implications of the technical problem:

JACK: And single node was what it was on yesterday which meant that . . .

. . .

JACK: Is . . . is the way that it comes up going to mean that performance is less than . . .

Sarah's refusal to explain the technical problem any further in layperson's terms reinforces the general awareness that she has exclusive access to a specialist knowledge within the company which is fundamental to its entire operation. While this imbues her with real authority as a speaker at this meeting because she can determine how much knowledge to make available, it simultaneously opens her expertise to challenge and contestation. There are at least three possible readings of Jack's need to cross-question Sarah in this extract. The *first* is that Jack feels he has a duty to interrogate Sarah's competing specialism on behalf of the company's culture of open dialogue in order to democratise her knowledge for the benefit of the others. In other words, the sharing of knowledge would help to equalise the power relationship between different specialisms: between Sarah as technical expert and her less technical colleagues. The *second* reading is that in terms of competing specialisms, Jack's sense of exclusion from an area of knowledge for which he has sales and marketing responsibilities is perceived as a professional threat; he may be unable to explain to clients why the website is experiencing difficulties. The *third* reading, suggested in the interview data, is that 'there is a question of trust in belief in competence':

RICHARD: Sarah and Jack have an element in their relationship [to do with trust] but it is more Jack drilling Sarah than the other way round. Jack pushes for more information, because he isn't entirely comfortable with what is happening ... and Sarah keeps on putting up the barriers.

Thus, Jack's cross-questioning signifies to Sarah that he does not trust her judgement. He is forcing her to account for her actions, rather than offering sympathy for her plight. While there is no obvious suggestion that this lack of trust has chauvinist or sexist connotations, Richard does imply that this is a *masculinised* response: Jack has distorted and masculinised the company discourse of open dialogue.

Ironically, the other aspect of Sarah's language which suggests that she is ambiguously powerful is her own masculinised speech style (e.g. use of interruptions, lengthy turns, talking over others, blocking statements, refusals to comply, bald assertions). While this might be described as a 'dominant' speech style, this does not imply that she always occupies a powerful subject position in the discussion. This is because she is herself subject to, and partially disempowered by, this very discourse of masculinisation. From an FDPA perspective, in the act of taking up a powerful subject position within the discourse of masculinisation, Sarah must negotiate its rules of engagement and terms of reference. As I have discussed in Chapter 6, this is not the same as being subject to a discourse of gender differentiation, as appears to be the case for the girls in the classroom study. Sarah is no obvious 'victim' of gender difference or discrimination, despite or perhaps because she is the only woman on the MT. In her interview, Sarah herself said, 'I don't think they necessarily treat me differently as a woman', although this denial of the influence of gender is known to be a common-sense perception of many successful business women (Halford and Leonard, 2000). Indeed, the discourse of masculinisation cuts across sex category differences, affecting all members of the team, male and female. Sarah's partial disempowerment is a result of the masculinised style of engagement which symbolically constructs any pair of speakers, male or female, as opponents in a fight. In my interview data, several participants described the discussion between different members of the MT using metaphors of fighting and aggression, drawing on the boxing ring, target practice and the battlefield. Indeed, this is a construction that is never entirely gender-neutral. There is little question that when this imagery is applied by a male colleague to Sarah, there are sexist connotations, of which she herself seems subliminally aware:

RICHARD: Sarah, under pressure, becomes very defensive at which point you don't get any more information out of her because she is just defending her territory, *not able to reason at this stage* (my italics)

. . .

RICHARD: Jack will back down very quickly when pushed by Keith, but will attack quite hard when he has Sarah on the ropes. He's comfortable with pushing her. He's not beyond sniping at anyone but he's cautious who his targets are. *He doesn't try to play that game with me* (my italics)

. . .

SARAH: I've noticed recently that the dynamics of the management team have changed enormously over the last year, and I think this has made me more defensive than I used to be. Before last year, there used to be two women on the board and this gave us a combined position of strength. Since then, I've noticed that the atmosphere in the team has become very 'boysy'.

In broad terms, these comments suggest that a discourse of masculinisation is increasingly affecting the terms of engagement of the management team, as evidenced in the second extract by Jack's failed attempts to 'attack' Sarah's handling of a technical problem, and Sarah's forceful attempts to resist the attack and 'defend' her own actions. With regard to Sarah in particular, she is constituted as a persuasive and influential speaker relative to Jack during this extract, largely because of her ascendant subject positions within the discourses of historical legacy and competing specialisms. But this ascendancy is contested and undermined by a discourse of masculinisation which has appropriated the meeting's terms of engagement (in the past, the domain of open dialogue), and cast Jack as 'goal attack' and Sarah as 'goal defence'. Sarah's ability to resist a verbal attack is an ambiguous achievement: she feels compelled to adopt the more masculinised terms of engagement in order to survive in the 'boysy' culture, while making it clear that she is far from comfortable with it:

SARAH: I think the reason why I've been feeling defensive lately is because of the feeling that I'm being marginalised by that boysy culture and that I have nothing much to contribute to it.

To sum up, at first glance Sarah appears to be assimilated within the 'boysy culture' of the management team, evidenced by her colleagues' deference to her subject position as a technical expert, and her dominant and masculinised style of interaction. However, Sarah's lack of ease with her own show of dominance is indicated both in her interview comments, and in her need to meta-analyse her contribution to the discussion at the end of the second extract. It is therefore possible that Sarah does adopt competing subject positions in the meeting which means that she is both assimilated within, and separated from, the 'boysy culture' or masculinised discourse she has identified. This possibility is signalled in the second extract by the way her show of dominance produces a strained silence among her colleagues at this meeting, tolerated but perhaps resented.

Meeting two

Extract one

Both the extracts below are situated towards the end of the meeting when the participants are discussing any other business (AOB) items. This extract begins about halfway through a contentious discussion of what the company should do about Christmas Eve. As it falls on a Monday, Keith, as managing director and chair of the meeting, has proposed that employees are 'encouraged' to take the day off. So far in the discussion, Keith has been quite oblique about what makes the issue contentious, namely, that he wants to avoid making this a formal day's holiday at company expense. Rather, he would prefer that employees are voluntarily 'encouraged' to take a day from their holiday entitlement. It is the skirting around this 'unsaid' issue that has hitherto caused a meandering and somewhat repetitive discussion.

SARAH: I actually think we should *say* that the office is going to be closed on Christmas Eve. Christmas Eve is traditionally a half-day anyway. That goes right through the shareholder business. Anyone who has any work to do can do it remotely. There is no reason for anyone to come into work. I would really question the value of people coming in on that day.

KEITH: (*SOUNDING IRRITATED AND OVERLAPPING FROM* 'There is no reason . . .')
We should have brought this out six months ago really. I think next year we are going to have to work this out much, much earlier so that if we are going to be closed, we can say that we want everyone to have the same day's holiday.

JACK: I'm just going to say to all my managers that we are going to be closed on that day and that it is a day's holiday, and people who haven't got a holiday left will have to take it out of next year's. If they really want to come in then fine.

KEITH: I'm just a bit dubious about *forcing* people to take a day off. This seems to be working against

729   Hook3 culture to be suggesting that we *force* people to take the day off at this late stage.

730   **JACK**: In that case, we just *encourage* them to take the day off . . .

731   **SARAH**: (*INTERRUPTING AND OVERLAPPING AS JACK CONTINUES. HIS TALK IS*

732   *INDECIPHRABLE.*) We'll end up with three people who come in because they haven't got any

733   holiday left.

734   **PETE**: And then they're be here until . . .

735   **SARAH**: And then you have to have another five people in to open up, support it, then they'll sit about

736   for half a day, do some filing, answer phones and go home.

737   **KEITH**: Shall we find out how big the problem is then, because if it's a dozen people, it's

738   different from two.

739   **SARAH**: Most of mine [won't be coming in].

740   **PETE**: Well, can we just make a decision?

741   **SARAH**: Yes, I think we should.

742   **PETE**: Let's just make a decision. Can we *please* just make a decision.

743   **KEITH**: (*WITH HEAVY EMPHASIS*) I don't think this is something we should be *forcing*

744   people to do. If we'd discussed this six months ago, then fine. If someone was *forcing* me to take a

745   holiday, I'd be pretty fed up. Let's find out how big the problem actually is.

746   **JACK**: (*IRONIC TONE*) You're not forcing *us* to take a holiday on Christmas Eve, are you,

747   Keith?

748   **PETE**: (*IRONIC TONE*) You're not *forcing* us to be available on Christmas Eve, are you,

749   Keith?

750   **KEITH**: I'm not forcing you to take a holiday, but I am forcing you to be available, that's

751   different. You're the management team (*SARCASTIC TONE*), I don't have to feel sorry for you.

Denotative analysis

The key speakers in this extract, Keith, Sarah, Jack and later, Pete, each have different perspectives on the issue. In her opening comment, Sarah appears to tackle the issue head on (ll. 716–20), although without raising the thorny subject of pay, by indicating that some decisive whole company action is necessary. She makes a clear and eloquent case for shutting the office, backing it up with reasons and suggesting a possible compromise: that if people are going to be paid for a day at home, they can still work 'remotely'. Keith shows his disagreement with this suggestion by talking over Sarah, although not so invasively that it sounds like a deliberate interruption. His comments are almost spoken to himself: he expresses regret about not planning the matter better (l. 722) and contemplates a future strategy (ll. 723–4), but he does not address the immediate issue. Keith's failure to direct the discussion and dictate strategy at this point seems to prompt Jack's next comment (l. 725), which is decisive, action-driven and takes matters into his own hands. The import of Jack's words seems to be that if Keith is not going to make a whole company decision, then he, Jack, will make the decision on his own team's behalf. Keith's reaction to this (ll. 728–9) suggests that this is not at all the subtle course of action he is looking for. While initially mitigating his disagreement with the hedge, 'I'm just a bit dubious...', Keith juxtaposes this with a strong statement about the company ethos. Taking the hint, Jack appears to back down. He modifies the wording of his earlier suggestion to fall in line with Keith's original proposal, even echoing Keith's own words: 'In that case, we just *encourage* them to take the day off...'.

From this point in the discussion, Jack makes no further attempt to challenge Keith, other than to tease him (ll. 746–7) later on. Instead, the focus of resistance switches to Sarah, who continues to argue for the office to be shut, and to Pete who 'just wants a decision'. In lines 731–6, Sarah suggests that Keith's proposal is an unworkable compromise by describing an undesirable scenario ('they'll sit about for half a day...'), and follows this with a flat refusal to comply (l. 739). Pete, who has played almost no part in the discussion so far, perhaps indicating a lack of interest in the issue, makes repeated requests (ll. 740, 742) for the meeting to reach a decision. Although Keith responds to Pete's demand by proposing an action to investigate the issue further, there is no real resolution of the issue. Jack and Pete's joky questions to Keith towards the end of this extract (ll. 746 and 748) signal a release of tension at the end of what has been a tense discussion of an apparently trivial issue. Keith's rejoinder (ll. 750–1), ending with, 'I don't have to feel sorry for you', although said humorously, gives him the last word in reminding the others that their senior team status carries both privileges *and* extra responsibilities, in other words, the day off is unlikely to apply to them.

Extract two

This extract constitutes the last AOB item of the meeting before it closes. As with the Christmas Eve issue, the discussion of a seemingly trivial and uncontentious matter becomes an opportunity for underlying tensions and micro-politics within the management team to surface.

788   **PETE**: Christmas cards? Who does all the administration of them? What do we want to do about them?

789   **RICHARD**: I think Keith reported a couple of weeks ago that Marketing was designing them.

790   **KEITH**: Well, normally each team do their own Christmas cards. They need to be within the next week

791   or so.

792   **PETE**: That's right, yeah.

793   **SARAH**: Sorry, I'm lost now.

794   **RICHARD**: So the design has been passed. It's been agreed in principle?

795   **PETE**: (*OVERLAPPING*) So they've been printed?

796   **SARAH**: (*WITH EMPHASIS*) We haven't seen them.

797   **JACK**: So you want to approve the Christmas cards now?

798   **SARAH**: (*SOUNDING PUT OUT*) No. I just would have liked to have seen the designs, not to

799   approve.

800   **JACK**: You think I get something out of marketing the Christmas cards . . . well, I don't.

801   **PETE**: (*SARCASTIC TONE*) The power of the marketing team . . . down to the Christmas

802   cards! (*LAUGHTER FROM THE OTHERS*)

803   **KEITH**: We've done the Christmas cards?

804   **SARAH**: (*SARCASTIC TONE*) Apparently.

805   **KEITH**: Who's done the Christmas cards?

806   **PETE**: (*TO KEITH*) Can you make sure they're printed in time this year.

Denotative analysis

The discussion opens quite routinely with a question from Pete in which he seeks information about the administration of Christmas cards. This information is provided by both Richard (l. 789) and Keith (ll. 790–1), which initially appears to answer Pete's query ('That's right, yeah'). It is at this point that Sarah indicates that she is either confused about, or dissatisfied with, presumably, Keith's answer (l. 793). It also provokes first Richard then Pete to ask further, rapid-fire, probing questions (ll. 794–5). Sarah's statement (l. 798) finally exposes the cause of her concern – she has not been consulted about the design of the cards prior, possibly, to printing. Jack's confrontational response to Sarah ('So you want to approve the Christmas cards now?') makes it clear that her somewhat proprietorial stance has annoyed him. As marketing manager, the subtext might go that this is surely Jack's area of responsibility anyway and nothing to do with operations. Rather than admitting to a proprietorial attitude, Sue tries to downplay her response to suggest an *interest* in the cards rather than a wish to be involved in decision-making (ll. 798–9). However, Jack's comment (l. 800) is in turn a defensive reaction to what he fears others may be thinking, that his assumption of responsibility for producing the Christmas cards means that he is on some sort of a 'power kick'. As if to confirm his fears, Pete immediately expresses this but defuses possible tension by turning his observation into a joke: 'the power of the marketing team ... down to the Christmas cards!' Keith's belated contributions to the discussion appear to suggest that he has not been listening (ll. 803, 805). The fact that he is reiterating the very questions asked by Pete, Sarah and Richard earlier tends to suggest that he too is 'miffed' that he has not been consulted about details on the printing. Pete's final comment before the meeting's close is a reminder that, despite all the hot air of the discussion, some form of action still needs to be taken.

FPDA commentary

In the first FPDA commentary, the analysis focused primarily on the interactions between three of the key speakers in the meeting, Sarah, Jack and Richard. The analysis aimed to show the extent to which the effectiveness of these speakers within this context (in terms of their influence and impact on others' opinions) was largely governed by the interplay of four competing discourses. The feminist perspective on the analysis strove to foreground the ways in which Sarah, as the only woman on the MT, was constituted as simultaneously powerful and powerless, both apparently assimilated within the MT and yet perceiving herself as separated from the masculinised company culture.

In the following FPDA commentary, I intend to foreground the more abstract issue of how different and competing gendered discourses position individuals within this management setting. I have argued that the discourse of masculinisation cuts across sex category differences, affecting all participants alike, both male and female. In other words, certain individuals, regardless of their sex categorisation, may gravitate towards particular values, beliefs and discursive practices which favour either a relatively masculinised or, alternatively, a relatively feminised management ethos. An FPDA approach is likely to be highly appropriate wherever one form of gendered discourse threatens to challenge, overturn or render silent another form of gendered discourse. This appeared to be the case in this management team setting where a discourse of masculinisation was seeking to challenge the feminised company discourse of open dialogue. From a strictly post-structuralist perspective, there is a hint of contradiction here: isn't the silenced voice usually that of the minority subculture rather than that of the establishment? While this is generally the case, I would argue that an FPDA approach is *not* concerned to consider binary oppositions between potentially opposing discourses. Nor is it concerned to support the interests of a feminised discourse against that of a masculinised one, as this merely endorses a traditional discourse of gender differentiation: namely, that sets of gender-stereotyped assumptions about language, behaviour and so on can be attached to each biological sex. Rather, FPDA is concerned to expose the ways in which individuals, females and males, can often be 'trapped' by their subject positioning within masculinised or feminised discourses and may seek ways of making shifts between them.

In order to demonstrate that a *male* research participant can be identified with a *feminised* discourse (just as a female research participant can be identified with a masculinised one), the focus of analysis will switch to Keith, CEO and chair of both meetings. As discussed above, Keith shared Sarah's founding vision for the company as open, egalitarian, democratic, collaborative and free-thinking, and was instrumental in constructing its mission statement. I have argued that this was a prototypically *feminised* vision, which both managers were keen to promote through the authorised company discourse of open dialogue. Given Keith's unique position as head of the company, how would he negotiate his speech in an MT meeting to be an effective leader, yet at the same time adhere to the feminised principles inscribing a discourse of open dialogue? How exactly would he position himself in relation to the competing discourse of masculinisation which was contesting his management style? In the light of his CEO/chairing roles, I will examine the ways in which Keith takes up constantly shifting positions of powerfulness and powerlessness that simultaneously construct and undermine his authority as a purveyor of a *feminised* corporate culture.

At first glance, both extracts appear to suggest that Keith occupies powerful subject positions within the discourses of open dialogue and historical legacy, here complementing each other, which should serve to reinforce, rather than undermine, his authority as CEO. Keith is powerful in terms of historical legacy because he has helped to found company policy and practices to reflect his democratic views of management and leadership. For example, there is a clear pattern to the way meetings are run which conforms to the authorised discourse of open dialogue: speakers are formally located as equally powerful within a general discussion, and a range of views are aired in order to reach a co-operative and collaborative decision. Voices from the interview data suggested that this meeting pattern was fine in the rhetoric but could be counterproductive in practice:

RICHARD: Keith is desperately keen to try and keep [the meeting] as a peer group session rather than him taking the chair. The control tends to pass round the room quite often with people taking turns to steer the conversation. I think one of the areas we were talking about was what to do if a supplier goes bust . . . It actually took an awful long time for anyone to steer us back on to track.

Here Richard hints at an oppositional reading of 'open dialogue': in the context of a management meeting, what may be regarded as fair-minded, co-operative and power-sharing by some, may also be perceived as a lack of leadership and clear direction according to a discourse of masculinisation. In the Christmas cards extract, Keith appears to take such a low profile in the discussion that at one point he appears not to be listening. He does offer one piece of information followed by an instruction (ll. 790–1), but otherwise does not obviously guide the discussion to a conclusion. That role is conspicuously taken by Pete, who both opens the subject, drives it along with a series of quick-fire questions, and then issues an instruction to Keith about the necessary action to be taken. In other words, the control has passed to Pete who has taken a turn to steer the discussion, but the interview data also revealed that this was not from any desire for open dialogue. Rather, Pete's actions constitute a form of *resistance* against the authorised discourse. According to a competing discourse of masculinsation with its emphasis upon firm leadership, delegation and goal-orientated action, Pete views open-ended discussion as a waste of his time. He simply wants an outcome:

PETE: I don't think any meeting is a successful meeting . . . we have this habit of sitting in meetings and discussing tiny details which are immaterial and not important to the company.

. . .

RICHARD: Pete is very action-driven. We had quite a waffly meeting here which frustrates him and he comes from a very structured background where he just wants to see people make decisions and almost to the extent where a bad decision is better than no decision because at least we are making progress.

The possibility that Keith's apparently powerful positions within the discourses of open dialogue and historical legacy are being contested is apparent in the Christmas Eve extract. Here, Sarah, Pete and Jack suggest in different ways that a decision must be taken 'from the top' about whether or not Christmas Eve should be an official day off. In other words, they are urging Keith to masculinise his approach to leadership. This is an approach Keith patently refuses to make, resisting attempts to masculinise his authority as CEO. For Keith, it seems that the consequence of a single, authoritative CEO decision is the erosion of the more feminised practice of open consultation. He is so concerned that the company ethos of open dialogue is being contested that he makes the point explicit on two occasions in this extract. Notice how often the word 'force' is used in this and subsequent quotations:

KEITH: I'm just a bit dubious about *forcing* people to take a day off. This seems to be working against Hook3 culture to be suggesting that we *force* people to take the day off at this late stage.
. . .

KEITH: (*WITH HEAVY EMPHASIS*) I don't think this is something we should be *forcing* people to do. If we'd discussed this six weeks ago, then fine. If someone was *forcing* me to take a holiday, I'd be pretty fed up.

As both CEO and chair, Keith is powerfully positioned here to champion the cause of the company ethos of open dialogue. But such a discourse cannot construct the practices of subjects without producing counteracts of resistance or supplementary challenges, according to an FPDA perspective. Keith is not simply reminding colleagues of company culture here, he is actively policing the boundaries of an authorised discourse that continues to construct him as CEO. The fact that he needs to do this is evidence that he may be aware of increasing *resistance* to both his own authority and the party line. Newer members of the MT in particular expressed a dissatisfaction, if not a dissension, with certain aspects of the feminised culture of Hook3 and a need to consider a change of approach:

RICHARD: There are an awful lot of people who really thrive in the culture we create but there are quite a few who find it overwhelming, so that, in some cases, what is space to be slightly free-thinking and what is space to form stronger teams and direction actually ends up as being lacking in direction in their view. There are quite a few areas where people would just like to be told what to do. For some people it is quite hard for them to get security from knowing where they fit.
. . .

PETE: One of the key guidelines we seem to operate from as a senior team is that people don't like being told what to do. But sometimes there are situations where, frankly, in companies you just have to do certain things, you don't have a choice. Obviously you tell them nicely of course, but a lot of people may not want to do it, then you have to *force* them to do it.

. . .

PAM: Generally the senior team are good at communicating with each other, but they are not very good at communicating with Keith. They are always ganging up together and not letting Keith know anything. He's always saying to me, 'I am the last one to know'.

What I would suggest is evident in these remarks, is that individual acts of resistance to the feminised discourse of open dialogue are being transformed into a covert counter-culture particularly comprising the newer colleagues of the MT. This counter-culture indicates the growing significance of the discourses of competing specialisms and masculinisation for this organisation. In terms of competing specialisms, interviewees proposed that the company should place a higher value upon the need for a lack of interference from the top; more autonomy for the individual team manager; clearer compartmentalisation between each team or specialism; and delegated decision-making. According to a competing discourse of masculinisation, interviewees suggested the need for a more assertive and authoritative style of management, and for systematic structures and processes for policy and decision-making. In the Christmas Eve extract we saw Keith's support for the company ethos of open consultation being contested by a discourse of masculinisation: most of the MT wanted to see a speedy decision from the top. In the Christmas card extract, Keith and Sarah's need to approve the design of the cards is contested both by the discourse of masculinisation (Pete's repeated plea for a speedy, top-down decision) and competing discourses (Jack's view that the job should be delegated to his specialist marketing team).

Thus, Keith's apparently powerful positions within the discourses of historical legacy (having an input on every decision) and open dialogue (not telling people what to do) are being continuously challenged and undercut by the growing counter-culture of masculinisation and competing specialisms. However, as with any feminist, post-structuralist analysis, this is not the whole story. Keith is not simply embodying one set of values (feminised) in a dialectical relationship with an opposing set of values (masculinised). It is one of FPDA's principles that individual subjects are themselves 'unfixed, unsatisfied . . . not a unity, not autonomous, but a process, perpetually in construction, perpetually contradictory, perpetually open to change' (Belsey, 1980: 132). Richard and Pete's resistance to Keith's feminised style of management isn't simply to do with lack of direction or time-wasting collaboration. It is also concerned with the way in which authorised, company discourse is mobilised in meetings by Keith as chair in order to empower his own subtextual agendas:

PETE: I think there is a pattern in meetings which isn't always healthy. We open up a debate where Keith will say, 'Let's look at X. What are everyone's views on it? and you know he already has a view on it which he is not willing to share for fear he'll be accused of manipulation. What he is hoping is that in the course of going round the room, we'll all come round to his point of view quite naturally and then he'll wrap it up. If all of us don't like X, he'll probably start to intervene as we go round to steer it. Actually, it's consultation without consulting.

Keith's surreptitious need to control final decisions within meetings, which appears to be in contradiction to his stated beliefs in open dialogue, is not necessarily hypocritical, self-deceiving, ill-intentioned or masculinisation by the back door. Like his colleagues, Keith is constantly negotiating for positions of power and resisting positions of powerlessness as his authority is continuously being reconstructed and undermined. But in addition, his subject position as the leader of a new, successful company is constituted by a work ethic that he creates and which creates him:

RICHARD: Keith is absolutely committed to team, beyond this being a job. Probably the most important thing he does in his life is to run the business. Therefore to come in at 7 o'clock and to leave at 10 o'clock at night is doing the job. That sort of thing is fantastic as head of the company but the difficulty lies in being able to understand that most people don't work like that.

In sum, Keith is seen to be multiply and somewhat ambiguously positioned as sometimes powerful and at other times powerless, within a range of competing discourses. From an FPDA perspective, he can be seen as a purveyor of a relatively feminised company ethos determined to resist the challenges of a more masculinised sub-culture, but this may also be a simplistic, dualistic reading of events.

Ultimately, perhaps, his powerful positions within the discourses of open dialogue and historical legacy continue to endorse and reinforce his position as the boss. Yet such a power base is constantly under contestation by the discourses of competing specialisms and masculinisation, as the newer members of the MT try to negotiate the conditions for a transformed company culture.

An evaluation of the study

In this final section, I briefly explore how the use of an FPDA approach enabled me to fulfil the aims of this study: namely, to consider the extent to which competing discourses position individual managers as relatively powerful or powerless in relation to the main purpose of their meetings: to solve business problems and make key decisions. In parallel with the classroom study, this study showed how the varying *discursive* ways in which these managers were positioned as powerful largely determined their ability to influence others and make decisions. Unlike the classroom study, there were no formalised criteria by which to judge speakers' effectiveness and, in the spirit of FPDA, no attempt at making such absolute assessments is made here. The kinds of observations an FPDA approach *can* contribute are insights and reflections on the kinds of speakers who are more likely to be key players in this setting, and the kinds of speakers who are less so.

In the context of this case study, there are no obvious winners and losers. Managers at this senior level have usually achieved their positions of responsibility on the basis that they are generally accomplished at speaking in public settings, able to persuade others to their point of view and to make collective decisions. All members of the MT appeared to be confident, articulate and socially skilled. None had a difficulty with speaking at length, chipping in to a discussion or confronting those with whom they might disagree. However, despite this base of professional accomplishment, it was evident that there were deep-seated disagreements and tensions within the team, and power struggles being negotiated between different interests and perspectives. Yet according to my analysis, those who came off best, in terms of their influence upon a meeting's decision-making processes, were more likely to be quite powerfully positioned across all four discourses at work in that setting.

Thus, a profile of a more powerful or effective speaker was likely to be an IT specialist, a founder member and a supporter of the firm's historical belief in open dialogue, but who was versatile enough to use masculinised speech strategies when a more assertive or confrontational style was deemed necessary. This profile potentially fitted all three founder members – Keith, Jack and Sarah – although none of them could be described as unambiguously powerful. Keith's subject position as MD formally gave him ultimate authority over the rest of the team, but his support of a philosophy of open dialogue often appeared to undercut his authority to take a final decision. Sarah's combined subject positions as company founder and an exponent of open dialogue were further empowered by her authority as the company's IT expert. While her position as the sole woman on the senior team could certainly not be construed as a disadvantage, nonetheless she was subject to insidious sexist judgements and criticisms. Finally Jack *appeared* to be powerfully positioned in terms of the way he exercised a kind of historical dominance over more recently appointed colleagues such as Richard and Pete. Yet, as the last appointed founder member, he was more accustomed to defer to Sarah and Keith.

Conversely, a profile of a less powerfully positioned speaker within this context was a more recently appointed member, without specific technical knowledge, who was prepared to challenge the company culture of open dialogue and compete for resources with colleagues in order to strengthen their own specialism. This description applied to both Richard and Pete in particular, who adopted resistant positions in challenging the old order. However, even this characterisation of more powerful and less powerful profiles is simplistic and inadequate. The masculinised discourse constituting Pete and Richard's resistance to the values supported by the founder members could hardly be described as positioning these two managers as powerless. In contradistinction, their challenge represented a serious threat to the status quo, which might ultimately seek to overturn the unusually collaborative culture of this dotcom company. This analysis presented me with quite a conundrum: from a post-structuralist perspective, resistant voices represented by the 'new' discourses (in this case, masculinisation and competing specialisms) are to be welcomed for their power to introduce fresher insights and further textual play. But from a feminist perspective, the voices that were being challenged were associated with a feminised culture, valuing listening, open dialogue, shared decision-making and collaborative styles of management. Yet if these voices have started to become reified within any 'community of practice' as a 'will to power', the contestation by resistant voices may lead to a revitalised cultural transformation. This particular conundrum is discussed further in Chapter 8.

8
Why Choose to Use FPDA?

So far I have demonstrated the way in which an FPDA approach can usefully be applied to analysing spoken discourse within classroom and business contexts. In this final chapter, I shall summarise the pragmatic benefits of the FPDA perspective in the hope that other researchers and practitioners will take the opportunity to apply the methodology to other discursive contexts. I have argued that FPDA can work alongside more widely recognised approaches such as conversation analysis (CA) or critical discourse analysis (CDA). However, its specific interest in the complex relationship between power, gender and discourse makes it a rigorous yet flexible framework for analysing any verbal and non-verbal interactions, and especially those conducted in public or institutional settings.

In assessing the supplementary contribution FPDA might make to the field of discourse analysis, I intend to show that there are at least four reasons why a discourse analyst might choose to use FPDA in preference to other discourse approaches. I have already argued in the context of the case study chapters (4–7) that FPDA can explain why certain speakers are judged more powerful, influential and effective than others in larger group contexts. In this chapter, I wish to explore how FPDA can also:

- make sense of the differences *within* and *between* girls/women (in terms of their verbal and non-verbal behaviour) including their experiences of the complexities and ambiguities of power
- open the way for a more complex, nuanced, searching understanding of spoken interactions by giving space to multiple and

competing voices and accounts, as well as to voices which have been silenced
- support transformative feminist projects within a post-structuralist paradigm provided these are specific, localised, action-driven and temporary.

In aiming to illustrate these reasons, which form the three section headings of this chapter, I refer to the two case studies which feature in this book. The first section draws upon the management team study; the second highlights the classroom study; and the third section assesses the implications of both studies for transformative action.

Differences within and between females

Feminist post-structuralism has sought to challenge the modernist myth that girls/women are universally and uniformly subordinated by a patriarchal order. With the decentring of the notion of essential identities has come the study of the multiplicity of gender identities and the realisation that there are different femininities and masculinities which are often culturally and historically specific. Such a perspective is able to offer an explanation for some of the theoretical complexities that have challenged feminism such as the multiple ways in which power is constituted both *between* men and women, and *between* individual women themselves. As Francis (1999: 383) has explained:

> Black, working class, gay and disabled feminists have drawn white, middle class, able-bodied, heterosexual feminists' attention to the fact that oppressive power relationships are not only dependent on gender, but can occur due to a host of other factors and can exist between women.

On the basis of this perspective, an FPDA approach is not entitled to make sweeping generalisations about what it is to be 'male' or 'female', as this tendency merely serves to reinforce and legitimise *differences* between men and women's social power. Politically speaking, I have discussed how FPDA *does* choose to privilege the category of 'female' and discourses of gender for the practical purposes of study, but it asks analysts to be constantly self-reflexive about making this a discursive choice. In any case, FPDA prefers not to view females as the *victims* of a patriarchal order, nor to view males as the *villains* of the piece, but to consider both biological sex categories in terms of their plurality or diversity. Plurality also implies that individuals, both female and male, are multiply positioned according to competing discourses, at times as powerful and at other times as powerless. As we have seen, the issue is often not one of difference but of gender 'polarisation' (Bing and Bergvall, 1998) or, in my own terms, the historically and culturally accreted discourse of *gender differentiation*. This phenomenon is aptly explained by Bem (1993: 2):

> It is thus not simply that women and men are seen to be different but that this male–female difference is superimposed on so many aspects of the social world that a cultural connection is thereby forged between sex and virtually every other aspect of human experience, including modes of dress and social roles and even ways of expressing emotion and experiencing sexual desire.

Implicated in and sustaining discourses of gender differentiation are unequal power relationships which have traditionally served the interests of males over females, making it easier to limit opportunities and exclude girls and women from education, public office and more senior positions in business and the professions. In counterpoint to this, girls and women in the Western world have attained far greater educational and career successes within the last 20 years, and are gradually taking on more prestigious public and occupational positions. Against this complex background, FPDA offers a means of unravelling the ways in which girls and women are on one level so heterogeneously positioned that it seems invidious to categorise them as a discrete group and yet, on another, are discursively implicated in a historical legacy of restrictive, gendered practices.

The management team study (Chapters 6 and 7) reveals some of the difficulties for FPDA practitioners of ever presuming that discourses of gender differentiation will govern spoken interactions. The study took place in a company renowned for its equal opportunities policies at all levels. Even in traditional areas such as computer programming, there were significant numbers of female employees, and women made up equal numbers with men on all managerial levels below the senior management team. Clearly, the sole presence of only one woman, Sarah, within a team of six male managers might constitute a gender issue for discourse analysts, particularly as this is broadly representative of the still relatively small proportion of women at senior levels in many Western countries (Halford and Leonard, 2001). However, such a perspective is leavened by the knowledge that it was Sarah who originally founded the company. From an FPDA standpoint, Sarah's historical reputation as the company's driving force meant that her minority status as a *woman* on the senior management team was unlikely to constitute her as a possible victim of gendered practices in the organisation. If anything, an FPDA approach might be more likely to explore the ways in which Sarah's spoken interactions in work settings have *helped* to constitute her as a success story, a role model to other women, rather than rationalised as a tokenist exception to the modernist feminist rule of institutionalised sexism.

The focus of the management team study was to examine what constituted effective speech during the course of a series of board meetings, with special regard to the effects of gendered discourses in this mixed-sex setting. My analysis showed that Sarah was more than capable of holding her own with her male colleagues and, moreover, that she was capable of silencing and peripheralising Jack, one of the more outspoken and confrontational members of the team. Sarah's relatively dominant manner in the meetings observed was being actively constructed by her powerful positions within the four discourses at work in this setting: historical legacy, open dialogue, competing specialisms and masculinisation. In more concrete terms, her authority was derived from her speech and actions as the founder member of the company, her espousal of the company's philosophy of open dialogue; her readiness to use a stereotypically masculinised style of engagement and finally from her highly specialised technical expertise. Despite this, Sarah could not be described as uniformly or unambiguously powerful. While there were no obvious signs of a discourse of gender differentiation governing the talk and behaviour of this group of managers, there were subtextual undercurrents. Like her male colleagues, Sarah's views and comments were constantly contested and continuously subjected to scrutiny. But there was a subtle difference in the nature of that contestation, evidenced in two ways. First, team members seemed unperturbed when a *male* manager made use of a 'masculinised' speech style but responded somewhat differently when *Sarah* made use of it. For example, when Sarah was being particularly assertive or confrontational in a discussion, this was followed by a non-response or extended silence from her colleagues (see p. 151), as if she were transgressing a speech norm for how female speakers should behave (e.g. Zimmerman and West, 1975). In contrast, when her male colleagues adopted a similarly assertive approach, the discussion continued with no obvious breaks, pauses or silences. Secondly, in my interviews with different managers, I noted a slight tendency among certain male managers to derogate Sarah's speech style in sexist terms ('Sarah, under pressure . . . is not able to reason at this stage . . .').

Had it been possible to extend this research study, I would have liked to investigate whether Sarah's relatively powerful position within this company constituted her as *different* from other female employees in the organisation. In contrast to Sarah was the case of Pam, personal assistant to all the members of the senior management team including the MD, who might be perceived as occupying a more traditionally subservient female position within the company. Pam was an entirely silent presence in the context of the board meetings, literally having no voice in terms of determining policy or making decisions. She was responsible for setting up the meeting, arranging the meeting room, fielding phone calls, organising the team's diaries and making coffee. I did not hear her speak or get any sense of her views until I interviewed her privately, when she seemed amazed that I should want to listen to her. Yet, while not officially ascribed as powerful, Pam's unrivalled subject position as a gatekeeper and 'private ear' to *all* the members of the senior team gave her privileged access to confidential information. While clearly having a lower occupational status to that of Sarah (in terms of authority, salary, having a voice), Pam was by no means powerless. Although aware of her agency to utilise such power, it was of course unlikely that she would do so. Pam's job description as a personal assistant behoved her to be discreet about any such confidential information, preventing her from exploiting her privileged access to such knowledge/power, as she herself acknowledged:

It would be easy to abuse my position but I try not to. All of the team tend to speak to me about different matters, some quite important and sensitive. I sometimes feel

I know more than I should. Sometimes I'm talking to one of them and know something about them that they have no idea I know. It is not always a comfortable feeling.

To sum up, the management study reveals some of the complexities
and ambiguities involved in aiming to make sweeping generalisations
about the experiences of female speakers in mixed-sex settings.
An FPDA approach enables practitioners to foreground the subtle or
more obvious distinctions between the experiences of girls and women,
but yet to be sensitive to the more entrenched ways in which gender-
differentiated practices continue to devalue female participation in
spoken discourse.

An understanding of spoken interactions

This book has argued for the value of a polyphonic approach to
discourse analysis that attempts to disprivilege the authorial voice in
order to give greater standing to a multiplicity of voices. In his
concept of supplementarity, Derrida (1976) advocated that there is
a subtle interplay between multiple-voices or texts that only comes
into being when each is heard or read in juxtaposition with the others.
Scott (1996: 154) wisely points out the dangers of automatically
'taking as read' that the polyphonic version of discourse analysis
necessarily leads to a more 'democratic' or deconstructed textual
representation when he suggests that, 'the authority of the author is
still sustained through his or her selection of voices, central role in
the data-collection process and choice of focus'. To this end, I have
argued that it is always vital to acknowledge the primacy of the
authorial voice when giving space to other voices and perspectives
within an analysis. This is because the FPDA practitioner has a meta-
analytical interest in demonstrating the ways in which speakers continuously shift between intertextualised and competing discourses.

But the inevitable primacy of the author's voice can be partially
offset by deploying 'writerly' (Barthes, 1977) strategies such as self-
evaluation or self-critique. In this spirit, I might ask of my own work
whether I am deluding myself in terms of my efforts to produce
a polyphonic analysis of classroom talk or management meeting discourse. Are the multiple-voices, readings and perspectives represented
in the two studies *genuinely* offering a polyphonic vision of speakers'
verbal and non-verbal interactions within their given contexts? Or is

this polyphonic representation merely an illustrative device, adding, at the very best, texture, colour, detail, multi-dimensionality and a spurious sense of realism to the 'authoritative discourse' of the author? While I am ready to accept that either (or both) evaluations of my work are possible, I would argue that both case studies adhere to a clear polyphonic focus, regardless of the way their outcome is interpreted, as I will go on to discuss. The crucial point about the FPDA approach is that it gives space to multiple and competing voices by aiming to identify and represent *sites of struggle* in stretches of spoken or textual interaction. A 'site of struggle' is usually taken to mean a discursive location (such as the family, motherhood, education, religion and so on) in which dominant discourses compete for ascendancy in their ceaseless endeavour to fix meaning (Simpson, 1997). Or, on a micro-analytical level, it might also mean significant moments in spoken discourse where meanings are negotiated and contested, manifested by differences of viewpoint, clashes of opinion or conflicting readings.

The classroom study particularly foregrounds the discursive location of *educational assessment* as a site of struggle in terms of the way various participants make competing judgements about the different ways that individuals speak and interact. On the formal level of awarding grades to students for their oral performances within a range of speech contexts, there are clearly set examination criteria defining and ultimately closing down the ways in which effective speech can be perceived and assessed. While this encourages some consensus of opinion, the basis upon which individuals make their competing judgements can nonetheless vary considerably. Thus, students, teachers and assessors in the classroom study individually interpreted the assessment criteria in multiple and diverse ways. This was not simply because they were *reading* the criteria in different ways; it was also because they were responding as *subjects* who were multiply located within competing discourses. The study was thus able to problematise the idea that speakers can be assessed and grades awarded on the basis of specified criteria alone, and, on a practical level, this meant that the assessors became much more self-reflexive about the ways in which they constituted their judgements.

Perhaps the most illuminating example of the value of a polyphonic perspective on the data was the case of Joe. As I discussed earlier, he was awarded a grade A (in an A* to G grading system) for showing that he could meet the examination criteria, which was to 'take command of the situation' and 'use language in a dynamic and influential way' (EDEXCEL, 1998). The FPDA approach needed to represent the conflicting ways in which the various research participants – students, class teacher and teacher assessors – construed his performance. It was also vital to represent the conflicts of opinion *within* a group of individuals such as the students. Thus, while Joe's status as a confident, popular boy appeared to guarantee the approval of most of his peers as an effective speaker, there remained a significant minority who were quite critical of his class performance. For example, girls such as Cathy and Kate, who were quite articulate about the workings of a discourse of gender differentiation in a classroom setting, were prepared to *contest* the dominant view that Joe was necessarily an effective speaker ('When Joe was talking and Damien was talking, Joe had to be right'). Also, boys like Michael who failed to fit dominant versions of teenage masculinity also expressed a resistant view ('[Joe and Damien] make sure everyone knows what they are saying').

Predictably, perhaps, it was the conflicting opinions of the teacher assessors on Joe's performance that most clearly signified educational assessment as a 'site of struggle'. As the analysis in Chapter 5 shows, the decision to award Joe a top grade was hotly contested by at least two of the eight assessors who felt that Joe was 'dominant', 'selfish', 'ridiculed others' and failed to listen to the opinion of others. In other words, these assessors were not happy solely to draw upon the formal examination criteria but preferred to evoke criteria from an alternative pedagogical discourse, a model of collaborative talk. Recently, I gained a supplementary perspective on Joe's performance when I showed the video-recording of the class discussion to a different audience, a workshop of postgraduate researchers studying approaches to discourse analysis (Baxter and Shaw, 2002). Perhaps because they were all students of language and gender, several of the researchers drew upon a discourse of gender differentiation to judge Joe's style of engagement as 'dominant' and 'masculinised' and therefore non-conducive to a successful whole class discussion. Yet they also recognised that Joe's performance met the assessment criteria for a grade A.

The FPDA approach to this type of data recognises that the business of making judgements about the educational construct of 'ability' inevitably coalesces into a significant site of struggle between competing or opposing discursive positions. In order to interpret the character and enactment of that struggle, the FPDA approach seeks to represent the different voices implicated and juxtapose the plural ways in which this significant moment within spoken discourse can be read. In the case of the classroom study, analysing how effective speakers are could never be a simple matter. Even though there is closure in the form of an agreed grade by a consensus of the participants, there are still a number of unresolved, underlying issues and tensions. By giving space to a range of different voices and perspectives, and representing the conflicts and connections between them, FPDA can produce richer insights into complex issues such as this.

A further dimension can be added to the polyphonic approach to analysis by representing *resistant* or marginalised voices and accounts or, in Bakhtin's (1981) words, heteroglossia (differently orientated voices). In the context of FPDA, this means aiming to spotlight and focus upon (especially) *female* voices and accounts which may be relatively silent or silenced compared to their more vociferous male or possibly female counterparts. It also means making space for voices that may have been repeatedly silenced by others, perhaps because they are attempting to contest or subvert the dominant view. In the classroom study, I was conscious that I did not *set out* to foreground the experiences of silent or silenced students. The original quest of the study was to examine what constituted 'effective' speech for the purposes of an oral assessment, and I chose to highlight the interactions of a selected group of students who were, 'likely to have something to say, and not likely to dry up in front of the video cameras' (Baxter, 2000b). It was only in the course of conducting the study that I became aware of a significant group of silent or silenced students, both male and female, who were very much at the margins of my *own* study.

In self-evaluation, if I were to conduct the study again, I would certainly take greater account of these 'silent' speakers, using FPDA to probe the reasons why they felt unable to contribute on an equal basis with their peers. However, what the analysis in Chapter 5 does achieve is to foreground some of the overshadowed voices in the whole class discussion and some of the *resistant* readings of this activity, for example, Cathy and Kate's irritation with the overbearing dominance of certain boys and the subservience of the girls;

Rebecca's sense that she is overlooked by the teacher for conforming to the rule of 'hands up'; Michael's difficulties with making contributions; assessor P's criticism of Joe's dominance; and assessor J's praise of Anne's stamina in seeing off male barracking tactics.

Transformative feminist projects

I have argued throughout this book that FPDA is not specifically concerned to work on behalf of girls or women who are 'oppressed' for political, economic or ideological reasons. It is not able to be involved in highly motivated ideological struggles or commit itself to a single liberatory cause, for fear that, in a Foucauldian sense, a 'will to truth' will lead to 'a will to power'. However, FPDA *is* concerned to create spaces to female voices that are being silenced or marginalised, if only because, as I have said, a greater richness of perspectives comes into play, promoting fresher insights and more complex understandings of problematic issues. In this spirit, I have argued that FPDA can and *should* contribute to transformative projects, provided that these are small-scale, localised, action-orientated and related to the specific needs of individuals, social groups or communities of practice (Elliott, 1996).

In both the case studies reported in this book, curricular and organisational transformation did follow in response to the FPDA commentaries, as I will now discuss by evaluating the various outcomes in more detail.

The classroom study

This study's aim to discover what constituted 'effective' speech, in the context of new British examination criteria, was in the first instance a theoretical question, although one that certainly had implications for teachers' practice. Indeed, the original conditions of access to the research context were strictly that the English department and its curricular practices should benefit. However, my feelings were initially ambivalent towards conducting a piece of action research, targeting curriculum development work on the assessment of speaking and listening. As I saw it, the problem with applying action research (e.g. Bryant, 1996; Kemmis, 1993) to educational practice involves a modernist quest of identifying a given problem, then jointly seeking to plan, implement and evaluate a course of action leading to improved educational practice. Additionally, although I had worked closely in the past with this school, my outsider status as a university researcher was not in the spirit of action research as described by Kemmis (1993: 183), who suggested that, 'only the practitioner can have access to the perspectives and commitments that inform a particular action as praxis'. Thus, I did not feel committed to the enlightenment spirit of much action research which 'views education as a historical and ideological process... shaped by the emancipatory intent to transform organisations and practices to achieve rationality and justice' (p. 177).

Yet I would suggest that action research *can* be reinterpreted and adapted for the purposes of a feminist post-structuralist approach, despite its overtly 'emancipatory intent'. Many of the principles that constitute action research – collaboration, participation, practicality, focus, self-reflection, a commitment to informed, committed and flexible action – can also play a part in many feminist/post-structuralist projects. Furthermore, both action research and FPDA perceive their work to be historical, localised and context-bound, their findings not automatically transferable to other settings or periods. Both approaches aim to increase understanding of participants' own practices and the situations in which these practices are carried out. However, while the emphasis in action research is upon achieving 'rationality and justice', the FPDA approach seeks to promote a greater plurality, openness and richness of perspectives as the basis for insightful action by the participants of the study.

The FPDA commentaries featured in Chapter 5 became the basis for transformative activities in the school setting. Rather than suggesting a course of action with clear goals, the FPDA commentaries sought to question habitual assumptions implicit within the practices of the English departmental team, stimulate new ideas, promote learning and offer possible routes for future curriculum development. As a consequence, there were changes of attitudes, policy and practices in the English curriculum of that school which had both immediate and long-term effects. First, the departmental team began to discuss their old, unquestioned adherence to the model of collaborative talk as the dominant model governing the ways in which they viewed students' oral achievements. The FPDA commentaries had never sought to suggest that the collaborative model was outdated, inappropriate or limited, but simply that there might be supplementary ways of teaching and assessing 'speaking and listening' that should not be discounted. The commentaries also drew the departmental team's attention to the rhetoric and constructs implied in the new criteria for assessing oral English. They prompted teachers to be quite critical of the discursive constructs and practices constituting 'dynamic and influential' speech (EDEXCEL, 1998). This led on to a discussion about the ways in which common-sense categories, such as self-confidence, popularity, peer pressure, male humour and outspokenness, were affecting the ways in which teachers formed judgements about students' oral skills. But it also had a practical effect on curriculum development. It was recognised that students needed to be taught how to meta-analyse their own classroom behaviour and discuss what *they* considered constituted effective speech in different contexts. This involved a follow-on analysis (Baxter, 2000a, b) of what distinguishes a dominant' speaker (e.g. the use of rule-breaking; a support group or sidekick; subversive or sexist humour) from an effective speaker (e.g. the ability to speak out and hold the floor; case-making skills; and inclusive humour). This helped the departmental team to devise new approaches to planning and teaching oral work.

Secondly, from a feminist perspective, the departmental team acknowledged that curriculum policy needed to take more account of the ways in which many girls (and certain boys) were being silenced and overlooked by particular classroom discursive practices. Policy needed to take account of the ways in which various subtextual practices in the classroom were impeding the ways in which girls might develop and practise their skills as speakers in public contexts. Furthermore, the staff raised a more general question about the recent boys and underachievement issue in British schools (e.g. OFSTED, 1993; QCA, 1998). They considered that this issue was in danger of being overplayed in their own school context in terms of the way extra resources were being deployed. For example, they discussed how female students in their school were unhappy with the positive discrimination being directed at boys, currently, the 'disadvantaged sex':

> *ASSESSOR J*: There is quite a strong feeling among certain girls in this school – and this is quite a recent thing – that their interests are being ignored. It's ironic because girls have only been achieving their so-called success relative to boys in the last few

years or so. We've had generations of privileging the boys and now it's happening all over again. My feeling is that we shouldn't be ignoring the girls or they will never be able to build on their recent achievements.

The management team study

As I explained in Chapter 6, I conducted the management team study in order to investigate the possibilities of applying the FPDA approach to social or professional contexts other than the school classroom. At the time I was conducting this study, a management consultancy company was also working with the management team (MT) to implement processes of management change. I saw this as an opportunity to explore whether an FPDA approach to analysing speech might provide *value* to the research participants themselves, in terms of increasing awareness about the discursive effects of spoken interactions and, as a consequence, potentially help to challenge and review their management practices. Working in partnership with one of the consultants, I was advised to reproduce the findings of the FPDA commentaries presented in Chapter 7, as a 'discourse map' (Appendix 3), translating the impenetrable (in their view!) academic rhetoric into more colloquial sound bites. This was supported by a detailed spoken explanation, followed by a question-and-answer session. Copies of the FPDA commentaries were also made available to those members of the management team who wished to read them.

As a consequence of the MT's response to the FPDA dissemination, there were a number of small-scale transformative effects on management practices which carried well beyond the conduct of meetings. The discourse map depicting the identity and intertextual relationships of the four discourses provided the MT with a set of insights into how the company culture might be perceived (by themselves and other employees), as well as a set of guiding principles for understanding where and how possible sources of conflict might take place within the organisation. It gave the MT a means of identifying their own discursive/political affiliations within the company culture and an explanation of why disagreements between individuals at different professional levels in the company tended to occur. It enabled individuals to examine their own managerial styles at some length and explore the cultural manifestations and constraints of such styles within the organisation as a whole. This set of guiding principles was therefore built into a broader consultancy programme for helping the company to manage change. The discourse map was used to enable the MT to examine what their particular business priorities were, consider what their priorities perhaps *ought* to be (by recognising whether or not they were 'trapped' within one discursive perspective or another) and hence reflect upon what changes might take place. One particular example of this was the business of 'naming' and 'outing' the discourses of masculinisation and competing specialisms. Until the research study took place, it was considered to be almost disloyal to take a resistant stance to the authorised discourse of open dialogue, with its emphasis on sharing of information and collaborative decision-making and egalitarian values. There had also been an unspoken policing of the discourse of historical legacy, in that it was assumed that MT founder members 'knew better' than more recently appointed managers. The process of *naming* the two subtextualised discourses allowed for the hitherto subversive recognition that *welcoming* some aspects of masculinisation and competing specialisms into management practices might be a good thing. For example, it was argued that the masculinised notions of 'tough love' and 'giving it to them straight' might enhance rather than undermine management credibility and provide a greater sense of security among employees that managers were able to 'own' the responsibility for taking more difficult decisions.

However, in the spirit of the post-structuralist principle of textual interplay, simply centring the marginal (that is, masculinisation and competing specialisms) and marginalising the central (historical legacy and open dialogue) remains an oppositional strategy and itself creates a dichotomy that needs overturning. In the context of the case study, managers recognised that there were two clear benefits in assimilating the concepts of the discourse map into management practices. The first was that they would be able to operate more freely upon their own discursive terrain without the fear that this would inevitably lead to disagreement and conflict with colleagues. This is because there should be a greater awareness and tolerance not only for colleagues' differing discursive affiliations but also an understanding of the intertextual connections between these positions. The second benefit was the recognition that individuals potentially have the agency to *shift between* different discursive positions according to need and circumstance. In suggesting this, I am not surreptitiously implying free will by another name; agency in this sense means having a greater *awareness* of the possibilities for discursive shifts. Agency in this context would particularly mean an individual's readiness to *resist* certain stereotyped or character-typed subject positions imposed upon them by the assumptions and expectations of others in the organisation.

From a *feminist* post-structuralist perspective, the dissemination of the discourse map with the MT allowed for greater reflection on the ways in which discursive affiliations help to construct gender-stereotyped attitudes and assumptions. Sarah, the only female member of the MT, confessed that she felt 'trapped' by perceptions that she was principally affiliated to the discourses of historical legacy and the more feminised discourse of open dialogue. In other words, she did not wish to be character stereotyped as the feminised voice of openness and co-operation. She wanted to feel that she could draw upon the values of a more masculinised discourse without fear of male prejudice that she was appropriating their terms of engagement. While not wishing to relinquish her reputation as a proponent of open dialogue, or conversely not wishing to be absorbed as a 'token male' into the growing 'boysy culture' of the MT, she wanted to feel that she could move more flexibly between different discursive positions as they fitted business needs. A measure of the success with which Sarah managed to achieve her wish to draw upon masculinised discourse without sacrificing her affiliation to open dialogue was indicated in my interview with Pam, the personal assistant to the MT:

> She is a very strong woman indeed. Last week, I heard her giving Pete a ticking off and she did it in front of everybody. He had missed a meeting she had arranged but hadn't told her he couldn't make it. She didn't shout or raise her voice or anything. She just said, 'If you are unable to make a meeting I've arranged, I would appreciate it if you would just come up to me and say, 'no'. People sitting around them started to become very uncomfortable and were making excuses to get up and leave. Then Pete said, 'Right, let's do the meeting now' so her words had an immediate effect. I was very impressed by her. There was no ranting and screaming.

While the actions Sarah takes here to deal with a tense moment are seen to constitute her as a role model in the eyes of more junior female employees like Pam, Sarah herself was aware that there were other unresolved issues in this organisation that would take more than the dissemination of a discourse map to solve. For instance, the imbalance of males and females on the MT might take years to correct, given the current swing towards discourses of competing specialisms and masculinisation in the corporate culture. Her exclusion from the 'boysy' social familiarity of the men was something she also felt unequipped or unwilling to negotiate. However, the ways in which the academically challenging and professionally disruptive concepts of the discourse map were seriously debated and assimilated by this senior management team, suggests that transformative feminist action within a post-structuralist paradigm is a real possibility within business settings.

Conclusion

Feminism and post-structuralism separately draw upon short but thoroughly diverse philosophical and epistemological traditions. Both movements, in their infinite variety, have as many detractors and critics as they do proponents. If you attempt to put these vast movements together as 'feminist post-structuralism' and then direct this apparently contradictory pair of theoretical perspectives to the field of discourse analysis, the implications for research practice may appear, initially at least, to be fraught with ambiguity, contradiction and a lack of clear mission or purpose.

The quest of this book has been partly to propose some 'productive contradictions' (Soper, 1993b) between the two theoretical discourses, and partly to demystify the presumed difficulties of applying FPDA to research practice. Despite the rather long-winded wordiness denoted by the acronym, I would argue that it is not a fanciful, pretentious or particularly esoteric approach to discourse analysis. On the contrary, I have aimed to demonstrate that FPDA is a strictly logical, organised, systematic and pragmatic approach to analysing spoken interactions. Although the approach certainly embraces complex and abstract post-structuralist principles such as deconstruction and supplementarity, I have aimed to show how these can be readily translated into lively new strategies for conducting discourse analysis, which may supplement, enhance or, indeed, undercut other more established methods. For example, data already analysed from a language and gender 'dominance' or 'difference' perspective might be usefully *reanalysed* from an FPDA perspective. In so doing, FPDA can produce a multi-faceted interpretation of spoken interactions that reveals rather than suppresses the discursive struggles to fix meaning according to different and competing interests. In educational contexts, FPDA can seek to explain why academically successful girls continue to have difficulties in commanding an audience or holding the floor in a whole class discussion. In work or professional contexts, it can move some way towards explaining why organisations with equal opportunities policies, which employ women in senior posts, still continue to be seriously male-dominated at executive or managerial levels.

On the basis of FPDA's focus upon gender, power and discourse, the approach is potentially transferable to a range of discursive settings for a variety of research purposes. For example, FPDA might be used to analyse the negotiation of complex power relations in more informal, mixed-sex conversations between groups of friends in homes, pubs, clubs, bars and restaurants. An FPDA approach might also be transferable to other mixed-sex, professional or public locations, such as hospitals, police stations, law courts, factory floors or local and national government, where power relations are routinely negotiated and contested through competing discourses.

Finally, FPDA is not just a form of theoretical analysis but may lead to tangible benefits on behalf of feminism as it becomes better known and more widely used. For instance, as a consequence of conducting the management team study (Chapters 6 and 7), I have recently been commissioned by a large, multi-national corporation to use the FPDA methodology to analyse some of the reasons why the senior management team ratio of men to women is 28:1, despite a long-term policy of recruiting equal numbers of males and females for management positions. This is an exciting departure for FPDA because it helps to forge a connection between post-structuralist scholarship and feminist transformative action. As I see it, there are now two questions for future practitioners of FPDA. Firstly, how can we work with the post-structuralist recognition of multiple-voices, plural readings of faceted, linked and echoed realities in a lived context, where people commonly believe that a modernist perspective offers the only way to understand complex issues or resolve difficult problems? Secondly, how can we best represent the successes, contradictions and diversity of female experiences whilst still working to transform the appalling inequities that so many girls and women continue to face?

Appendix 1
Glossary of Terminology used in the Denotative Analyses

Interruptions: 'violations of the turn-taking rules of conversations'; that is, the 'next speaker begins to speak while current speaker is still speaking at a point in current speaker's turn which could not be defined as the last word' (Coates, 1993: 109). This definition was questioned by Beatlie (1981).

See also Esposito, 1979; Swann and Graddol, 1988; Zimmerman and West, 1975.

Minimal responses: short responses to a question, often barely a word, for example: *mmh, yeah, oh, right.*

See Coates, 1993; Fishman, 1980; Zimmerman and West, 1975.

Mitigated directives: a 'directive' is a speech act which gets someone to do something, a command. A 'mitigated directive' takes 'the form of proposals for future activity rather than an explicit command' (Graddol and Swann, 1989: 80–1), often including the speaker, for example: *'Let's'*, or *'we could'*.

See Goodwin (1980, 1990).

Open and closed questions: an open question does not presuppose a given answer, for example: 'Tell me about yourself'.

A closed question usually presupposes a given answer, for example: 'What did you put for number one?'

Overlaps: 'instances of slight over-anticipation by the next speaker: instead of beginning to speak immediately following current speaker's turn, next speaker begins to speak at the very end of current speaker's turn, overlapping the last word' (Coates, 1993: 109), or last few words.

See Zimmerman and West, 1975.

Appendix 2
Transcription Conventions

Standard layout

Following Simpson (1997), the practice of feminist post-structuralist discourse analysis does not require me to display speaking turns as units of analysis, that is, as the basis for identifying different types or categories of talk. Rather, I wanted a simple method of presentation that would depict the whole picture as well as capture the nuances and detail of both verbal and non-verbal interaction within a large group. I therefore elected to use a 'standard layout' (Swann, 1993), which is set out rather like a dialogue for a play, with speaking turns shown as following one another in sequence.

'Stage directions' (in brackets and italicised caps) indicate:

- all instances of non-verbal behaviour, for example: laughing, head-nodding, finger-pointing and so on, of the speaker
- metalanguage: volume, pitch, stress, intonation and so on
- pauses, hesitations by the speaker
- interruptions and overlaps by other speakers
- descriptions of group behaviour affecting the speech of the speaker.

Phonetic transcription

Following Swann's advice (1993: 41), I have avoided the danger of trying to represent the phonetic quality of people's speech, and have only used a phonetic transcription in cases of well-recognised variations of words (e.g. 'yeah'). On the other hand, I have opted to use as little punctuation as possible in order to capture the greater fluidity and spontaneity of speech compared to writing.

Appendix 3
The Discourse Map

(a) Discourse combination

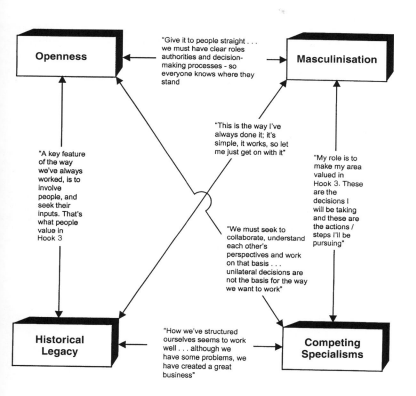

(b)   Discourse tension

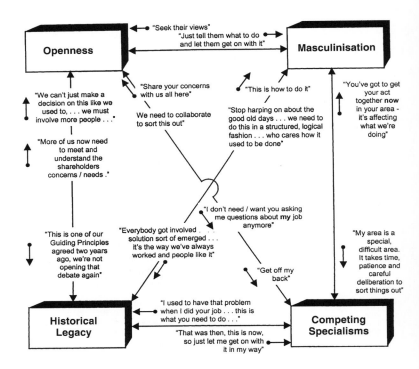

Bibliography

Althusser, L. (1971) *Lenin and Philosophy and Other Essays* (London: New Left Books).

Bakhtin, M. (1981) *The Dialogic Imagination: Four Essays* (TX: University of Texas).

Balbus, I. (1987) Disciplining women: Michel Foucault and the power of feminist discourse. In S. Benhabib and D. Cornell (eds), *Feminism as Critique* (London: Polity Press).

Barnes, D., Britton, J. and Rosen, H. (1965) *Language, the Learner and the School* (Harmondsworth: Penguin).

Barthes, R. (1973) *Mythologies* (London: Granada).

Barthes, R. (1977) *Image-Music-Text* (New York: Hill & Yang).

Baxter, J. (1999) Teaching girls to speak out: the female voice in public contexts. *Language and Education*, 13(2), pp. 81–98.

Baxter, J. (2000a) Going public: teaching students to speak out in public contexts. *English in Education*, 34(2), pp. 26–34.

Baxter, J. (2000b) Teaching girls to speak out: an investigation of the extent to which gender is a pertinent discourse for describing and assessing girls' and boys' speech in public contexts. Unpub. PhD thesis, University of Reading.

Baxter, J. (2000c) Jokers in the pack: why boys are more adept than girls at speaking in public settings. *Language & Education*, 16(2), pp. 81–96.

Baxter, J. (2002a) A juggling act: a feminist post-structuralist analysis of girls' and boys' talk in the secondary classroom. *Gender & Education*, 14(1), pp. 5–19.

Baxter, J. (2002b) Competing discourses in the classroom: a post-structuralist analysis of girls' and boys' speech in public contexts. *Discourse & Society*, 13(6), pp. 827–42.

Baxter, J. and Shaw, S. (2002) Analysing Spoken Discourse. A workshop at the IGALA 2 Conference, University of Lancaster, April 2002.

Beatie, G. (1981) Interruption in conversational interaction and its relation to sex and status of interactants. *Linguistics*, 19, pp. 15–35.

Beauvoir, S. de (1972) *The Second Sex*. H.M. Parsley (trans.) (Harmondsworth: Penguin).

Belsey, C. (1980) *Critical Practice* (London: Methuen).

Bem, S. (1993) *The Lenses of Gender: Transforming the Debate in Sexual Equality* (New Haven: Yale University Press).

Benwell, B. (2002) Is there anything 'new' about these lads?: the textual and visual construction of masculinity in men's magazines. In L. Litosseliti and J. Sunderland (eds).

Bergvall, V.L. (1998) Constructing and enacting gender through discourse: negotiating multiple roles as female engineering students. In V.L. Bergvall, J.M. Bing and A.F. Freed (eds), pp. 173–201.

Bergvall, V.L. (1999) Towards a comprehensive theory of language and gender. *Language in Society*, 28, pp. 273–93.

Bergvall, V.L., Bing, J.M. and Freed, A.F. (eds) (1996) *Rethinking Language and Gender Research* (Harlow: Longman).

Billig, M. (1999) Critical discourse analysis and conversation analysis: an exchange between Michael Billig and Emmanuel A. Schegloff. *Discourse & Society*, 10(4), pp. 543–82.

Billig, M. (2000) Towards a critique of the critical. *Discourse & Society*, 11(3), pp. 291–2.

Bing, J.M. and Bergvall, V.L. (1998) The question of questions: beyond binary thinking. In V.L. Bergvall, J.M. Bing and A.F. Freed (eds), pp. 1–30.

Bousted, M. (1989) Who talks? *English in Education*, 23(3), pp. 41–51.

Bryant, I. (1996) Action research and reflective practice. In D. Scott and R. Usher (eds), pp. 106–19.

Bucholtz, M. (1999) Bad examples: transgression and progress in language and gender studies. In M. Bucholtz, A.C. Liang, and L. Sutton (eds), *Reinventing Identities: the Gendered Self in Discourse* (New York: OUP), pp. 3–24.

Butler, J. (1990) Gender trouble, feminist theory, and pyschoanalytic discourse. In L.J. Nicholson (ed.) *Feminism/Postmodernism* (London: Routledge).

Butler, J. (1991) *Gender Trouble: Feminism and the Subversion of Identity* (New York: Routledge).

Cain, M. (1993) Foucault, feminism and feeling: what Foucault can and cannot contribute to feminist epistemology. In C. Ramazanoglu (ed.) pp. 73–95.

Callaway, H. (1981) Women's perspectives: research as re-vision. In P. Reason and J. Rowan (eds) *Human Inquiry* (New York: John Wiley).

Cameron, D. (1997a) Performing gender identity: young men's talk and the construction of heterosexual identity. In S. Johnson and U.H. Meinhof (eds), pp. 47–64.

Cameron, D. (1997b) Theoretical debates in feminist linguistics: questions of sex and gender. In R. Wodak (ed.) *Gender & Discourse* (London: Sage).

Cameron, D. (2001) *Working with Spoken Discourse* (London: Sage).

Cheshire, J. and Jenkins, N. (1991) Gender issues in the GCSE Oral English examination: Part 2, *Language and Education*, 5(1), pp. 19–40.

Chouliaraki, L. and Fairclough, N. (1999) *Discourse in Late Modernity: Rethinking Critical Discourse Analysis* (Edinburgh: Edinburgh UP).

Coates, J. (1993) *Women, Men and Language*. 2nd edn (London: Longman).

Coates, J. (1995) Language, gender and career. In S. Mills (ed.) *Language and Gender* (London: Longman).

Coates, J. (1998) *Woman Talk* (Oxford: Blackwell).

Cooper, R. (1989) Modernism, post-modernism and organisational analysis 3: The contribution of Jacques Derrida. *Organisation Studies*, 10(4), pp. 479–502.

Corson, D. (1997) Gender, discourse and senior education: Ligatures for girls, options for boys? In R. Wodak (ed.), pp. 140–64.

Crawford, M. (1995) *Talking Difference: On Gender and Language* (London: Sage).

Daly, M. (1978) *Gyn/Ecology the Meta-ethics of Radical Feminism* (London: The Women's Press).

Davies, B. (1997) The subject of post-structuralism: a reply to Alison Jones. *Gender & Education*, 9, pp. 271–83.

Davies, B. and Banks, C. (1992) The gender trap: a feminist post-structuralist analysis of primary school children's talk about gender. *Curriculum Studies*, 24(1), pp. 1–25.

Derrida, J. (1976) *Of Grammatology* (Baltimore: John Hopkins Press).

Derrida, J. (1978) *Writing and Difference* (London: RKP).

Derrida, J. (1982) *Margins of Philosophy* (London: Harvester).

Derrida, J. (1987) *A Derrida Reader: Between the Blinds* (Brighton: Harvester Wheatsheaf).

DES (1989) *English in the National Curriculum* (London: HMSO).

DfEE (2000a) *The National Curriculum for England and Wales* (London: DfEE).

DfEE (2000b) *Removing Barriers: Raising Achievement Levels for Minority Ethnic Students. Key Points for Schools* (London: DfEE).

Drew, P. and Heritage, J. (1992) *Talk at Work: Interaction in Institutional Settings* (Cambridge: Cambridge University Press).

Eagleton, T. (1983) *Literary Theory: An Introduction* (Oxford: Blackwell).

Eckert, P. (1989) The whole woman: sex and gender differences in variation. *Language Variation and Change*, 1, pp. 245–67.

Eckert, P. and McConnell Ginet, S. (1992) Think practically and look locally: language and gender as community-based practice. *Annual Review of Anthropology*, 22, pp. 461–90.

Eckert, P. and McConnell Ginet, S. (1995) Constructing meaning, constructing selves: snapshots of language, gender and class from Belten High. In K. Hall and M. Bucholtz (eds), pp. 469–507.

Eckert, P. and McConnell Ginet, S. (1999) New generalisations and explanations in language and gender research. *Language in Society*, 28, pp. 185–201.

Eco, U. (1990) *The Limits of Interpretation* (Bloomington: Indiana University Press).

Edelsky, C. and Adams, A. (1990) Creating inequality: breaking the rules in debates. *Journal of Language and Social Equality*, 9(3), pp. 171–90.

EDEXCEL (1998) *GCSE Syllabus 1999: English* (London: EDEXCEL Foundation).

Elliott, A. (1996) *Subject to Ourselves* (Oxford: Polity Press).

Epstein, D., Elwood, V. and Maw, J. (1998) *Failing Boys? Issues in Gender and Achievement* (Buckingham: Open University Press).

Esposito, A. (1979) Sex differences in children's conversations. In *Language and Speech*, 22(3), pp. 213–20.

Fairclough, N. (1992) *Discourse and Social Change* (Cambridge: Polity Press).

Fairclough, N. and Wodak, R. (1997) Critical Discourse Analysis. In T. van Dijk (ed.) *Discourse as Social Interaction* (London: Sage), pp. 258–84.

Fishman, P. (1980) Conversational insecurity. In G. Howard, W.P. Robinson and P.M. Smith (eds) *Language: Social Psychological Perspectives* (Oxford: Pergamon Press), pp. 127–32.

Foucault, M. (1972) *The Archaeology of Knowledge and the Discourse on Language* (New York: Pantheon).

Foucault, M. (1979) *Discipline and Punish* (Harmondsworth: Penguin).

Foucault, M. (1980) *Power/Knowledge* (Brighton: Harvester Press).

Foucault, M. (1984) What is enlightenment? In P. Rabinow (ed.) *The Foucault Reader* (London: Penguin).

Fox-Keller (1985) *Reflections on Gender and Science* (New Haven: Yale University Press).

Francis, B. (1998) *Power Plays: Children's Constructions of Gender, Power and Adult Work* (Stoke-on-Trent: Trentham Books).

Francis, B. (1999) Modernist reductionism or post-structuralist relativism: can we move on? An evaluation of the arguments in relation to feminist educational research. *Gender & Education*, 11(4), pp. 381–93.

Fraser, N. and Nicholson, L. (1990) *Feminism/Postmodernism* (London: Routledge).

Frater, G. (2000) *Securing Boys' Literacy* (London: The Basic Skills Agency).

Gal, S. (1995) Language, gender and power: an anthropological review. In K. Hall and M. Bucholtz (eds).

Garfinkel, H. (1967) *Studies in Ethnomethodology* (Englewood Cliffs, NJ: Prentice Hall).

Gold, R.L. (1958) Roles in Sociological Fieldwork. *Social Forces*, 36, pp. 217–23.

Goodwin, M.H. (1980) Directive-response speech sequences in girls' and boys' task activities. In S. McConnell-Ginet, R. Borker and M. Furmar (eds) *Women and Language in Literature and Society*. New York Praeger, pp. 157–73.

Goodwin, M.H. (1990) *He-Said-She-Said: Talk as Social Organisation among Black Children* (Bloomington: Indiana University Press).

Graddol, D. and Swann, J. (1989) *Gender Voices* (Oxford: Blackwell).

Gray, J. (1992) *Men are from Mars, Women are from Venus* (New York & London: Thorsons).

Grimshaw, J. (1993) Practices of freedom. In C. Ramazanoglu (ed.), pp. 51–72.

Halford, S. and Leonard, P. (2001) *Gender, Power and Organisations* (Basingstoke: Palgrave).

Hall, K. and Bucholtz, M. (eds) (1995) *Gender Articulated: Language and the Constructed Self* (London & New York: Routledge).

Halliday, M. (1989) *Language, Context and Text: Aspects of Language in a Social-semiotic Perspective* (Oxford: Oxford University Press).

Hammersley, M. (1990) What's wrong with ethnography? The myth of theoretical description. *Sociology*, 24(4), pp. 597–615.

Hammersley, M. and Atkinson, P. (1995) *Ethnography* (London: Routledge).

Hannan, G. (1991) *Equal Opportunities: Gender* (Oxford: Blackwell).

Hartsock, N. (1990) Foucault on Power: A Theory for Women? In L.J. Nicholson (ed.), pp. 155–75.

Heritage, J. (1984) *Garfinkel and Ethnomethodology* (Cambridge: Polity Press).

Hodge, C. and Kress, G. (1993) *Language as Ideology*. 2nd edn (London: Routledge).

Holmes, J. (1992) Women's talk in public contexts. *Discourse & Society*, 3(2) pp. 131–50.

Holmes, J. (1995) *Women, Men and Politeness* (London: Longman).

Honigmann, J. (1973) Sampling in ethnographic fieldwork. In R. Burgess (ed.) *Field Research: A Sourcebook and Manual* (London: Allen & Unwin), pp. 79–90.

Howe, A. (1992) *Making Talk Work* (London: Hodder & Stoughton).

Hutchby, I. (1996) Power in discourse: the case of arguments on a British talk radio show. *Discourse & Society*, 7(4), pp. 481–97.

Irigaray, L. (1985) *This Sex which is not One*. C. Porter and C. Burke (trans.) (New York: Cornell University Press).

Jenkins, N. and Cheshire, J. (1990) Gender issues in the GCSE oral examination: Part 1, *Language & Education*, 4(4), pp. 261–92.

Johnson, B. (1995) *In the Wake of Deconstruction* (Oxford: Blackwell).

Johnson, S. and Meinhof, U.H. (eds) (1997) *Language and Masculinity* (London: Blackwell).

Jones, D. (1980) Gossip: notes on women's oral culture. In C. Kramarae (ed.) *The Voices and Words of Women and Men* (Oxford: Pergamon Press).

Jones, P. (1988) *Lip-service: The Story of Talk in Schools* (Milton Keynes: OUP).

Jones, A. (1993) Becoming a 'girl': post-structuralist suggestions for educational research, *Gender & Education*, 5(2), pp. 157–66.

Jones, A. (1997) Teaching post-structuralist theory in education: student resistances, *Gender & Education*, 5(2), pp. 261–9.

Julé, A. (2002) *Gender, Language and Silence in an ESL Classroom*. Unpub. PhD thesis, The University of British Columbia.

Kehily, M.J. and Nayak, A. (1997) 'Lads and laughter': humour and the production of heterosexual identities. *Gender & Education*, 9(1), pp. 69–87.

Kelly, J. (1991) A study of gender differential linguistic interaction in the adult classroom. *Gender & Education*, 3, pp. 1–23.

Kemmis, S. (1993) Action research. In M. Hammersley (ed.) *Educational Research: Current Issues* (Milton Keynes: Open University Press), pp. 177–90.

Kristeva, J. (1984) Woman can never be defined. In E. Marks and I. de Coutivron (eds) *New French Feminisms* (New York: Schocken).

Kuhn, T. (1970) *The Structure of Scientific Revolutions* (Chicago: University of Chicago Press).

Lafferty, J.C. and Pond, A. (1989) *The Desert Survival Situation*. 4th edn (Hampshire: Human Synergistics-Verax).

Lakoff, R. (1975) *Language and Woman's Place* (New York: Harper & Rowe).

Lather, P. (1991) *Getting Smart: Feminist Research and Pedagogy with/in the Postmodern* (London: Routledge).

Linstead, S. (1993) From post-modern anthropology to deconstructive ethnography. *Human Relations*, 45(1), pp. 97–120.

Litosseliti, L. and Sunderland, J. (eds) (2002) *Gender Identity & Discourse Analysis* (Amsterdam/Philadelphia: John Benjamins Press).

Lyotard J.F. (1984) *The Post-modern Condition* (Manchester: Manchester University Press).

Mac An Ghaill, M. (1994) *The Making of Men: Masculinities, Sexualities and Schooling* (Buckingham: Open University Press).

Marshall, B. (1998) Boys go to Jupiter to be stupider, girls go to Mars to be superstars. *Critical Quaterly*, 40(2), pp. 95–103.

McElhinny, B. (1997) Ideologies of public and private language in sociolinguistics. In R. Wodak (ed.) (London: Sage).

McNay, L. (2000) *Gender and Agency: Reconfiguring the Subject in Feminist and Social Theory* (Malden, MA: Polity Press).

McNeil, M. (1993) Dancing with freedom: feminism and power-knowledge. In C. Ramazanoglu (ed.), pp. 147–75.

McWilliam, E. (1997) Performing between the posts: authority, posture and contemporary feminist scholarship. In W.G. Tierney and Y. Lincoln (eds) *Representation and the Text: Reframing the Narrative Voice* (Albany: State University of New York Press), pp. 219–32.

Mercer, N. (1995) *The Guided Construction of Knowledge: Talk Among Teachers and Learners* (Clevedon: Multilingual Matters).

Middleton, S. (1993) *Educating Feminists* (New York: Teachers' College, Columbia University).

Millard, E. (1997) *Differently Literate: Boys, Girls and the Schooling of Literacy* (London: Falmer Press).

Miller, J. (1996) *School for Women* (London: Virago).

Millett, K. (1977) *Sexual Politics* (London: Virago).

Mills, S. (2002) Third Wave Feminism Linguistics and the Analysis of Sexism and Naming Practices. Plenary lecture at IGALA 2, University of Lancaster, UK.

Mitchell, J. (1974) *Psychoanalysis and Feminism* (Harmondsworth: Penguin).

Moi, T. (1985) Power, sex and subjectivity: feminist reflections on Foucault. *Paragraph*, 5, pp. 95–102.

Moi, T. (1999) *Feminism of Freedom: Simone de Beauvoir* (Oxford: Oxford University Press).

Moi, T. (2000) *What is a Woman?* (Oxford: Oxford University Press).

NEAB (1996) *English Syllabus for the 1996 Examination* (Manchester: NEAB).

NEAB (1999) *Syllabus for 1999/2000: English* (Manchester, NEAB).

Norris, C. (1990) *What's Wrong with Post-modernism: Critical Theory and the Ends of Philosophy* (London: Harvester Wheatsheaf).

Ochs, E. and Taylor, C. (1992) Family narrative as political activity. *Discourse & Society*, (3), pp. 301–40.

OFSTED (1993) *Boys and English* (London: HMSO).

Ohrn, E. (1991) Gender patterns, in classroom interaction. *Goteburg Studies in Education Sciences 77* (University of Goteburg.)

Olsen, T. (1978) *Silences* (New York: Delacourt Press).

Pease, A. and Pease, B. (2001) *Why Men Don't Listen and Women Can't Read Maps* (London: Orion Books).

Pickering, J. (1997) *Raising boys' achievement* (Network Educational Press).

QCA (1998) *Can Do Better: Raising Boys Achievements in Literacy* (London: HMSO).

Ramazanoglu, C. (ed.) (1993) *Up Against Foucault: Explorations of some Tensions between Foucault and Feminism* (London: Routledge).

Ransom, J. (1993) Feminism, difference and discourse: the limits of discursive analysis for feminism. In C. Ramazanoglu (ed.) (London: Routledge).

Riley, D. (1988) *Am I that Name? Feminism and the Category of 'Women' in History* (Basingstoke: Macmillan).

Sacks, H., Schegloff, E.J. and Jefferson, G. (1974) A simplest systematics for the organisation of turn-taking. *Language*, 50(4), pp. 696–735.

Sadker, D. and Sadker, M. (1994) *Failing at Fairness: How America's Schools Cheat Girls* (New York: Touchstone).

Saussure, F. de (1974) *A Course in General Linguistics* (London: Fontana).

Sawaki, J. (1991) *Disciplining Foucault: Feminism, Power and the Body* (London: Routledge).

Schegloff, E.J. (1997) Whose text? Whose context?, *Discourse & Society*, 8(2), pp. 165–87.

Schegloff, E.J. (1999) Schegloff's texts as Billig's data: a critical reply. *Discourse & Society*, 10(4), pp. 558–70.

Scott, R. (1996) Ethnography and education. In D. Scott and R. Usher (eds), pp. 143–58.

Scott, D. and Usher, R. (eds) (1996) *Understanding Educational Research* (London: Routledge).

Shaw, S. (2000) Language, gender and floor apportionment in political debates. *Discourse & Society*, 11(3), pp. 401–18.

Showalter, E. (1989) *Speaking of Gender* (London: Routledge).

Simpson, A. (1997) 'It's a game! The construction of gendered subjectivity. In R. Wodak (ed.) *Gender and Discourse* (London: Sage).

Skeggs, B. (1994) Situating the production of feminist ethnography. In M. Maynand and J. Purvis (eds) *Researching Women's Lives from a Feminist Perspective* (London: Taylor & Francis), pp. 72–92.

Skelton, C. (1998) Feminism and research into masculinities and schooling. *Gender & Education*, 10(2), pp. 217–27.

Skidmore, D. (1999) Discourses of learning difficulty and the conditions of school development. *Educational Review*, 15(1), pp. 17–28.

Soper, K. (1993a) Postmodernism, subjectivity and the question of value. In J. Squires (ed.) *Principled Positions: Postmodernism and the Rediscovery of Value* (London: Routledge).

Soper, K. (1993b) Productive contradictions. In C. Ramazanoglu (ed.) pp. 30–49.

Spender, D. (1980) *Man-made Language* (London: Pandora Press).

Spender, D. (1982) *Learning to Lose* (London: The Women's Press).

Stam, R. (1988) Mikhail Bakhtin and left cultural critique. In E. Ann Kaplan (ed.) *Post-modernism and its Discontents* (London: Verso), pp. 116–43 .

Steinem, G. (1992) *The Revolution from Within: A Book of Self-esteem* (London: Bloomsbury).

Swann, J. (1992) *Girls, Boys and Language* (Oxford: Blackwell).

Swann, J. (1993) Observing and recording talk in educational settings. In D. Graddol, J. Maybin and B. Steirer (eds) *Researching Language and Literacy in Social Context* (Clevedon: Multilingual Matters and OUP), pp. 26–48.

Swann, J. (2002) Yes, but is it gender? In L. Litosseliti and J. Sunderland (eds), pp. 43–68.

Swann, J. and Graddol, D. (1988) Gender inequalities in classroom talk. *English in Education*, 22(1), pp. 48–65.

Swann, J. and Graddol, D. (1995) Feminising classroom talk? In S. Mills (ed.) *Language and Gender* (London: Longman).

Talbot, M. (1998) *Language and Gender: An Introduction* (Oxford: Polity Press).

Talbot, M., Atkinson, K., and Atkinson, D. (2003) *Language and Power in the Modern World* (Tuscaloosa: University of Alabama Press).

Tannen, D. (1992) *You Just Don't Understand: Women and Men in Conversation* (London: Virago).

Tannen, D. (1995) *Talking from 9 to 5: Women and Men at Work: Language, Sex and Power* (London: Longman).

Thornborrow, J. (2002) *Power Talk: Language and Interaction in Institutional Discourse* (London: Pearson Education).

Thorne, D. and Henley, N. (1975) *Language and Sex: Difference and Dominance.* MA: Newbury House.

TTA (2000) *Raising the Attainment of Minority Students* (London: TTA).

Urquhart, I. (1998) 'You see all the blood come out': Popular culture and how boys become men. In M. Hilton (ed.) *Potent Fictions* (London: Routledge).

Usher, P. (1996) *Feminist Approaches to Research.* In D. Scott and R. Usher (eds), pp. 120–42.

van Dijk, T. (1986) *Racism in the Press* (London: Arnold).

van Dijk, T. (2001) Multidisciplinary CDA: a plea for diversity. In R. Wodak and M. Meyer (eds) *Methods of Critical Discourse Analysis* (London: Sage), pp. 95–120.

Walkerdine, V. (1990) *Schoolgirl Fictions* (London: Verso).

Walkerdine, V. (1998) *Counting Girls Out: Girls and Mathematics* (London: Falmer Press).

Walsh, C. (2001) *Gender and Discourse: Language and Power in Politics, the Church and Organisations* (London: Pearson Education).

Wareing, S. (1993) *Co-operative and Competitive Talk: The Assessment of Discussion at Standard Grade.* Unpub. PhD thesis, The University of Strathclyde.

Weedon, C. (1997) *Feminist Practice and Post-structuralist Theory.* 2nd edn (Oxford: Blackwell).

West, C. (2002) Peeling an onion: A critical reply to 'Competing Discourses'. *Discourse & Society*, 13(6), pp. 843–52.

Wetherell, M. (1998) Positioning and interpretative repertoires: conversation analysis and post-structuralism in dialogue, *Discourse & Society*, 9, pp. 387–412.

Wilkinson, A., Davies, A. and Berrill, D. (1990) *Spoken English Illustrated* (Milton Keynes Open University Press).

Willis, P. (1977) *Learning to Labour* (London: Saxon House).

Winter, J. (1993) Gender and the political interview in the Australian context. *Journal of Pragmatics*, 20, pp. 117–39.

Wodak, R. (1989) Introduction. In R. Wodak (ed.) *Language, Power and Ideology* (Amsterdam: John Benjamins), pp. i–ix.

Wodak, R. (1996) *Disorders of Discourse.* London: Longman.

Wodak, R. (ed.) (1997) *Gender and Discourse* (London: Sage).

Wodak, R. (2002) Interdisciplinarity, Gender Studies and CDA: Gender Mainstreaming and the European Union. Plenary lecture at IGALA 2, Lancaster University, UK.

Wodak, R. and Meyer, M. (2001) *Methods of Critical Discourse Analysis* (London: Sage).

Wolf, M.A. (1992) A Thrice-told tale: *Feminism, Post-modernism and Ethnographic Responsibility* (Stanford CA: Stanford University Press).

Zimmerman, D. and West, C. (1975) Sex roles, interruptions and silences in conversation. In D. Thorne and N. Henley (eds) *Language and Sex: Difference and Dominance* (Rowley, MA: Newbury House) pp. 105–29.

Index

Adams, A., 81, 82
agency, 26, 27, 30–1, 195
Althusser, L., 26
Atkinson, P., 85, 86, 87, 88,
    134, 138

Bakhtin, M., 36, 38, 65, 67, 68,
    69, 70, 77, 153, 189
Balbus, I., 23
Banks, C., 27, 43
Barthes, R., 6, 51, 61, 75, 78, 186
Baudrillard, L., 5
Baxter, J., 33, 44, 81, 82, 83,
    101, 124, 188, 189, 192
Beauvoir, S. de, 5, 15
Belsey, C., 26, 177
Bem, S., 183
Benwell, B., 33
Bergvall, V.L., 12, 15, 17, 29, 30,
    43, 49, 51, 65, 98, 183
Billig, M., 3, 43, 44, 47, 53,
    54, 55, 56, 59
Bing, J.M., 12, 65, 98, 183
Bousted, M., 83
Bryant, I., 84, 190
Bucholtz, M., 4, 15, 28, 30
Butler, J., 5, 9, 10, 12, 17, 20,
    29, 32, 35, 59

Cain, M., 35, 39
Callaway, H., 12
Cameron, D., 2, 7, 15, 17, 29,
    30, 42, 45
Cheshire, J., 101, 120, 121, 125
Chouliaraki, L., 5, 30
classroom study
    aims of, 83
    evaluation of, 123–7
    feminist post-structuralist analysis,
        99–100

identifying discourses, 89–99
methods followed in, 85–9
outcome of, 190–3
overall purpose of, 81–3
research setting, 83–5
close linguistic analysis, 47–8
Coates, J., 20, 81, 98, 143,
    147, 148, 162
competing discourses, 9, 26
competing specialisms, 128, 139,
    141, 143–7, 149, 153, 159–60,
    161, 163–4, 166, 169, 176, 178,
    180, 184, 194, 196
competing voices and accounts
    see heteroglossia
consciousness-raising, 16, 18
conversation analysis (CA), 2–3,
    42
    see also FPDA
Cooper, R., 63, 67
Corson, D., 83
Crawford, M., 4, 10
critical discourse analysis (CDA),
    3, 42
    see also FPDA

Daly, M., 15
Davies, B., 12, 23, 27, 35, 43
deconstruction, 33–4, 63–4, 196
deconstructive criticism, 6, 24
deconstructive movements
    (strategies), 63
Derrida, J., 3, 6, 23, 24, 28, 36,
    43, 62, 71, 77, 186
differance, 24, 62
discourse
    definition of, 7, 45–6
    in classroom setup, 89–99
    in management setup, 137–50
    intextuality, 8

211